BUSINESS
PLANNING

A Comprehensive Framework and Process

WESLEY B. TRUITT
Foreword by
José de la Torre

QUORUM BOOKS
Westport, Connecticut • London

Library of Congress Cataloging-in-Publication Data

Truitt, Wesley B., 1939–
    Business planning : a comprehensive framework and process / Wesley B. Truitt;
foreword by José de la Torre
        p. cm.
    Includes bibliographical references and index.
    ISBN 1–56720–475–9 (alk. paper)
    1. Business planning 2. Business enterprises—Planning. I. Title.
    HD30.28.T776 2002
    658.4'012—dc21   2001019593

British Library Cataloguing in Publication Data is available.

Library of Congress Catalog Card Number: 2001019593
ISBN: 1–56720–475–9

First published in 2002

Quorum Books, 88 Post Road West, Westport, CT 06881
An imprint of Greenwood Publishing Group, Inc.
www.quorumbooks.com

Printed in the United States of America

The paper used in this book complies with the
Permanent Paper Standard issued by the National
Information Standards Organization (Z39.48–1984).

10 9 8 7 6 5 4 3 2 1

Contents

Figures

Foreword

Business planning in today's environment is indeed a challenging assignment. On the one hand, the twin forces of globalization and technological change are making the job of forecasting future conditions extremely difficult for any business, be it large or small. Second, the arrival of alternative business models and new competitors brought about by the Internet revolution requires constant updating of business strategies. Finally, most businesses are finding that the speed of change and complexity of the competitive landscape necessitates the use of business alliances and other forms of intercorporate collaboration that call for enormous flexibility and diversity in operations.

Wesley Truitt's approach to business planning is unique in that it takes into account all of this complexity and yet renders it manageable. By following a systematic and incremental approach, he provides an excellent guide to the do's and don'ts of planning. The book is rich in examples that bring realism to the principles and tools that he advocates, making them user-friendly and practical. Yet Dr. Truitt's prescriptions and advice are firmly anchored in solid academic research. His own background in industry, research and academia is clearly at the foundation of this considerable value added.

In addition to synthesizing much of the current literature on strategic planning, the book also combines principles, analytical techniques and examples from other relevant areas of management science, economics, political science, history and public policy. It incorporates these disciplines in ways that mutually reinforce and underpin the planning process, and are designed to stimulate the reader to consider alternative perspectives and insights. This eclectic interdisciplinary approach makes the book a valuable addition to the body of literature on corporate planning.

Two other things are especially noteworthy in Dr. Truitt's treatment of the subject. First, he builds the planning process step by step, from broad issues involving corporate vision and values to the nitty-gritty of integrating operational plans into an overall strategy, and on to detailed suggestions for control and implementation. Second, the book has enormous breadth, as Chapter 4 on environmental assessment illustrates. It ranges from the role of industry transformations in autos and computers (including the strategies of some key players in both) to detailed examples of how changes in the "rules of the game" in countries ranging from Russia to France affect the planning process. This chapter alone is worth the price of admission.

In conclusion, I found this book to be an extremely useful and practical guide to the critical task of strategic planning in our new economic environment. As the title implies, it is both comprehensive and relevant. I recommend it with equal fervor to someone starting a new business, to an experienced executive overseeing a global business unit, or to a business student who aspires to be either one of these.

José de la Torre
Professor of International Business Strategy
Anderson Graduate School of Management at UCLA

Preface

All organizations set goals and work to achieve them. Some succeed but many do not. The purpose of this book is to equip leaders with a valuable management tool to increase their probability of success by providing a comprehensive planning process. When you plan for success, the chances are greatly increased that you will achieve it. When you do not plan, or plan for anything less than success, the outcome will likely be self-confirming.

A plan is like a road map, laying out a route to get you from where you are now to where you want to be. Arriving at "where you want to be" is "success." This is the achievement of your objective, fulfillment of your goal. A properly laid-out business plan is, like a road map to a motorist, an invaluable guide for decision making throughout the journey—identifying the end point, plotting the route, checking your progress as you travel from place to place, correcting your course as external (weather or road) conditions may change, and providing a means for estimating the cost of resources (tanks of gasoline) and time (miles per day) needed to arrive at the end. Would you start a trip without a map? Would you start a business without a plan?

"Hope for the best and plan for the worst" is an adage that has no place in the management of an enterprise. Always plan for success. No general enters a battlefield without a battle plan, and no battle plan is a plan for defeat. All battle plans are plans for victory. Leaders must plan to succeed in war and in business. Successful leaders embrace success. They understand it represents achievement of a goal, the result of a plan fulfilled.

Planning for success also requires the application of all the resources necessary to achieve the chosen goal. Some individuals and many businesses say they want to achieve a particular objective, but they fail to do all the things within their means necessary to make it happen. Success requires commitment. Making the commitment to invest enough capital into the business, to hire enough employees to operate the business properly, to lease enough space, to spend enough money on advertising—all are examples of committing to succeed. Take the risk of becoming a success.

This book is designed to be a useful, practical guide for practitioners of business planning. It provides a comprehensive process and framework for undertaking the planning task from beginning to end. The book will assist managers of any size firm, from start-ups and small businesses to large established corporations, in both their preparation and use of a business plan. Managers of international businesses will benefit from the global applicability of the approach and the international examples presented.

Others, such as nonbusiness organizations, not-for-profits, and government agencies, will find this approach relevant for their purposes. It will be particularly useful for those hoping to enter the field of business planning. Students of business administration will benefit from the comprehensive approach to business planning presented here to learn how to construct business plans for class assignments and how to use them later in the operation of the firm. Finally, the general business reader should find the book thought-provoking.

This book blends the author's experiences from three areas:

(a) It benefits from the author's experiences in developing and writing business plans as a consultant for small and large companies in diverse industries, for not-for-profit organizations, and for federal government agencies.

(b) It builds on the author's experiences as the Manager-Planning and Analysis for a major division of a Fortune 100 company and also, on the corporate headquarters staff of the same firm, as Corporate Director-Policy Analysis and as Executive Assistant to the Chairman of the Board & Chief Executive Officer, reviewing all the divisional plans and participating in the preparation of the composite corporation-wide plan.

(c) Finally, the book synthesizes more than twenty years of teaching business planning and international business management to MBA and Executive MBA students at the Peter F. Drucker Graduate School of Management at Claremont Graduate University, at the Anderson Graduate School of Management at UCLA, and at the College of Business Administration at Loyola Marymount University in Los Angeles, where the author currently teaches Business Planning to MBA and Executive MBA students.

Over the past two decades the author has reviewed hundreds of business plans prepared by MBA students for class assignments and midcareer Executive MBA students for their own firms. The book benefits from this breadth of experience and is peppered with relevant real-world examples.

Every business plan should be a plan for success—for the successful implementation of the plan and ultimately for the success of the firm's business. Your success does not depend on using a particular style or format of planning material. It does depend on your careful, disciplined, insightful approach to each element of the process. Because formats are not central to success they are not emphasized in this book, and most firms prefer to use their own.

For those needing formats, there are ample planning books and software programs readily available to provide any number and type of formats—charts, spreadsheets, graphs, etc.—you could possibly need. The following books have useful formats:

William L. Megginson, Mary Jane Byrd, Charles R. Scott, Jr., and Leon C. Megginson, *Small Business Management: An Entrepreneur's Guide to Success*, 2nd ed. Toronto: Irwin, 1997.

Harold J. McLaughlin, *The Entrepreneur's Guide to Building a Better Business Plan: A Step-by-Step Approach*. New York: Wiley, 1992. (Contains software.)

Michael O'Donnell, *Writing Business Plans that Get Results: A Step-by-Step Guide*. Chicago: Contemporary Books, 1991.

Patrick D. O'Hara, *The Total Business Plan*, 2d ed. New York: Wiley, 1995. (Contains software.)

The specific objectives of this book are to provide the practitioner with (a) an understanding of the importance of business planning to the enterprise, (b) suggestions and information on how to approach the planning process and where to find resources, (c) a step-by-step guide and framework to prepare a business plan and use it to operate the company, and (d) examples drawn from real firms' businesses to illustrate key points. The book is written from the perspective of a practitioner who has written business plans to help you do the same.

In short, what you can expect to gain from this book is a clear understanding of what a business plan is, why it is needed, how to prepare it, and how to use it as a management tool to operate the firm. This is a comprehensive planning process for your enterprise's success.

Introduction to
Business Planning

This chapter is a general introduction to the planning process, answering the questions what is the purpose of planning, what are its major benefits, how important is it to plan, what is a definition of planning, how is a plan organized, what is included, and who should do it and why?

PURPOSES OF BUSINESS PLANNING

Business planning has three basic purposes. First, it provides a structure for identifying and examining alternative future courses of action open to an organization. Managers are usually too time-limited in the course of daily work to withdraw from current tasks and problem solving to take a long view—to stop to focus on the future, on the fact that there are choices available to the organization for its future, and to rationally and coolly evaluate those choices. The planning process provides that opportunity for careful reflection on at least an annual basis.

Second, planning provides the organization with a frame of reference for making current decisions. How often managers, when confronted with a major decision today, need to know where the company is headed in the longer run—to enable them to choose the course that leads down the chosen road. Thus, the plan provides a context for current decision making.

Finally, a purpose of planning is, within a vision of the organization's future, to establish objectives in the near term and the longer term to achieve that vision. Establishing goals in financial terms, by other quantitative measures (e.g., increasing the number of customers by x percent), or on qualitative criteria (such as quality improvement or customer satisfaction improvement) is an important purpose of planning because these goals become the yardstick for measuring performance. Establishing quarterly, annual, and five-year objectives for the organization provides management with a clear set of signposts for direction and a means of evaluating their own progress along the chosen path.

BENEFITS OF PLANNING

What are the benefits or values of business planning? Why do it?

1. Planning requires the organization to be conscious of the future. The process of performing a regularly scheduled planning activity requires the firm to examine its assumptions about the future in an orderly way and puts the organization's leaders in a "future-oriented" frame of reference. This is especially important for start-up firms and young companies whose focus is typically on today's problem—closing a sale, meeting an immediate cash flow problem, obtaining an urgently needed patent to protect emerging intellectual property, getting ready for a trade show, etc. Rarely is there time to think about next week, much less about next year.

2. Planning disciplines an organization to be conscious of the future, disciplines the organization to rationally evaluate its choices and prospects, disciplines members of the organization to work together to prepare the plan and more importantly to execute it together, and the process of planning helps transform entrepreneurial start-ups into more mature business organizations.

3. Planning emphasizes choice. If there were not a number of alternatives for the firm, there would be little value in performing a planning activity. Every firm, indeed every individual, has a myriad of choices for future activity. Identifying alternative paths, evaluating them, and then choosing a particular route is the essence of planning. As a process, planning keeps managers focused on the most critical issues and on the most important priorities—and stimulates choice making among them.

4. Planning helps to rationally structure present decisions in light of their future consequence. The process of planning reminds management of the futurity of present decisions and helps evaluate present decisions in light of their future consequence and impacts on the firm. It establishes a useful structure and guide for day-to-day decision making.

5. The planning process creates an orderly framework for consideration of present and future actions based on an assessment of the business environment. The process helps managers identify future opportunities and risks that stem from current unchanged behavior, from changed behavior, and from trends in the business environment that affect any chosen course of action. Clear, open-eyed evaluation of the emerging business climate affecting the organization is a critical task and provides important benefits

to managers. Careful analysis of the external environment will expose future opportunities as well as risks and will help "close the loop" in the planning process by using outcomes from that assessment to strengthen the planning process itself.

6. Planning reminds management that it has to manage. Top management must take the helm of the firm and steer. The act of steering is choice making. Management has choices, it must make choices, and whatever choices are made have future consequences and impacts on the firm. Making no choice is also a choice (letting go of the helm), which has impacts as consequential as those consciously made. Therefore, planning imposes a discipline on management to make choices by setting goals, choosing particular courses of action, and consciously determining its own fate as much as possible. The context of the planning process helps managers make choices that are rational and realistic, inspire achievement, and take into account risks and opportunities.

7. The business plan provides a means of communicating up, down, and across the organization the strategic direction managers have chosen. Everyone who is exposed to the plan is informed by it of management's direction. This act of communication is itself critical to the successful implementation of the plan down the path management has chosen to take. In this context, the process of planning will also surface and clarify issues that require management attention.

8. Planning inspires confidence and credibility. Managers gain confidence and self-assurance through the process of planning—gaining the security that they have a strong handle on their business and its direction. And confidence is gained in the execution of the plan—by knowing that there is a road map to follow and an organized way to track progress. Confidence is also inspired in others—suppliers, customers, investors—that the managers know what they are doing, have a clear sense of purpose, direction, and control over their business.

9. Planning provides a marketing tool for obtaining capital. Most venture capitalists, commercial banks, investment banks, other institutional lenders, and individual investors require a business plan before putting money into a new venture or before providing a line of credit for an ongoing operation.[1]

An example is Alcon Entertainment, a company Federal Express Founder and Chairman Fred Smith established in the late 1990s with his personal money. Alcon was the result of a 220-page business plan prepared by two young Princeton graduates, Andrew Kosove and Broderick Johnson, which Fred Smith said was "one of the most well-thought-out plans I had ever seen."[2] Their plan was essentially a strategy for lowering risks and increasing the odds for profitability in the motion picture business. The first movie, *Lost & Found*, lost money, but the second, *My Dog Skip*, was a hit, grossing $14.1 million in its first weekend of release, more than paying for its

$7 million production cost. Alcon then signed a five-year, ten-picture deal with Warner Bros. "The movie business," Smith stated, "is much more adaptable to business principles than most people believe it is."[3]

10. Planning makes managers think. Careful analysis of the business environment and rational choice making with respect to it requires thought. Knee-jerk reactions to current events and day-to-day business conditions place the firm in jeopardy. There needs to be a carefully considered path for the company's future growth to guide managers through challenging times. Plans are the product of thought and keep leaders and managers thinking—and focused. As the planner of a food services firm commented in a Conference Board report on changes in planning, "Less activity, more thinking; less form, more substance; less medium, more message."[4]

PLANNING DEFINED

There are numerous definitions of planning, though none has been universally accepted.[5] A particularly useful definition was coined by Peter F. Drucker as follows: Planning "is the continuous process of making present entrepreneurial (risk taking) decisions systematically and with the best possible knowledge of their futurity, organizing systematically the efforts needed to carry out these decisions, and measuring the results of these decisions against the expectations through organized, systematic feedback."[6]

Let us examine Drucker's definition. Planning is a process. It is not a single act of a manager, but rather it is a series of actions that occur over a period of time, taking into account numerous inputs from as many individuals as management is comfortable with. The process involves establishing objectives for the firm, defining detailed strategies and policies for implementing them, implementing decisions once options have been identified, reviewing the organization's performance against the plan, and incorporating observed performance into the next planning cycle. President Dwight Eisenhower, once the Army's top planner, is reported to have said, "Plans are nothing, planning is everything."[7]

The process is continuous. Drucker cautions that once the plan is made and published, management is not through with it; it cannot be safely tucked away on a bookshelf. On the contrary, the plan should be USED. The plan represents a critical path that has been chosen. Now the task is to go down that path and act on the decisions made in the plan, monitor progress, and continue implementation.

The planning process, according to Drucker, is systematic. It is not haphazard but careful, not casual but formal, not occasional but regular, not benign but active. This is a structured process that utilizes all available quantitative referents available to organize the firm's future behavior. Planning is comprehensive—systematic throughout the entire organization.

The process produces decisions. Without these, the process would have little value to the business. Decisions are the result of the process of analysis and choice making. Decisions need execution. In the process of execution, myriad additional decisions are made at all levels of management.

Finally, Drucker instructs that the process requires measuring. The measurements are performance against expectation, actual against planned. Without the plan there is no road map; without measurement of performance in an organized, systematic way there is no evaluation of progress against a metric. The plan is a road map for getting from point A to point B within a certain time period; constant reference to the chosen route of travel is essential as any journey progresses.

Christopher Columbus had no map to chart his first great voyage going west from point A (Spain) to find a new route to point B (the Indies in Asia). He arrived instead at point C—the New World, not Asia. The discovery of the Western Hemisphere was a great achievement, but Columbus failed in his mission without knowing it at the time. Indeed, Columbus made four voyages "without ever knowing where he had really been."[8] He had a goal that he did not achieve, but he serendipitously made an even more valuable discovery. And he did it all on government money.

Having defined what planning is, it is important to understand what planning is not. "Planning is not forecasting."[9] The two are closely tied together, but they are not identical. Forecasting is the projection of trends into the future or prediction of future events. "Planning," says George Steiner, "is not making future decisions." Planning requires "making current decisions in light of their futurity."[10] Decisions are made in the present to shape events in the future—that is the essence of planning. Planning does not eliminate risk; it enables managers to "choose rationally among risk-taking courses of action" to better understand and manage risks that devolve from today's decisions.[11] "The goal of planning is to create the future, not to forecast it."[12]

THE PLAN ITSELF

The business plan itself varies with the type of organization, the type of goals being set, and the scope of the plan in terms of time and overall coverage. Plans vary with the stage of the firm's development with respect to the plan's focus and content. All plans, regardless of these variations, can follow the same basic format—i.e., be structured similarly, even though the content will vary with respect to emphasis. Slavish adherence to a particular sequence in the format is not needed, provided all the elements are included somewhere in the plan. The sequence presented here is recommended because it works.

Entrepreneurial companies—those just getting started—would produce a plan that is focused on two goals: getting the company organized, up and

running, and focused toward obtaining capital. Such plans tend to be relatively brief, have considerable information regarding the nature of the
proposed business, define a business structure, contain biographical information regarding the firm's principals, and provide financial information
delineating the capital requirements and projected sales, earnings, and potential return on investment, together with a balanced evaluation of the
risks associated with that investment.

More mature organizations' plans will likely have the same structure but
contain different emphasis under each heading. Goals will be set, an analysis of the firm's strengths and weaknesses is essential, but ongoing companies need typically to spend more time and attention evaluating the
changing business environment, the competitive environment, and carefully
reevaluating their internal control and review mechanisms to ensure that
the plan is faithfully executed by all levels of management. Execution of
crisply defined operating goals in light of surrounding business conditions
is the essential task of the mature organization's plan.

All plans need to include strategic planning as well as tactical (or operating) planning. Strategic plans, sometimes called master strategy, lay out
the entire pattern of the basic company mission and the means to pursue
it.[13] Strategic plans include any change in the organization's mission, objectives, policies, and specific means to deploy resources in order to succeed
in a new direction.[14] "Strategic planning is, simply put, the process of positioning an organization so that it can prosper in the future."[15]

Tactical or operating plans provide for "the detailed deployment of resources to achieve strategic plans."[16] They define the specific resources
needed in particular areas of activity to achieve specific objectives, employing them in ways that are somewhat determined by circumstances and by
performance to date. Simply put, strategic plans provide the grand strategy
and operating plans provide the detailed steps to achieve it.

The structure of a typical business plan is fairly straightforward. It con-
sists of a number of sections or chapters each of which focuses on a particular aspect of the business for which the plan is written. The outline of
the plan that the author has developed, tested, and perfected for over two
decades for companies large and small, young and mature is presented
below in Figure 1.1. If you are more comfortable altering that sequence,
for example by beginning with the Mission Statement and then writing the
Vision Statement, by all means do it in that order. There is nothing magic
in the sequence presented. It is offered as a guide to the process, providing
a framework for your use. What is critical is that all the elements of the
plan be included in the final product—in whatever sequence makes the
most sense for your business.

The purpose and content of each of these chapters is explained in its
relevant chapter in this book. This is the sequence of the book's organization. Startup companies or those seeking financing using their plan as a

Figure 1.1
Outline of a Business Plan

Chapter	Title	Content
	Executive Summary	Concise summation of the plan's highlights
1	Vision	Long-term intent; what the firm wants to be
2	Goal/Mission/Strategy	Business purpose, objectives, and approach/focus
3	Resource Audit	Critical self-analysis of strengths and weaknesses
4	Environmental Assessment	Business climate within its industry and beyond
5	Competitive Assessment	Competitors within and outside its industry
6	Operational Plans	Specific objectives and pro forma
7	Control and Review	Mechanism and schedule for performance evaluation
8	Implementation	Procedures for plan's rollout and change management

marketing tool should also include a Fact Sheet about the business, a Company History, a Biographical Profile of the Principals, and a Summary of Intellectual Property (patents owned, key technologies, and unique processes).[17]

PLANNING IS A POWERFUL MANAGEMENT TOOL

Top management is often viewed as having an almost unlimited number of tools available to it for use in achieving its objectives. From the perspective of a Chief Executive Officer, this is a numbingly inaccurate overstatement. Surprisingly, many top executives perceive they have relatively few tools available for their direct use. A list of some of the most important top-level management tools follows:

- Hiring and firing: bringing fresh talent into the organization, removing marginal or unacceptable performers from the organization.
- Rewarding and punishing: providing financial compensation in the form of greater salary, bonus, stock, perks, and promotion to higher levels within the

organization with more elevated titles; or reducing compensation, removing perks, lowering organizational standing, transferring to less attractive locations or job circumstances.

- Providing positions of opportunity or denying them: promoting a person to higher levels within the organization to enable the person to have greater resources to demonstrate greater achievement, empowering the subordinate to additional accomplishment; or demoting the individual to lesser levels of influence within the firm and perhaps to less important geographic locations or to less important tasks.

- Providing social/psychological status: providing intangible but nevertheless real rewards to a favored individual by name recognition at an event, by entering a meeting room with the person or sitting with him/her during a meeting or at a company meal or other function, or being known to value the person's advice as an informal advisor or counselor; or by denying an employee any of the above by ignoring or isolating him or her and never providing any form of overt social recognition.

- Communicating within and without the organization: top management is provided a pulpit unlike anyone else in the organization to communicate downward within the company and to audiences on the outside the vision of the firm, its goals, mission, successes, new products and services, and other critical items of information.

- Acquiring or divesting: only top management has the authority within the firm to make decisions, with the board of directors' approval if a publicly held firm, to make acquisitions for the company, or to sell portions of the company.

- Affecting the external and internal business environments: top management more than anyone else within the organization has the levers of power needed to change the climate within the company and, if the company is large enough or important enough within its industry group, to possibly alter the external business climate for the good or ill of the firm.

- Planning: the planning process provides top management with a vehicle for obtaining input from the organization to mobilize their ideas and energies, to systematically evaluate a roster of choices for the firm's future, to evaluate the options carefully and rationally, to establish and communicate courses of action in a clear implementation program that itself provides yardsticks for measuring success or failure against the chosen course of action, and a means to discipline the organization to adhere to top management's direction.

Planning is one of the most powerful tools of management available to the organization's leadership. Using it carefully and regularly can provide immense benefits. Failing to use it or using it improperly denies oneself a most important weapon in management's arsenal.

STRATEGIC PLANNING

No business today can afford to simply wait for events in the larger business environment to occur and react to them, whether those events are new opportunities for growth and profit or whether they represent forces that will negatively impact their business operations or future prospects. Strategic planning is the technique used to try to understand the complexities of the longer-term external business environment and to chart a path through it for the sustained health and viability of the firm. A critical purpose of strategic planning is to enhance the organization's vision and business mission in light of management's understanding of future trends.

Businesses that are multinational or that seek to become global have a special need to undertake strategic planning because of the increased complexities and risks associated with international business conditions over those present in a purely domestic setting.[18] Multinational companies have unique choices of strategies to deal with unique circumstances they face in multiple business settings.[19]

David Aaker has labeled strategic planning "strategic market management" to emphasize that "strategy development needs to be driven by the market and its environment rather than being internally oriented. It also points out that the process should be proactive rather than reactive, and that the task should be to try to influence the environment in addition to responding to it."[20] Aaker identifies a number of potential benefits that accrue to the firm if it undertakes strategic market management or strategic planning. These benefits are:[21]

- Precipitate the consideration of strategic choices. Avoid being absorbed in day-to-day issues and letting the firm drift strategically by addressing strategic issues and making strategic decisions in a timely manner.
- Force a long-range view. There are strong pressures to manage with a short-term focus, which frequently leads to strategic errors.
- Make visible the resource allocation decision. Elevating the resource needs of all parts of the business to management attention and clearly focusing on resource needs will help avoid inertia in decision making (the same as last year), decisions being made by the accounting system, or by the political prowess of key managers.
- Provide methods to help strategic analysis and decision making. Numerous models and other techniques are now available to enable businesses to collect and analyze information and make difficult strategic choices.
- Provide a strategic management and control system. Managing a business strategically requires a focus on assets and skills needed, based on the strategic thrusts that have been chosen.
- Provide a communication and coordination system both horizontally and vertically. Problems and proposed strategies can be communicated up, down, and across the organization using strategic planning; the planning vocabulary adds precision to the communication process.
- Help a business cope with change. Most businesses today face rapidly changing and increasingly unpredictable environments, and the need for them to approach

the future by coping strategically is crucial. For businesses in highly stable markets facing little likelihood of change, the need is less critical.

Strategic planning will provide these benefits to any firm, large or small, domestic or global. It has particular value for businesses that:[22]

Need multifunctional strategies by using marketing strategies in a strategic role for functions other than marketing.

Need to achieve synergy among multiple markets.

Need to coordinate the strategies of multiple brands.

Need to coordinate among complex markets in multiple or layered channels, regional variations, or multiple elements of the marketing mix.

Many companies have these needs, but those that particularly have them are firms that are becoming international in their activities either by design or by chance. These companies especially need to focus on global strategy making.

George Yip believes a total global strategy has three separate components:[23]

- Developing the core strategy. This is the basis of sustainable strategic advantage. Without a sound core strategy, a worldwide business need not bother with global strategy.
- Internationalizing the core strategy. This is done through international expansion of activities and adaptation of the core strategy. Firms need to have mastered the basics of international business before attempting a global strategy.
- Globalizing the international strategy. The firm must integrate the strategy across countries by systematically analyzing industry conditions, "industry globalization drivers," by evaluating the costs and benefits of globalization, and by understanding the different ways in which a globalization strategy can be used through "global strategy levers."[24]

Thus, whether the firm is domestic, international, or global, it needs to undertake strategic planning. This is an essential part of the management task. It is the particular duty of top management to participate in this vital activity.

THE ROLE OF TOP MANAGEMENT IN STRATEGIC PLANNING

Planning is a top management responsibility. It is one of the essential tasks that a CEO or other organization's leader must perform. As George Steiner warned, "There can and will be no effective comprehensive corporate planning in any organization where the chief executive does not give it firm support and make sure that others in the organization understand his depth of commitment."[25]

Recent research indicates that the role of the top manager or the top management team in the development of long-range planning strategy is a more complex matter than generally perceived. Top managers may not "own" the strategy-making process as forthrightly as it might appear. One study sees four possible ownership postures that members of top management may take: mature involvement, abdication, frustration, and detachment.[26]

- Mature involvement includes strong acceptance of strategic responsibility for the firm by top management; top management engages in robust debate, respects their colleagues' contributions, and accepts the outcome of the strategy debate.
- Abdication is the form of involvement in the strategy debate where top management does not internalize it, prefers not to take responsibility for setting strategic direction, will critique strategies suggested by others, and largely passes the buck to other executives.
- Frustration is a process in which the chief executive desires to take ownership of the strategic planning process but feels excluded from the real debate and real decisions, resulting in frustration, anger, subversion of the strategy, or simple disillusion and resignation.
- Detachment is a process that excludes the top executive from the process, but he is comfortable with that, preferring operational or other forms of executive activity and hoping strategy issues will "go away" or be handled by others.

Only in the case of "mature involvement" will top management perform its role in the strategic planning process properly—by participating in it fully, "owning" the process, and ensuring that the outcome of the process is a strategy that will be supported and implemented. In the other three cases, the strategy-planning process will be undermined, top management may be perceived as threatening to the process, and the implementation of the strategy could be sabotaged by top management. Top management has to have a "felt inclusion in the strategy process" and has to internalize "the responsibility for setting and implementing strategy."[27]

The proper role of top management is critical in today's planning process, which has become more team-based, more participatory, and more democratic. The annual planning cycle, led by a large corporate planning staff, has largely been replaced during corporate downsizing of the 1980s and early 1990s by a new structure centered on debate by several levels of management on strategic issues. The General Electric Company's "Workout" process and 3M Company's "Templates on the Screen" process are examples of companies making wider use of teams, greater use of strategy software, and moving toward real-time strategy.[28]

Since all strategy is made under uncertainty,[29] top managers not only need to be personally involved, "own" the process, and use teams to ensure participation in the formulation and execution process of the strategy; they also need to equip themselves with the latest tools to assist in the process.

Some of the most recent developments in management science that can be quite helpful to top management in this new age of high-risk/high-payoff decision making in incredibly complex, uncertain times are the following:[30]

- Scenario planning. These techniques provide managers help in planning strategy under conditions of uncertainty.[31]
- Game theory. These techniques provide understanding for uncertainties based on competitors' conduct.[32]
- Agent-based models. These techniques provide simulation models to help understand complex interactions in a variety of situations, including markets.[33]
- Real options. These valuation models help to correctly value investments in learning and flexibility.[34]

With the aid of these and other recent developments and methodologies, senior management can approach the strategic-planning task with greater confidence in the success of the outcome.

STRATEGIC PLANNING TODAY

The process of strategic planning has evolved over the past half-century from detached central corporate staffs to greater involvement by all levels of management.[35] Strategic planning as a legitimate, necessary business function has survived attacks on its costs and numbers and even attacks by some on the very heart of its assumed role.[36] It has evolved, refocused, and become more iterative and interactive. By the late 1990s, it had been "reinvented," wrote Gary Hamel. "The challenge is to invent anew the conduct of strategy in ways that make it intensely important to companies struggling to maintain their vitality in the innovate-or-die environment of the new economy."[37]

The MOST process is typically used in strategy classes and is still employed in some large corporations today: it involves Mission, Objectives, Strategy, and Tactics. This process suggests there is an orderly structure to the development of strategy that managers should follow. First, choose a mission, then define the near-term objectives to move toward the mission's fulfillment, and then develop a strategy to achieve the objectives using short-term operating decisions or tactics to implement the strategy. Yet, "[t]he process of developing a winning strategy is much more messy, experimental, and interactive; and it is driven from the bottom up," say two management experts.[38]

The MOST process's seemingly textbook order with rigid timetables should rarely be followed because it will likely not generate the profound insights and fundamentally new ideas needed by today's firms. What is needed is for managers to define a purpose, discover insights, and combine the two into a strategy. This is a puzzling process that confounds us often because people are prone to impose timetables for strategy preparation that do not allow for the development of insights and their inclusion in the process.[39]

Gary Hamel distinguishes planning from strategizing, saying the latter is "revolutionary" and "subversive" in that it should challenge orthodoxy and become a "quest" for new ideas and models.[40] To close in on the deep secrets of the process of corporate vitality and self-renewal, he has identified five preconditions for the emergence of strategy:[41]

1. New voices: Expand the participation in the process, bring in new constituencies where diversity lurks, especially young people; the process should be pluralistic and deeply participative.
2. New conversations: "Opportunities for new insights are created when one juxtaposes previously isolated knowledge in new ways."
3. New passions: Unleash the deep sense of discovery that lies within people to invest their energies in finding new wealth-generating strategies and to share in an exciting future.
4. New perspectives: Put new conceptual lenses on people to gain new perspectives about themselves, their customers, and competitors to "reconceive" their opportunities.
5. New experiments: Launch small, risk-avoiding experiments in the marketplace to maximize the company's rate of learning about which strategies will and won't work.

STRATEGIC LEADERSHIP

Today, strategic planning has emerged in the form of strategic leadership. After a period of downsizing and reengineering, firms recognize the essential need for strategic thinking, for focus, and for leadership.[42] Strategic planning is a useful way for leaders to gain learning skills such as conceptualization and imagination through scenario building, raising the capacity of leaders to think strategically.[43]

Critical elements in the process of strategic leadership, as illustrated by Jack Welch, CEO at General Electric, are the following:[44]

- Strategy is not conducted as an annual event but as a continuous dialogue taking place throughout the year. For example, after being GE's CEO for just three years, Jack Welch scrapped the company's fabled but laborious strategic-planning system because it kept managers from doing their main job, running the business, and because it took too long for serious issues to reach the top. His new planning system was based on operating plans that could be changed without formal meetings if circumstances warranted, plus a system of running reviews and the long-standing monthly financial reporting system.[45]

• Strategy discussions are focused on a few strategic issues, not operational plans. As Welch said, "By the time [the problem] gets to the top, it has become a solution, not a problem."[46] Welch's new approach was "real time planning," centering on a five-page strategy playbook that had simple one-page answers to five questions relating to current market dynamics, competitors' activities, GE's responses, and the most important competitive threat over the upcoming three years, together with GE's planned response.[47]

• Corporate strategy staffs are replaced by corporate teams at the director level who work on corporate projects like strategic alliances and joint ventures, entry into new markets, etc. These are small staffs that work closely with senior executives at headquarters and divisions. If more manpower is needed, external consultants are brought in. Welch's "lean and agile" dogma at GE included the reduction of the 200-person corporate strategic-planning staff he inherited, which in a highly symbolic move he cut by 50 percent.[48]

• Strategy consultants work with top management teams to benchmark performance, identify trends, do thinking outside the box, and help formulate corporate vision. Consultants help identify gaps between corporate vision and strategies that are being discussed by various business units.

• Management then undertakes to align the organization behind the strategy, developing policies and processes, new structures, information systems, and people consistent with it.

• The task then shifts to implementation of the strategy:
—Initiate or deepen management training in shareholder value or balanced scorecard approach.
—Develop learning companies that focus on developing human assets.
—Adopt participative management and employee empowerment.
—Adopt techniques that encourage upward feedback, individually and in groups.

Strategic leadership is the new model for success. It depends on a clear personal commitment to the process by the CEO and the top management team, and it also depends on all levels of management "buying in" to the process to have the feeling of ownership of its outcome. This is a powerful process that can harness the creative instincts and the insights of line managers as well as staff personnel to help top leaders focus the firm toward a clear path into the future and together to achieve it. It is especially applicable for global firms.

CONCLUSION

Although there is no single right way to plan—a best practice based on a particular time-tested process—all effective planning processes share three critical common features. They are clear about the value they are trying to create, have well-defined objectives based on their leaders' insights, and provide a mechanism for winning buyin throughout the business.[49] "Structure follows strategy," wrote Peter Drucker. "Strategy determines what the key activities are in a given business."[50] And strategy charts the course for the firm to steer successfully into the future.

Now let us turn to the actual writing of the business plan. The material that follows is in the sequence recommended for your plan's presentation. The actual sequence you use to undertake the writing of the plan is up to you. Develop the plan's chapters in the order that makes most sense for your firm and in the order in which the insights come to you most easily and productively. At the end of the creative process, the plan should be complete—that is, have all of the chapters that follow, preferably in the sequence presented for ease of reading and understanding by your audience, beginning with the Executive Summary and concluding with Implementation.

EXECUTIVE SUMMARY OF THE BUSINESS PLAN

This is the most important part of the plan's presentation. If you cannot grab the reader's attention here, he or she may not read on. The executive summary simply must be a well-written, clear, and fair representation of what is included in the complete plan—in summary form.

What follows is a checklist of the characteristics of a well-crafted executive summary:[51]

- Be brief. Keep it to one or two pages. It is a summary after all. You do not have to make your entire case in these few paragraphs. This is intended for executive reading, to provide a quick overview of the entire plan. It is not the plan itself. It takes time to write a good, short executive summary; long ones are written quickly.

- Be focused. Confine the discussion to the main, essential points of the plan. Rambling narrative, self-congratulatory commentary, detailed exposition of some scientific breakthrough are inappropriate in a summary.

- Be persuasive. Write your summary based on your belief in the plan. Use simple declarative sentences. Be positive. Your purpose is to entice the reader to want more. This plan is going to be a success, and you want that message to come through.

- Be honest. If there are major problems or weaknesses in the firm that the plan identifies or there are serious shortcomings in the plan itself, state them to alert the reader that they exist in the longer narrative that follows. The summary is not just the "good stuff." It is also a summary of the problems and critical issues and how they will be overcome, if possible.

- Be precise. State for whom the plan is intended. Name the intended audience for the plan: managers, employees, investors, etc. Typically, a plan targets a number of audiences. If the plan's main purpose is to raise capital, state that clearly and outline the terms of the deal, equity or debt financing, payback period, rates of return, etc.

- Be factual. Outline the facts: what is your product or service? why are they unique or important? what are your markets? who is the competition? why you believe you can beat it? what are your planned revenues and returns? what are your strengths and weaknesses? who will manage the business? in what stage of development is the business?

The summary is like a headline: briefly announce the chosen strategy, why it was selected, the ways and means it will be implemented, why it is important to the reader, and telegraph that message—which is explained fully in the body of the plan.

NOTES

1. See Patrick D. O'Hara, *The Total Business Plan*, 2d ed. (New York: Wiley, 1995), for a discussion of using a business plan as a marketing tool for obtaining financing.

2. Claudia Eller and James Bates, "FedEx Chief Banks on Film-Making Package," *Los Angeles Times*, March 14, 2000, p. C1.

3. Ibid., p. C1.

4. Rochelle O'Connor, *Facing Strategic Issues: New Planning Guides and Practices* (New York: A Research Report from the Conference Board, Report No. 867, 1985), p. 5.

5. George A. Steiner, *Top Management Planning* (New York: Macmillan, 1969), p. 5. For a number of definitions, see George A. Steiner, *Strategic Planning* (New York: The Free Press, 1979), pp. 346–47.

6. Peter F. Drucker, "Long-Range Planning," *Management Science 5* (April 1959), pp. 238–39, cited in Steiner, *Top Management Planning*, p. 7. Italics deleted. In another work Drucker uses essentially these same words to define "strategic planning"; see Peter F. Drucker, *Management: Tasks, Responsibilities, Practices* (New York: Harper & Row, 1973), p. 125. From *Management: Tasks, Responsibilities, Practices* by Peter F. Drucker. Reprinted by permission of Butterworth Heinemann.

7. Quoted in David A. Aaker, *Developing Business Strategies*, 4th ed. (New York: Wiley, 1995), p. 3.

8. Norman Davies, *Europe: A History* (New York: Oxford University Press, 1996), p. 511. For a more complete discussion of Columbus's voyages, see J. H. Parry, *The Age of Reconnaissance: Discovery, Exploration and Settlement, 1450–1650* Berkeley, CA: University of California Press, 1981.

9. Steiner, *Top Management Planning*, p. 17. Drucker makes the same point; Drucker, *Management: Tasks, Responsibilities, Practices*, p. 123.

10. Steiner, *Top Management Planning*, p. 18.

11. Drucker, *Management: Tasks, Responsibilities, Practices*, p. 125. From *Management: Tasks, Responsibilities, Practices* by Peter F. Drucker. Reprinted by permission of Butterworth Heinemann.

12. O'Connor, *Facing Strategic Issues*, p. 27.

13. William H. Newman, "Shaping the Master Strategy of Your Firm," *California Management Review* 8 (spring 1967), p. 77. See also Alfred D. Chandler, Jr., *Strategy and Structure* (Cambridge, MA: MIT Press, 1962), p. 13.

14. James Brian Quinn defines strategy as follows: "A strategy is the pattern or plan that integrates an organization's major goals, policies, and action sequences into a cohesive whole. A well-formulated strategy helps to marshal and allocate an organization's resources into a unique and viable posture based on its relative internal competencies and shortcomings, anticipated changes in the environment, and contingent moves by intelligent opponents." James Brian Quinn, *Strategies for Change: Logical Incrementalism* (Homewood, IL: Irwin, 1980), p. 7.

15. Clark Holloway, *Strategic Planning* (Chicago: Nelson-Hall, 1986), p. 16.

16. Steiner, *Top Management Planning*, p. 37.

17. For useful formats for these items, see Michael O'Donnell, *Writing Business Plans that Get Results* (Chicago: Contemporary Books, 1991), pp. 21–34.

18. Hans Schollhammer, "Long-Range Planning in Multinational Firms," *Columbia Journal of World Business* VI, no. 5 (September–October 1971), pp. 79–86.

19. Yves L. Doz, "Strategic Management in Multinational Companies," *Sloan Management Review* (winter 1980), pp. 27–46; the article identifies strategies MNCs can use to address the conflict between the economic and political imperatives within a business in differing national settings.

20. Aaker, *Developing Business Strategies*, p. 13.

21. Ibid., pp. 17–18.

22. George S. Yip, "Who Needs Strategic Planning?" *Journal of Business Strategy* 6 (fall 1985), pp. 30–41, cited in Aaker, *Developing Business Strategies*, p. 18.

23. George S. Yip, *Total Global Strategy: Managing for Worldwide Competitive Advantage* (Englewood Cliffs, NJ: Prentice-Hall, Business School Edition, 1995), p. 4.

24. Ibid., p. 6. Yip's entire book is devoted to the third bullet.

25. Steiner, *Top Management Planning*, p. 88; see pp. 90–95 for a discussion of the CEO's role. Indeed, the title of Steiner's seminal work is Top Management Planning (emphasis added).

26. Cliff Bowman and Andrew Kakabadse, "Top Management Ownership of the Strategy Problem," *Long Range Planning* 30, no. 2 (April 1997), p. 200.

27. Ibid., p. 200.

28. Bernard Taylor, "The Return of Strategic Planning—Once More with Feeling," *Long Range Planning* 30, no. 3 (June 1997), p. 334. For GE's "Work-out" process, see Robert Slater, *Jack Welch and the GE Way* (New York: McGraw-Hill, 1999), pp. 149–56.

29. Hugh Courtney, Jane Kirkland, and Patrick Viguerie, "Strategy under Uncertainty," *Harvard Business Review*, November–December 1997.

30. Cited in Courtney, Kirkland, and Viguerie, "Strategy under Uncertainty," p. 78.

31. See Kees van der Heijden, *Scenarios: The Art of Strategic Conversation* (New York: Wiley, 1996). See also Pierre Wack, "Scenarios: Uncharted Waters Ahead," *Harvard Business Review*, September–October 1985, and Pierre Wack, "Scenarios: Shooting the Rapids," *Harvard Business Review*, November–December 1985.

32. See Adam M. Brandenberger and Barry J. Nalebuff, "The Right Game: Use Game Theory to Shape Strategy," *Harvard Business Review*, July–August 1995.

33. See John L. Casti, *Would-Be Worlds: How Simulation Is Changing the Frontiers of Science* (New York: Wiley, 1997).

34. See Timothy A. Luehrman, "What's It Worth?" *Harvard Business Review*, May–June 1997.

35. Ronald N. Paul, Neil B. Donavan, and James W. Taylor, "The Reality Gap in Strategic Planning," *Harvard Business Review*, May–June 1978, pp. 124–30 for a discussion of the evolution of planning.

36. See Henry Mintzberg, *The Rise and Fall of Strategic Planning* (Englewood Cliffs, NJ: Prentice-Hall, 1994). Professor Mintzberg has written, "Strategic planning isn't strategic thinking. One is analysis, and the other is synthesis." Also, "the most successful strategies are visions, not plans." Henry Mintzberg, "The Fall and Rise of Strategic Planning," *Harvard Business Review*, January–February 1994, p. 107.

37. Gary Hamel, "Strategy Innovation and the Quest for Value," *Sloan Management Review*, winter 1998, p. 10.

38. Andrew Campbell and Marcus Alexander, "What's Wrong with Strategy?" *Harvard Business Review*, November–December 1997, p. 46.

39. Ibid., pp. 46, 51.

40. Gary Hamel, "Strategy as Revolution," *Harvard Business Review*, July–August 1996, p. 71.

41. Hamel, "Strategy Innovation and the Quest for Value," pp. 12–13; the quotation is on p. 12.

42. Act like a leader, not a manager, urges GE's CEO, Jack Welch; see Slater, *Jack Welch and the GE Way*, pp. 15–29.

43. Arie de Geus, "Planning as Learning," *Harvard Business Review*, March–April 1988.

44. Taylor, "The Return of Strategic Planning," pp. 342–43.

45. Howard Banks, "General Electric—Going with the Winners," *Forbes*, March 26, 1984, p. 102.

46. Ibid., p. 102.

47. Christopher A. Bartlett and Meg Wozny, "GE's Two-Decade Transformation: Jack Welch's Leadership," Harvard Business School, Case No. 9–399–150, Rev. January 6, 2000, p. 3.

48. Ibid., p. 2.

49. Andrew Campbell, "Tailored, Not Benchmarked: A Fresh Look at Corporate Planning," *Harvard Business Review*, March–April 1999, p. 42.

50. Drucker, *Management: Tasks, Responsibilities, Practices*, p. 75. From *Management: Tasks, Responsibilities, Practices* by Peter F. Drucker. Reprinted by permission of Butterworth Heinemann.

51. For an extensive checklist of items for an executive summary and worksheets, see Michael O'Donnell, *Writing Business Plans that Get Results: A Step-by-Step Guide* (Chicago: Contemporary Books, 1991), pp. 13–21.

Chapter 1

Vision Statement

The vision statement is a brief declaration of management's long-term intention for the firm's success. It is expressed in positive terms. For start-up firms the statement is a bit like a child's declaration of what he/she wants to be when he/she grows up. For a mature company, the statement declares management's intention for the long haul. In a sense the vision statement is an announcement of management's concept of the endgame—how managers hope things will turn out for the organization and where the firm will arrive in its chosen industry.

The vision is a broad, general statement announcing the focus and long-term strategic direction the firm intends to take. The statement can be qualitative, quantitative, or a mix of the two. The statement crystallizes the purpose and intended direction of the business. It declares "the dream" of the company's future—the dream realized. The statement may also give a sense of the values of the firm (for example, operating the company with a high sense of integrity), and it may declare a simple operating philosophy (for example, putting customers first).

The statement is useful as a means of communicating to employees, customers, and other stakeholders what the company is about. The statement should also challenge and inspire in its fundamentals—setting a lofty goal for future achievement, such as becoming the "best" in your industry.[1]

CORE VALUES OF THE FIRM

The vision for the future of the enterprise must be grounded in the fundamental core values of the firm. "Core values are the essential and en-

Figure 1.2
Core Purpose Is a Company's Reason for Being

Company	Core Purpose
3M	To solve unsolved problems innovatively
Cargill	To improve the standard of living around the world
Fannie Mae	To strengthen the social fabric by continually democratizing home ownership
Hewlett-Packard	To make technical contributions for the advancement and welfare of humanity
Mary Kay Cosmetics	To give unlimited opportunity to women
McKinsey & Co.	To help leading corporations and governments be more successful
Merck	To preserve and improve human life
Nike	To experience the emotion of competition, winning, and crushing competitors
Sony	To experience the joy of advancing and applying technology for the benefit of the public
Wal-Mart	To give ordinary folk the chance to buy the same things as rich people
Walt Disney	To make people happy

during tenets of an organization. A small set of timeless guiding principles, core values require no external justification; they have *intrinsic* value and importance to those inside the organization."[2] In addition to basic principles such as having an ethical operating style and concern for customers' welfare, the fundamental core values of the firm are typically expressed in the purpose of the firm, a summary phrase explaining the firm's reason for being. Examples of the core purpose of some leading organizations appear in Figure 1.2.[3]

Your enterprise needs to think through very carefully what its core values and purposes are and base its vision statement on them.

VISION AS A MOTIVATING FACTOR

The vision, based on enduring core values and purposes, should be "big, hairy, audacious" to inspire, stimulate, and motivate—"a big commitment that when people see what the goal will take, there's an almost audible gulp."[4] The vision should have a long time frame (ten to thirty years); be clear, compelling, and easy to grasp; and connect to the core values and purposes of the organization.[5] A corollary to having a bold, positive vision to stimulate achievement is the quest for power, to enable the achievement of the vision.[6]

Fear is also a motivator. When a leader asserts a vision to be achieved, that leader then becomes hostage to all the factors that can prevent the realization of the vision. Yet, once the leader has openly committed himself or herself to the vision, a sense of determination sets in to work hard to make the dream come true, despite all the scary possibilities that could produce failure.

Mike Grillo, Head of Production at DreamWorks SKG, illustrates this when describing the dynamics of the motion picture industry.[7] Once a producer commits him/herself to making a movie, lines up the financing, obtains the backing of a studio or independent production company, and has the leading actors under contract, the great motivator then becomes fear. In this instance the fear is that the audience will not find the storyline compelling, that the director will not do as good a job as hoped, that the stars will not perform to their prior levels of excellence, that the set locations chosen will not work out for any number of reasons, that on the opening day of release a competing film will siphon off the audience, and for these reasons the investors will lose money. The ultimate fear is that the film will be a flop, and you might not be invited back to make another. These fears motivate you to work harder to achieve your vision of a hit movie.

WHAT BUSINESS *SHOULD* YOU BE IN?

The vision statement should answer Peter Drucker's fundamental questions: What business will you be in? What business *should* you be in?[8] The "should" answer needs to precede the "will" answer, for to do otherwise might put the firm in a business that it possibly should not be in.

Examples of industries that a company might wish it were not in could include those that:

- generate a possible health risk for their customers (tobacco)
- have an ethics issue (employing children in offshore facilities)
- deal with an enemy country or potential enemy (oil production in Libya or Iraq)
- are based on technologies that could become obsolesced by new technologies (buggy whips versus automobiles)
- provide services that may no longer be needed, become economically nonviable, or become technologically irrelevant (ushers in movie theaters, tellers in banks, telephone switchboard operators).

Thus, determine what industry the firm should be in, and then plan to be in that industry. Crafting a wonderfully worded vision statement to direct the company into an abyss is a foolish and dangerous exercise.

HOW TO EXPRESS THE VISION

The vision statement requires the company to actually have a vision to express. Coming forward with some vague remark like former President George Bush made during the 1992 election campaign about "the vision thing" makes it clear that the firm has no vision of its future and that President Bush had no "vision" of America's future.

His son, however, stated a clear vision for government's role in America's future. In his first address to a joint session of Congress, President George W. Bush stated, "Our new governing vision says government should be active, but limited, engaged, but not overbearing." Earlier in the speech Bush had said, "Year after year in Washington, budget debates seem to come down to an old, tired argument: on one side, those who want more government, regardless of the cost; on the other, those who want less government, regardless of the need."[9]

George W. Bush staked out his vision squarely in the middle ground of the American political spectrum, spurning the Reagan Republican view that government is the problem and also rejecting the philosophy of the liberal wing of the Democratic Party that government is the major solution to domestic problems. President George W. Bush's crisply stated vision is centrist and pragmatic: use government when it can be useful and use private means when those are more appropriate.

Some eschew writing statements about vision, preferring foresight. "Vision connotes a dream or an apparition," write Hamel and Prahalad, "and there is more to industry foresight than a blinding flash of insight."

Industry foresight is based on deep insights into trends in technology, demographics, regulations, and lifestyles, which can be harnessed to rewrite industry rules and create new competitive space. While understanding the potential implications of such trends requires creativity and imagination, any "vision" that is not based on a solid foundation is likely to be fantastical. For this reason industry foresight is a synthesis of many people's visions.[10]

Others believe the vision is the statement of the "dream" of the firm's leader.[11] Just as a dream for a brighter future or a better day is usually expressed simply and briefly, so too should a vision statement. The Rev. Dr. Martin Luther King, Jr., in his famous speech on August 28, 1963 at the Lincoln Memorial in Washington, DC, stated, "I have a dream that one day the nation will rise up and live out the true meaning of its creed

. . . all men are created equal."[12] His dream was that *all* people would be accorded value not by the color of their skin but by the content of their character.[13]

This is a fine example of a vision statement expressed as a dream—it is clear in its meaning, simple and elegant in its presentation, focused in its message, and inspiring to others to want to achieve its fulfillment. Note Dr. King did not say on the steps of the Lincoln Memorial, "I have a strategic plan." He would have lost his audience and his message would not have been heard. What he did was communicate a vision as a "dream," a statement of hope for a future yet to come.

Examples of Firms' Visions

Some firms' names give instant information as to what businesses the organization is engaged in while others do not. "Sara Lee Corporation" provides insight into what that company does by using one of its best-known brand names as the moniker for the entire corporation. That brand name is well known for food products, especially baked goods. The vision statement for that company need not even mention the product line of the firm.

Similarly, Xerox, Exxon, and The Boeing Company do not need to mention their products/services in their corporate name because their company name is their well-recognized brand name, communicating instantly what industry they are in. Hilton Hotel Corporation and Hershey Foods Corporation have their industry's name included in their corporate name for immediate recognition of the nature of the business they are in—those brands being synonymous with hotels and chocolate.

General Dynamics Corporation is a company name less familiar to the general public, it is not a brand name, and it provides no help in identifying its industry or product line. Unless you know the company, you would not know it builds submarines and tanks.[14] Similarly, Navistar, Rockwell, and AMR need to identify themselves as builders of heavy trucks, industrial equipment, and the parent of American Airlines, respectively.

A firm that has its industry name included in its brand name is Bank of America. Hugh L. McColl, Jr., Chairman of the Board and CEO of Bank of America, following the acquisition of the previous BankAmerica Corporation by NationsBank, announced the fulfillment of his long-standing vision in the first Annual Report of the new, combined firm: "We achieve the dream of nationwide banking."[15] The newly merged bank is the largest bank in the country, has assets of $617 billion, retail branches in twenty-two states and the District of Columbia, serves clients in 190 countries, and does business with 80 percent of the *Fortune* Global 500.[16] McColl stated, "We took giant steps [in 1998] toward fulfilling our vision of providing a consistent and exceptional banking experience to all our clients and customers throughout the world."

The vision of the new Bank of America is summarized by McColl:

[I]t will be a nationwide bank with a strong position in all the country's best growth markets and the most comprehensive corporate client base in the industry. It will have the power and reach to serve these corporate clients anywhere in the world. It will have the scale and the capital power to invest in systems and products that will make banking easier and better for all its customers. And it will be a valued financial partner to individuals, small business and large corporations, creating broad, deep relationships over customers' lifetimes. This is the bank we're building.[17]

Motorola Inc. of Schaumburg, Illinois, has a clearly stated vision, which in its case is expressed as a "goal": "to provide customers with what they want, when they want it, with Six Sigma Quality and best-in-class cycle time."[18] Six Sigma means 3.4 defects per million, and it has been adopted by Motorola, GE, DuPont and other major firms as the foundation in their drive toward quality improvement. In Motorola's case the trophy achievement was their winning in 1988 the first Malcolm Baldridge National Quality Award. A decade later, in 1998, Motorola began applying Six Sigma "concepts to the realm of consumer preference—of delighting the customer."[19]

In 1984, while a freshman at the University of Texas, Michael Dell had a bold vision: to establish a company to make personal computers to a customer's exact specifications and to sell them directly to the customer avoiding the markup by retailers. He founded Dell Computer Corporation with $1,000. He quit college after one year, and two years later he was doing $60 million in sales.[20] From 1989 to 1999, Dell stock gained 36,000 percent, having repeatedly been the single best-performing stock in the Standard & Poor's 500, making Michael Dell a billionaire by age thirty.

Dell's vision forced industry leaders such as IBM, Apple, and Compaq to change the way they do business, and he stimulated a rival direct seller, Gateway, into the marketplace.[21] By first quarter 1999, Dell accounted for 12 percent of all computer industry sales and 55 percent of all industry profits[22] and was the second largest personal computer maker with 9.2 percent of the world's market share, behind Compaq with 13.4 percent. IBM had slipped to third place with 8.4 percent and continued to sell PCs at a loss.[23]

Fred Sands Realty, one of the nation's largest real estate brokers, had a vision statement: "To be recognized by the consumer and the industry as the most professional, ethical and highest quality real estate organization."[24] This simple "qualitative" statement sets a high standard for the thousands of associates in the firm and inspires client confidence.

CHARACTERISTICS OF A VISION STATEMENT

On a practical level a vision statement should have the following characteristics:

- Begin with the verb "to be," expressing a longer-term future outcome.
- Be brief: keep the statement to a sentence or two, no longer than a short paragraph.
- Focus the statement on a future point, where the organization wants to arrive.
- Do not focus on how to get to the end point; state only what it is.
- Be elegant in language to add inspiration and motivate achievement.
- Be bold, even daring, in your aspiration for future success.
- Be qualitative ("to become the best") and/or quantitative ("achieve 1,000 percent growth").
- Declare what business the firm should and will be in.
- Provide information as to the nature of the business or industry, if that is not clear from the company's name or brand.

By following these guidelines, top management can craft a well-thought-through, simple declaration of their dream and communicate that dream to inspire others.

The Fred Sands Realty vision statement is an excellent example of one that is very well crafted: one sentence in which the firm's leader announced his intent to be "recognized" as the best by his entire industry and by his customers in the areas of activity that are important in his industry—highest ethical performance, solid professionalism, and excellence in the quality of services provided. All of this is implied and communicated in a single sentence.

Another clear-cut example is Bell Atlantic, which had revenues of $33 billion and operating income of $8.4 billion in 1999. This is a communications company, now Verizon after the merger with GTE, which provides wired phone service for domestic local and long-distance, domestic wireless, global wireless, high-speed data, Internet access, and numerous international communications partnerships, and is the world's largest publisher of directory information. Bell Atlantic's vision statement: "To be the customer's first choice for communications and information services in every market we serve, domestic and international."[25]

APPROACH TO WRITING A VISION STATEMENT

How do you get started writing your vision statement? A useful approach is to begin with Michael Porter's three "generic strategies" and determine which one is appropriate for your company.[26] For clarity and consistency, select only one generic strategy.[27]

- Cost leadership. Achieve low-cost producer in your industry and compete on an industry-wide basis.
- Differentiation. Develop features of a product or service that distinguish it from competitors' and compete on an industry-wide basis.
- Focus. Serve only a segment of the market by cost leadership or differentiation, rather than competing in most or every segment of the market.

Cost leadership in the computer industry is the generic strategy in Michael Dell's vision. He could price his product lower than the competition by tailoring it to the specifications of the customer and by direct selling via the telephone or Internet, as opposed to selling through retailers who would add their markup. Further, he drove down the cost of production through streamlined factory operations, outsourcing virtually all components, having just-in-time delivery, and fierce inventory control. Dell stated that Hewlett-Packard had sixty to seventy days of inventory in the last quarter of 1998, whereas Dell Computer had six days of inventory. "That difference accounts for a measurable problem. If the value of inventory declines at a half a percent or 1% a week," said Mr. Dell, "that means that the customers have to pay quite a bit more or HP loses money. . . . That's without factoring in the cost of the dealer, which is an added markup."[28]

In general, says Porter, "[a] firm has a cost advantage if its cumulative cost of performing all value activities is lower than competitors' costs," as well as potential competitors' costs.[29]

Differentiation requires the firm to do something unique from its competitors that is valuable to buyers. This strategy "stems from uniquely creating buyer value."[30] The strategy requires the firm to develop attributes of a product or service that are differentiated from or superior to competitors' products or services—or are simply perceived to be so. The underlying objective is to earn superior returns on investment through a pricing policy that takes advantage of the real or perceived superiority stemming from the differentiation.

Caterpillar follows a differentiation strategy, emphasizing superior quality, reliable products, a strong dealer organization able to support the products in the field, and the capability to deliver anywhere in the world quickly.[31] Many consumer brand name products' manufacturers follow a differentiation strategy, spending considerable sums of money advertising the virtues of their brand over others that may be priced lower to develop and reinforce consumer brand loyalty.

Focus strategy serves the needs of a particular market segment and can be achieved either through cost leadership or by differentiation. A focus strategy can be a means for achieving cost advantage because it rests on using focus to control cost drivers, reconfiguring the value chain, or both.[32] This strategy enables a firm that lacks the capability or determination to compete industry-wide to successfully position itself in the limited market segment it has chosen.

By employing a focused regional strategy *and* a reconfigured value chain emphasizing strict cost control, Southwest Airlines adopted the vision of a focus strategy—limited passenger service, very low ticket prices, high air-craft utilization, frequent departures, lean and productive crews—which enables it to successfully compete, gain, and sustain market share profita-bly.[33]

Top management must be quite clear which of these three strategies it is choosing. To be successful, only one strategy should be chosen, and once chosen must be pursued relentlessly for the firm to have continuing success. This selection process is a critical precursor to writing the vision statement, and the selected strategy should be inculcated in that statement as the core business strategy for the firm. Fred Sands Realty based its vision on "dif-ferentiation," i.e., providing superior service.

Bear in mind that the ultimate objective is the growth and viability of the enterprise. That can be achieved only through earning a satisfactory return on investment on a continuing, sustained basis.[34] The generic strat-egy selected must have this as its objective because a profit stream is the sole means by which a business is compensated for risk. The selected core strategy expressed or implied in the vision is the pathway to that profit stream.

CONCLUSION

Writing the vision statement is the most intellectually challenging part of the planning process. It can take hours and hours, spread over many days to think it through, write the statement, review it, test it, and make certain it crystallizes the dream and communicates it with spirit and accuracy. Even though this is the shortest part of the plan, the vision statement is the most critical. This is the first element of the plan and its bedrock. You have to drill deep to get it just right at the beginning or the rest of the plan will be ungrounded and an unreliable guide into the future for the company's man-agement.

Some firms begin the planning process by writing not the vision statement but rather the mission statement, others with the goal or strategy statement, still others with an evaluation of their strengths and weaknesses. Each of these approaches has merit, and each clearly is necessary at some point in this "messy" planning process. There is no magical benefit to doing things in any particular order, beginning either with the vision statement or with one of the other statements. Do them in whatever order is most comfortable and productive for you—as long as you write all of them before the plan is completed.

Experience has taught that the firm's vision is what motivates, inspires, and coalesces the management team. Defining it well at or near the beginning of the process encapsulates the entire raison d'être of the business and makes the remaining portions of the planning task easier and more consistent.

NOTES

1. Gerard H. Langeler, "The Vision Trap," *Harvard Business Review*, March–April 1992, p. 42, warns: "Grand, abstract visions can be *too* inspirational. The company may wind up making more poetry than product."

2. James C. Collins and Jerry I. Porras, "Building Your Company's Vision," *Harvard Business Review*, September–October 1996, p. 66. For a discussion of core values, see Jim Collins and Jerry I. Porras, *Built to Last: Successful Habits of Visionary Companies* (New York: HarperBusiness, 1994).

3. Adapted from Collins and Porras, "Building Your Company's Vision," p. 69.

4. Collins and Porras, "Building Your Company's Vision," pp. 72, 75. Example: Wal-Mart in 1990 aspired to become a $125 billion company by the year 2000.

5. Jim Collins, "Turning Goals into Results: The Power of Catalytic Mechanisms," *Harvard Business Review*, July–August 1999, p. 72.

6. David C. McClelland and David H. Burnham, "Power Is the Great Motivator," *Harvard Business Review*, (January–February 1995. "A good manager is not one who needs personal success or who is people oriented—but one who has a need for power," p. 126.

7. Remarks by Michael Grillo at Western Academy of Management, annual conference, March 25, 1999, Redondo Beach, California.

8. Peter F. Drucker, *Management: Tasks, Responsibilities, Practices*, 4th ed. (New York: Harper & Row, 1973), pp. 74–94. From *Management: Tasks, Responsibilities, Practices* by Peter F. Drucker. Reprinted by permission of Butterworth Heinemann.

9. *New York Times*, February 28, 2001, p. A14.

10. Gary Hamel and C. K. Prahalad, "Competing for the Future," *Harvard Business Review*, July–August 1994, p. 128.

11. For a discussion on the idea that a winning strategy begins with the CEO's vision, see Robert Michael, *Strategy Pure and Simple II*, rev. ed. (New York: McGraw-Hill, 1998), p. 22ff.

12. Rev. Dr. Martin L. King, Jr., cited in Arthur M. Schlesinger, Jr., ed., *The Almanac of American History* (New York: Barnes and Noble Books, 1993), p. 564.

13. For a discussion of Dr. King's speech, see Taylor Branch, *Parting the Waters: America in the King Years, 1954–63* (New York: Simon & Schuster, 1988), pp. 881–83.

14. General Dynamics also builds destroyers and business jets, and is adding defense electronics and communications to its business lines; *Los Angeles Times*, June 23, 1999, p. C3.

15. Hugh L. McColl, Jr., Chairman and CEO, Bank of America *1998 Summary Annual Report*, undated, p. 2.

16. Ibid., pp. 16, 20.

17. Ibid., p. 3.

18. Cited in Bernard Taylor, "The Return of Strategic Planning—Once More with Feeling," *Long Range Planning* 30, no. 3 (June 1997), p. 339.

19. Motorola, Inc., *1998 Summary Annual Report*, undated, p. 5.

20. Michael Dell, *Direct from Dell: Strategies that Revolutionized an Industry* (New York: HarperCollins, 1999), pp. 12–13, 26.

21. *Los Angeles Times*, March 8, 1999, p. C1.

22. *Los Angeles Times*, June 23, 1999, p. C3.

23. *Los Angeles Times*, April 24, 1999, p. C2.

24. Fred Sands Realty, Los Angeles, CA, fact sheet, dated December 1997. In December 2000 Fred Sands agreed to be acquired by Coldwell Banker; *Los Angeles Times*, December 2, 2000, p. C1.

25. *Bell Atlantic 1999 Annual Report*, dated March 2000, p. 2.

26. Michael E. Porter, *Competitive Strategy* (New York: Free Press, 1980), pp. 35–40. Adapted with the permission of The Free Press, a Division of Simon & Schuster, Inc., from *Competitive Strategy: Techniques for Analyzing Industries and Competitors* by Michael E. Porter. Copyright © 1980, by The Free Press.

27. It is possible to combine two of the strategies (cost leadership and differentiation) because of recent advances in production technologies enabling firms to gain the benefits of both strategies; see Charles W. L. Hill and Gareth R. Jones, *Strategic Management: An Integrated Approach*, 5th ed. (Boston: Houghton Mifflin, 2001), pp. 210–11.

28. *Los Angeles Times*, March 8, 1999, p. C8. For a more complete discussion of Dell Computer's business strategies, see Dell, *Direct from Dell*.

29. Michael E. Porter, *Competitive Advantage* (New York: Free Press, 1985), p. 97. Adapted with the permission of The Free Press, a Division of Simon & Schuster, Inc., from *Competitive Advantage: Creating and Sustaining Superior Performance* by Michael E. Porter. Copyright © 1985, 1998 by Michael E. Porter.

30. Ibid., p. 150. Adapted with the permission of The Free Press, a Division of Simon & Schuster, Inc., from *Competitive Advantage: Creating and Sustaining Superior Performance* by Michael E. Porter. Copyright © 1985, 1998 by Michael E. Porter.

31. Thomas J. Peters and Robert H. Waterman, Jr., *In Search of Excellence* (New York: Warner Books, 1984), p. 318.

32. Porter, *Competitive Advantage*, pp. 111–18. Adapted with the permission of The Free Press, a Division of Simon & Schuster, Inc., from *Competitive Advantage: Creating and Sustaining Superior Performance* by Michael E. Porter. Copyright © 1985, 1998 by Michael E. Porter.

33. Michael E. Porter, "What Is Strategy?" *Harvard Business Review*, November–December 1996, p. 73.

34. For a discussion, see George A. Steiner, John B. Miner, and Edmund R. Gray, *Management Policy and Strategy*, 3rd ed. (New York: Macmillan, 1986), p. 145.

Chapter 2

Goal, Mission, and Strategy Statement

In this chapter the organization's grand strategy to successfully achieve its business goals and business mission is presented. Goals are provided in quantitative and/or qualitative terms, and the mission is articulated crisply and clearly for those inside and outside the company to understand unambiguously what this business is about. "Only a clear definition of the mission and purpose of the business makes possible clear and realistic business objectives," wrote Drucker. "It is the foundation for priorities, strategies, plans, and work assignments."[1] This chapter answers the questions: what business are we in, what do we want to achieve, and how will we do it?

GOAL STATEMENT

The goal statement announces what the organization wants to achieve. This statement identifies the objectives of the organization over a time horizon—one year, five years, etc.—expressed typically in quantitative terms. For example, Company X will achieve sales of $1 million by year one of the plan and sales of $5 million by year five, representing a 500 percent improvement over the planning period. Qualitative goals are also appropriate, such as improvements in productivity, customer satisfaction, or quality to the point where the company aspires to win the Baldridge National Quality Award. A combination of qualitative and quantitative goals may also be appropriate.

Figure 2.1
Process Development of a Goal Statement

Step	Statement	Criteria	Comment
1	To achieve improved planning	Single, identifiable main theme	Improved planning is the stated goal
2	To use improved planning to achieve better financial results	Results oriented	"To" followed by a verb shows "why"
3	To increase planning participation through-out the organization	Clarity and specificity	The "what" is stated
4	To increase planning participation by April 30, 2002	Provides measure-ment	The "when" is stated
5	To have 90% of managers participate in the process by September 30, 2002	Attainable measure-ment	States "who" and im-proves ability to measure attainment
6	To achieve "best of class," have 100% of all managers partici-pate in improved planning process by January 1, 2003	Inspiring, motivating	Real goal of attaining "best" in industry by a date certain is stated as underlying purpose for improving the planning process

Approach to Writing the Goal Statement

How do you go about writing the goal statement? Typically, the top management team works together over a few days in an iterative process to craft words that best capture their objectives. As an example, Figure 2.1 uses "planning improvement" as a goal in a six-step process.[2]

Through an iterative process, the goal statement has been defined, re-fined, and transformed from a simple assertion for improvement of the planning process into a well-crafted, results-oriented statement of goal that answers the who, what, when, and why questions. It is realistic, attainable, and measurable, and it provides a lofty purpose for the organization. This step-by-step technique is straightforward: begin each interaction with the preposition "to" followed by an action verb, answer the four "w" questions each in turn, and make sure the goal is measurable and inspiring.

Evaluating the Goal Statement

General Electric Company used the RAM test to determine whether a goal statement was crafted appropriately. This useful template could be applied to any statement of goals developed by a start-up firm or those sent to a corporate office from an operating unit to determine whether the statement is Realistic, Achievable, and Measurable.

"Realistic" means there is reality to the goal—that the company or particular business unit is engaged in that type of business, could reasonably expect to perform the needed work to the level aspired to, and the competitive environment is such that the business unit has an honest chance for success.

"Achievable" means the goal, as stated, could literally be achieved—that the task laid out is such that it could be accomplished, even though a real stretch might be required.

"Measurable" means the goal statement has to have built into it a way of knowing whether or not it is achieved—i.e., a yardstick included in the goal statement such as "achieving 100 percent increase in sales in two years." At the end of the second year anyone could measure whether the operating unit had in fact achieved an increase in sales of 100 percent or not. The RAM test is a practical, useful guide to crafting an effective goal statement.

George Steiner has identified ten guides for preparing long-range planning objectives to test and evaluate goal statements; these are not mutually exclusive:[3]

- Suitable. Achievement of the established objective must move the firm in the direction identified by management and must support the basic purpose and mission of the enterprise, not conflict with it or make no contribution to it.

- Measurable over time. Expression of objectives in concrete terms for specified periods of time enables their achievement to be measured objectively in quantitative terms (dollars of sales growth per year) or qualitative terms (quality improvement per year).

- Feasible. Objectives should be possible to achieve, not unrealistic or impractical, in light of internal capabilities and external business environment over the time period selected.

- Acceptable. People in the organization must be willing to accept the chosen objectives as compatible with their business ethics and value system, be within their risk tolerance to incur costs and effort to achieve them, and represent an acceptable goal in terms of market share, profit, and the like.

- Flexible. The objective should be clear enough to assure direction for the firm, yet it should be possible to modify it in the event of unforeseen contingencies.

- Motivating. Specific objectives that are difficult to achieve, if accepted, motivate and increase performance better than easy-to-achieve goals or those that are clearly out of reach.

- Understandable. State objectives in clear and simple terms to avoid misunderstanding and miscommunication.

- Commitment. Once agreement is reached on the objectives, there should be full commitment by everyone to do what is necessary and reasonable to achieve them.

- People participation. Best results are achieved when those who are responsible for achieving objectives have participation in determining them; this not only motivates performance but also provides valuable inputs into the goal-setting process.

- Linkage. Objectives should be linked to overall business purposes and mission, they should be consistent between top management and different operating units of the firm, and there should be appropriate linkage of objectives within operating units.

Example of Goal Statement: John F. Kennedy. President John F. Kennedy's goal statement for the space program, delivered in person on May 25, 1961 before a joint session of Congress, provides an excellent example of a goal statement for national policy that passed the RAM test and met Steiner's guidelines. Kennedy said, "I believe that this nation should commit itself to achieving the goal, before this decade is out, of landing a man on the moon and returning him safely to the earth."[4] This statement meets the criteria cited above: as a statement of goal it is brief, clearly understood, realistic, achievable, and measurable in terms of time and deed, and it is lofty and inspiring.[5]

In this one sentence the President established a national purpose and objective for the entire country for the decade of the 1960s, and he also set a major spending priority: a stunning 25 percent of U.S. civilian R&D dollars was absorbed by the space program in the 1960s.[6] Indeed, a year after his speech, Kennedy declared the moon goal is "among the most important decisions that will be made during my incumbency in the office of the Presidency."[7] And, as everyone knows, when Neil Armstrong stepped foot on the surface of the moon in July 1969 the goal was achieved (fully achieved at splashdown several days later when he returned safely!).

Oddly, there was considerable concern among the scientific community at the time Kennedy announced this goal regarding the "achievability" issue. In 1961 America's rocket technology was incapable of lifting a payload as heavy as the moon capsule that would be required for carrying three men to and from their destination. Kennedy was in fact advised that a manned moon mission was not feasible at the time. Two things had to happen: make a more powerful rocket to lift and carry the capsule out of Earth's atmosphere and reduce the weight in the capsule.

Each element of this two-pronged approach required a major technology effort whose outcome was speculative. Advancements in rocket technology were further along than weight reduction, and Kennedy chose the course of quickly completing the rocket improvement, which became the Saturn rocket, and then investing in the technologies needed to reduce weight in the capsule, rather than investing in further advancements in rocket lift capacity. He believed the longer-term payoffs in science and engineering from the effort to miniaturize electronics to make it less heavy would be greater for the country than that needed to improve booster strength. His moon shot goal statement therefore carried great risk of failure, and Kennedy bet heavily that his chosen R&D course could be fulfilled by NASA and industry in time to achieve his stated goal.[8]

Kennedy had a clear appreciation of these "technical" risks, and he also understood the "market" risks inherent in articulating this goal. He had to "sell" the goal to Congress to obtain the necessary funds (which he estimated to be $7 to $9 billion over five to seven years), and he had to "sell" the goal to the American people to gain their backing for "a firm commitment to a new course of action."[9] Kennedy had another level of "market" risk concern—stating goals for the nation in a bold and decisive manner was simply not done, except in time of war. "We have never specified long-range goals on an urgent time schedule, or managed our resources and our time so as to insure their fulfillment," Kennedy admitted. "[T]he facts of the matter are," he added, "that we have never made the national decisions or marshaled the national resources required for such leadership."[10]

Kennedy was breaking new ground in America with the moon goal statement. Before him, Presidents typically did not make goal statements, opening themselves to the risk of failure and consequent loss of face. He understood and accepted the technical risks inherent in this decision and used them to challenge and inspire the nation to undertake a great new enterprise. He personally reviewed and approved the scientific and technical strategies to be pursued. And he used the "bully pulpit" of the Presidency to "market" the program to the nation at every level he could, delivering the commitment statement personally to a joint session of Congress and subsequently lobbying on hundreds of occasions on behalf of the commitment privately and publicly. This is quintessential leadership: decide on a course of action, announce it, and work to achieve it.

Example of Goal Statement: Michael Dell. Michael Dell provides two vivid examples of goal setting at Dell Computers. First, in 1986, when the company was only two years old and had sales of $60 million, Dell set its goal for 1992 (essentially a five-year plan) to achieve sales of $1 billion. Achievement of this highly ambitious goal was based on a three-pronged strategy: target large companies, give the best support to win them, and go global—targeting Canada, Germany, the United Kingdom, and France. By the end of that planning period, 1992, Dell had achieved sales more than twice the $1 billion goal.[11]

Second, in 1994, the company was preparing a three-year plan and saw it had the potential to grow between 40 and 50 percent a year over that period. "That meant," wrote Mr. Dell, "that the company would more than double in size every two years. We were challenged running a $3 billion business. It was clear that to get to $7 billion or $10 billion we would need to hire and develop lots of additional talent."[12] Achieving this highly ambitious goal was principally a question of talent: "to show how leveraging talent can prove to be an invaluable competitive advantage."[13] How do you do that? Michael Dell answers, "[M]y goal has always been to make sure that everyone at Dell feels they are part of something great—something special—perhaps something even greater than themselves."[14]

Role of Top Management

Setting goals is one of top management's major responsibilities. It is also one of top management's levers of power. By establishing goals for the business, the CEO is essentially setting the strategic direction for the organization and motivating it toward its achievement. One former chairman/CEO stated that, at the end of the day, the most important thing the planning process produces is a "compass heading" for the firm—i.e., setting a course toward a destination, establishing a goal.[15] Being the one to set the "compass heading" is power. Using the plan to achieve it makes the plan a powerful rudder.

MISSION STATEMENT

The mission statement encapsulates the purpose of the business. This statement identifies the basic reason the company is in business. It answers in some detail the fundamental questions: What business are we in? What business should we be in?[16]

"To know what a business is we have to start with its *purpose*," advised Drucker. "Its purpose must be outside of the business itself. In fact, it must lie in society since business enterprise is an organ of society. There is only one valid definition of business purpose: *to create a customer*."[17]

The Purpose of the Business

To answer these questions properly, the plan needs to answer other important questions:

- Who is the customer?
- Where is the customer?
- What customer needs are satisfied by the firm?

- What is of value to the customer?[18]
- What does/can the firm do to satisfy those needs over time?

This analysis will reveal to the firm's managers the fundamental raison d'être of the firm, which is to satisfy a customer's need. In the future tense, the analysis will help management realize that customer groups may change, may already have changed, and certainly will change over time, and that the firm needs to reevaluate its products and services over time to ensure that it remains of value to its customers. Adaptation to change by abandoning unneeded product lines, providing new products and services and new ways of providing them and delivering them, and using new technologies and processes is essential over time to keep the business strong and prevent obsolescence and competitive decline.

Example: Delphi Automotive Systems. In 1999, Delphi Automotive Systems separated from General Motors and became an independent company. It combined a number of former GM and Delco Electronics activities, becoming instantly the world's largest supplier of automotive component and systems technologies, with 1999 revenue of $29.1 billion and net income of $1 billion.[19]

Delphi has nearly 200,000 employees and operates 169 plants, 40 joint ventures, and 27 technical centers located in 36 countries. Its world headquarters is in Troy, Michigan, and it has regional headquarters in Paris, Tokyo, and São Paulo. Its major products include chassis systems, engine management systems, steering systems, electrical systems, communications systems, thermal systems, and interior systems. Its customers include virtually every major manufacturer of cars and trucks in the world, including heavy truck manufacturers and the aftermarket.[20]

"Delphi's vision is to be recognized by its customers as their best supplier.[21] Its goals are (a) to maximize the opportunities its independence provides to become customer-focused and responsive, (b) to achieve 10 percent earnings growth annually through superior technical innovation and customer satisfaction, and (c) to implement lean manufacturing processes."

Its mission is fivefold:

Be a global automotive systems supplier with component excellence;

Achieve the passionate pursuit of customer satisfaction through technology, quality, cost, responsiveness, and attitude;

Grow revenue across a diversified customer base;

Increase stakeholder value through revenue growth and superior returns;

Create an environment where every employee can contribute and excel.[22]

These statements of vision, goals, and mission are very well crafted to provide clarity of business purpose, intent, and anticipated reward to any of the new firm's stakeholders, especially investors in the new company's stock, which was on the verge of being issued through an initial public offering when these words from General Motors were written to their shareholders.

The Need for Sustained Success

Whether the firm is a mature company in an established industry or an entrepreneurial start-up, its sustained success depends on its management keeping in focus the value it provides to its customers by continually generating new ideas and new techniques for satisfying customer demand.

"Businesses grounded in the old model will become obsolete and die. At Monsanto," said its CEO, Robert Shapiro, "we're trying to invent some new businesses around the concept of environmental sustainability. We may not know exactly what those businesses will look like, but we're willing to place some bets because the world cannot avoid needing sustainability in the long run."[23] Monsanto's mission was consistent with Michael Porter's analysis of six industries in which innovations were made resulting in both economic gains and environmental benefits. Environmental regulation and environmental innovation can have clear competitive implications.[24]

Monsanto was one of four companies (plus DuPont, Intel, and Xerox) studied by RAND to learn how environmental concerns are being incorporated into overall corporate planning, especially product development. Monsanto attempted to create products that have less environmental impact because they fulfill multiple purposes—for example, plants that bear fruit and provide biomass as feedstock for plastics. Driven largely by environmental concerns, the company's product research shifted to biotechnology and agriculture—to engineer crops that will survive its herbicides or crops that will not be attacked by a particular pest.[25]

In 1987 Nestlé, Kraft/General Foods, and Procter & Gamble owned nearly 90 percent of the U.S. coffee market, and they assumed their business model, based on low price and a dominant distribution system through retailers, would assure continued success in the $18 billion U.S. coffee market.[26]

Howard Schultz had a different idea and a different mission—Starbucks. His mission was to sell premium coffee at a premium price in a coffee store. In ten years, Schultz turned a commodity into a premium brand, developed direct distribution channels through 2,100 retail outlets and growing, and had captured 25 percent of the business at retail coffee stores and 4.4 percent of all coffee sold in supermarkets. In 1998, Kraft signed an agreement to distribute Starbucks' whole beans and ground coffee to over 20,000 grocery stores. Yet, Howard Schultz worries about the skeptics:

"that's one of the things that have [*sic*] always driven me." Looking at negative forecasts for the firm's future is "a humbling reminder of what other people think."[27]

Will Starbucks go the way of Planet Hollywood (which filed for Chapter 11 bankruptcy protection after its stock dropped in value in two years from $28.50 per share to $.75 per share and its owners announced it will be unprofitable for five years[28]), Rainforest Cafe (which lost 70 percent of its value in one year), and Boston Market (the once-high-flying IPO that filed for bankruptcy in 1998 and was bought out by McDonald's)?[29] Probably not, because, unlike the other stores, Starbucks has loyal customers. Yet Schultz, constantly searching for new ideas, is not complacent.

Nor are other successful entrepreneurs. Bill Gates, the richest man in the world because he implemented new ideas through a new company with a clear mission, worries about Microsoft's sustainability: "Will we be replaced tomorrow? No. In a very short time frame, Microsoft is an incredibly strong company. But when you look to the two- to three-year time frame, I don't think anyone can say with a straight face that any technology company has a guaranteed position." Andy Grove, Intel's former CEO, put it this way, "Only the paranoid survive."[30] Intel's motto is "quick or dead"—a reflection of the fact that its product lines are completely retooled every two years to sustain growth.[31]

"Creativity is the new business currency."[32] Businesses constantly have to generate new ideas to have an edge in the future. They must dare to break the rules: like Fred Smith when he challenged the U.S. Post Office to deliver mail by founding Federal Express; like Steve Jobs, George Eastman, and Isaac Singer, who designed personal computers, cameras, and sewing machines for home use and mass-marketed them to customers; and like Lunsford Richardson, Vick's VapoRub's inventor, who convinced the Post Office to allow him to send mail addressed only to the "boxholder" or "occupant" and not by name, thus inventing direct-mail advertising. Each of these ideas broke the previous mold and became the heart of a fresh, new business's mission.

Mission statements are quite prevalent, widely used, and are generally developed with top management involvement. They have become an obligatory part of a company's portfolio of literature. But more than mere boilerplate, they can be valuable as a tool for getting senior managers to discuss their differences and arrive at a common view.[33] In a recent survey of large Canadian firms it was found that their mission statements were used for a variety of purposes, and the majority of firms surveyed were satisfied with the statements and the process they used to create them.[34] Mission statements need to be reviewed periodically to ensure their relevancy—for sustained success.

Genuine Business Mission

The planner should be careful not to insist on stating a purpose for the firm if one does not exist; "[f]or many large diversified companies, there is no purpose beyond creating shareholder value." Campbell and Alexander continue, "The best purposes give long-term, directional stability without pushing the organization into an unrealistic box."[35]

Derek Abell sees a business mission defined in three dimensions: customer groups, or who is being satisfied; customer functions, or what is being satisfied; and technologies, or how customer needs are satisfied.[36] Using this approach, the firm gains the advantage of identifying clearly the alternatives available to it in each of these key dimensions and the future position the firm may hold in each dimension as it is revealed, and the firm is reminded that changes in technologies and customer groups and needs regularly occur.

The mission needs to be stated broadly enough to enable the firm to reposition itself over time to meet changing conditions in its chosen industry, in the economy, in technology, in taste and culture. The statement should be brief. It can be combined with the goal statement; this is especially useful in young firms to focus and clarify the business's principal purpose and objectives. The simple and compelling mission statement of the world's largest Internet service provider, America Online, is this: "Our mission is to build a global medium as central to people's lives as the telephone or television . . . and even more valuable."[37]

STRATEGY STATEMENT

Having stated the company's goals and business mission, the firm's leaders need to state how they intend to achieve their business objectives successfully. It is here that the "strategy" discussion presented in the Introduction comes into the plan. This is the statement of grand strategy by top management.[38] It springs off from the decision made in the Vision statement regarding which generic strategy will be adopted: cost leadership, differentiation, or focus.[39] Having chosen a generic strategy, the next step is determining the how of that core strategy's achievement.[40]

Establish Strategic Direction

The strategic objectives of the firm need to be stated clearly to provide direction to all employees of the firm and to provide information to the firm's customers, suppliers, shareholders, creditors, and other stakeholders. Strategic objectives should:[41]

- Correlate with and facilitate the achievement of the business goals and mission
- Be compatible with the philosophy and culture of the business
- Be robust, yet attainable, to stretch, motivate, and inspire the enterprise
- Emerge from a consensus-building discussion by all levels of management to attain "buyin"
- Be communicated to and understood by all levels of the organization for execution
- Contain target dates and quantitative and /or qualitative targets for measurements
- Have consistency with social, legal, and ethical codes of conduct

The grand strategy for World War II for the United States and Great Britain was decided at the Newfoundland meeting of President Roosevelt and Prime Minister Churchill in August 1941—four months before the United States entered the war after the attack on Pearl Harbor.[42] That strategy met the tests presented above: in the name of the principles of democracy stated in the Atlantic Charter, the two countries decided to wage war against and defeat Hitler's Germany as the first priority and against Japan as the second priority because Hitler was viewed as the more dangerous enemy of the two. This key decision established priorities for the allocation of millions of men, vast quantities of materiel, and military operations to the North Atlantic theater of war first and to the Pacific theater second. This was truly grand strategy—to wage global warfare against two great powers at once in the name of freedom!

Global Strategy: General Electric. In 1981 Jack Welch, at age forty-five, became Chairman and CEO of the General Electric Company. At that time GE was viewed as a model company, a true icon of American industry since Thomas A. Edison had founded it nearly a hundred years earlier. In 1980 GE's sales were $25 billion and profits were $1.5 billion. Despite this appearance of success, Welch saw major problems ahead stemming from high inflation and serious competitive threats from Asia. He set out to transform GE into a high-growth, efficient, new model company. When he took over, GE had 350 business units, of which few were leaders in their markets.

Welch's strategy was simplicity itself: either be the market leader in your industry or, by being number two, have the chance to become the leader; otherwise, get out of that business.[43] In 1986 Welch globalized the strategy.[44]

Following this strategy, by 1998, GE had $100.5 billion in sales, $9.3 billion in earnings, had grown to become the fifth largest company in America with a market value of $360 billion, was named *Fortune* magazine's "Most Admired Company in America," and the *Financial Times* had declared it "The World's Most Respected Company." During Welsh's then-18-year tenure, GE averaged 24 percent per year total return to its share owners,[45] sales grew 3.7 times, profits rose 5.7 times, and the company became truly global. GE's European businesses in 1999 had become nearly as large as was all of GE when Welch became CEO—and he intends to do the same in Asia, only faster.[46]

In 1999 GE's total revenues rose 11 percent to $112 billion, earnings increased 15 percent to $10.7 billion, operating margin rate grew to 17.8 percent, and working capital turned 11.5 times—all records. In 1999 GE won "The Most Admired Company" and "The World's Most Respected Company" awards for the second consecutive year, and it also won *Time*'s plaudits as "The Company of the Century."[47] In the mid-1980s when globalization began, GE derived more than 80 percent of its revenues from the United States; by 1999 41 percent of revenues were from outside the United States and moving toward a majority sometime in the decade of 2000.

"Globalization evolved from a drive to export," wrote Welch, "to the establishment of global plants for local consumption, and then to global sourcing of products and services. Today, we are moving into its final stages—drawing upon intellectual capital from all over the world." One of Welch's "biggest and longest-running dreams [is]—a truly global GE."[48]

International Strategy: Wal-Mart. In 1991 Wal-Mart, the world's largest retailer, adopted an international strategy, opening its first store in Mexico. By the end of 1998 the company operated 2,884 stores of all types in the United States and 716 stores abroad in eight countries, with more on the way.[49] Over 90 percent of company sales and profits were still generated in the United States.[50] In the fourth quarter of 1998, international sales rose by 26 percent and profit surged by 33 percent, while total company sales gained 15 percent and total company net income rose 21 percent. Wal-Mart, whose total sales for all of fiscal year 1998 were $137.6 billion with earnings of $4.4 billion, stated it wants to have its international unit generate a third of annual sales and earnings over the next few years.[51] For 1998, the international division generated sales of $12.2 billion and a profit of $551 million.[52] In 1999 Wal-Mart became the second largest company in America when sales reached $166.8 billion, with a profit of $5.3 billion.[53]

Global Strategy: General Motors. General Motors, America's largest company with 1999 sales of $176.5 billion and profit of $6 billion (after spinning off Delphi), has had an international strategy almost from its beginning.[54] In the 1990s, under Chairman/CEO Jack Smith, it expanded and refocused its international strategy into a global strategy. As of May 2000, GM had operations in forty countries, accounted for 25 percent of the world's auto output, and its chairman relished the new meaning of its acronym—"Global Motors."[55]

"The top priority is global integration of our talents, resources, and business systems and processes," Smith declared. "Global integration is the biggest lever we have to get more competitive and profitable and at the same time grow the business."[56] In 1998, for the first time in its history, GM combined its worldwide automotive operations into a single global unit under a single individual, GM's President and Chief Operating Officer. "This will make GM more focused, faster, and more innovative in responding to diverse customer needs," wrote Jack Smith.[57]

Together with this restructure and to capitalize on the growth potential in emerging markets, General Motors launched the largest production expansion in its history—in emerging markets, where the company viewed the potential for growth to be the most substantial. These markets include Latin America, the Middle East and Africa, Asia/Pacific, and central and eastern Europe. Total "emerging market" growth over the decade beginning in 1998 is forecast at 8.4 million cars and trucks, representing a growth rate of 72 percent. By contrast, the growth forecast in traditional markets (North America, western Europe, Japan, and Australia) over the same period is projected at seven million units, representing a growth rate of 19 percent.

Between 1994 and 1997 alone, GM announced, broke ground, or started production at new plants in eight countries, including Russia, Argentina, Indonesia, India, and China (including opening a new Buick assembly plant in Shanghai valued at $1.5 billion for nonexport), plus the following:

Thailand: $750 million investment in an Opel assembly plant to produce 100,000 vehicles per year

Hungary: DM235 million for an Opel cylinder-head plant, tripling its investment in Hungary in five years

Poland: DM470 million for an Opel plant to produce 70,000 cars annually.

In 2001, GM announced a deal valued at $100 million for a Chevrolet SUV joint venture with Avtovaz in Russia.[58]

" 'Global' is definitely where the growth markets are," declared Mr. Smith. "To succeed and grow in the auto industry, you must be competitive on a global—not just a regional—basis."[59]

International Strategy: Coca-Cola. Another example of a company with a clear international strategic focus is Coca-Cola, the world's largest soft-drink company, which had net operating revenue in 1998 of $18.8 billion, operating income of $4.9 billion, and a market valuation of $165 billion.[60] "Now and always" is how the company views its business. "That dual vision," wrote Douglas Ivester, then Chairman and CEO, "simultaneously nearsighted and farsighted, is only natural for a Company with our history and our future." For this 113-year-old company with a presence in nearly 200 countries, " 'always' . . . is more than an advertising slogan: it's a business plan. As we manage through the day-to-day concerns of our business, we work to stay mindful of the long term."[61]

Coca-Cola's "strategic focus" for its largest region, North American Group, is as follows:

- Build brands locally
- Focus on local market management
- Develop marketing programs for all thirst occasions
- Reinforce strong customer partnerships

The success of this strategic focus is this: for nine consecutive years through 1998, Coca-Cola increased its share of soft-drink sales in the United States, averaging 6 percent increases annually versus the rest of the industry at 2 percent. In 1998, North America with 30 percent is the largest regional market in the world for unit case volume in a worldwide total of 15.8 billion cases; Coke had 44.5 percent of the U.S. market to Pepsi's 31.4 percent.[62] In 1999, however, Coca-Cola's market share slipped .4 percent to 44.1 percent, while PepsiCo's remained at 31.4 percent; real growth in 1999 was in Cadbury Schweppes and Cott Corp., a private-label bottler.[63]

Coca-Cola has recently experienced a long list of other problems. Following the death of CEO Roberto Goizueta in 1997 and his replacement by Douglas Ivester, the former CFO,[64] Coca-Cola had strained relations with one of its major customers, Walt Disney Company; a racial discrimination lawsuit; difficulty with key acquisitions abroad (Schweppes and Orangina); poor handling of its largest product recall in history—17 million cases in France and Belgium;[65] a $16 million antitrust fine by an Italian court;[66] a high-profile investigation by four European governments (Britain, Germany, Austria, and Denmark) of charges of illegal trade practices;[67] a 14 percent decline in earnings in 1998; steeper earnings decline in 1999 due to slowing demand in Asia and the health scare in Europe;[68] and a 10 percent decline in net income in 2000.

Exposure to problems outside the United States is a major concern for Coke because three-fourths of its profits and two-thirds of its sales come from overseas, where most of these serious problems have arisen.[69] After two and a half years on the job, Ivester announced his retirement. Douglas N. Daft, an Australian Coca-Cola marketing veteran, succeeded him.[70]

For the Minute Maid Company, a Coca-Cola subsidiary, the company also has a clear strategic focus in a worldwide juice beverage business that has more than $40 billion in sales annually and growing. Ivester's stated vision was this: "The destination of The Minute Maid Company is to be The Coca-Cola Company of juices, worldwide, and capture category growth with global brands, premium products and a superior business system." The strategic focus for the Minute Maid Company is:

- Create healthy, sustainable base businesses with superior consumer and customer fundamentals

- Create long-term economic value through innovation and new business models
- Build competitive advantage through enhanced organizational capabilities
- Build superior financial fundamentals throughout our business[71]

Given Coca-Cola's clarity of vision, strategic focus, and global business experience, the Minute Maid Company should be a major contender in the juice beverage business, but its full potential has not been realized. Perhaps this is part of the reasoning behind Mr. Daft's move to put juices into a joint venture with Procter & Gamble—to harness P&G's unmatched ability to generate new products and to exploit existing brand strength.[72]

For Coca-Cola and Minute Maid, the strategies stated above are "market share building" strategies, based on a grand strategy of growing these businesses globally by gaining market share in each product sector. This is one of nine fundamental strategies that could have been adopted.

Fundamental Strategies

Top management has the strategic choice of any one or a combination of nine fundamental business strategies, which are outlined in Figure 2.2 under the conditions for which each would be relevant.[73]

Management of a firm that has a single or dominant line of business has the choice of any one of these nine fundamental strategies as the key to its implementation of one of the three generic strategies it has chosen: cost leadership, differentiation, or focus. As time goes by, management may elect to alter its fundamental strategy because it may have achieved success or anticipates failure with that strategy, or it has determined that a new course is needed, given altered circumstances.

For multiproduct firms or diversified businesses, management will likely have several of these strategies at work simultaneously, one for each major line of business. Indeed, it may be a management goal of a diversified company to have at least one business unit active in each of several of these fundamental strategies at the same time.

For example, a business unit may have a commanding position in a mature industry that exhibits little potential for future growth; this business unit would be a likely candidate for "cash cow" status under a "market share holding" or "market share harvesting" strategy. Another business unit could be in a growth mode in a young, promising industry, which would mandate a "market share building" strategy. Still other business units' industries may have declined to the point where "liquidation" or "divestiture" would be appropriate to generate resources to nourish units with greater potential.

Example: Seagram. Occasionally the reverse situation occurs. A diversified firm seeks to focus itself into one primary industry and divests those

Figure 2.2
Fundamental Business Strategies

---

1. Market share building
    —Firm wants to expand and has resources to do so
    —Opportunity for market share expansion exists
        —Market is growing
        —Firm has new product or has extended life cycle of present product
        —Market is declining but firm is committed to remaining in industry
            —Horizontal merger is possible in industry consolidation
    —Firm has achieved lower costs than competitors
        —Firm is willing to lower price
    —Revenue gained from market share expansion will exceed cost of market share expansion within acceptable time frame at acceptable risk
2. Market share holding
    —Firm has attained leadership position and wants to hold it
        —Routinely develops new products for mature market
    —Market represents core business for firm
        —Key product is in early stage of lifecycle—will hold market share
        —Firm routinely develops new products to hold market share
    —New competitive pressures are emerging, foreign or domestic
3. Market share harvesting
    —Key product may be entering declining phase of life cycle
    —More promising business units may be emphasized
    —Firm no longer committed to the business
    —Firm may be considering divestiture
        —Firm will make no further investment in the product
4. Divestiture
    —Business unit is marginal in its industry
    —Heavy investment needed to modernize
        —Resources better used elsewhere
    —Firm has redefined its business mission
    —Product has been superseded by new technology
    —Firm wishes to exit the business

5. Liquidation

—Market is too small, has disappeared, or has been overtaken by competition

—Business unit has little or no economic viability

—Plant and equipment are too old

—Too much investment needed to modernize

—Assets have been reduced to scrap value

—No buyer for a harvested or undesired business unit

6. Diversification

—Desire for growth

—Desire to enter new lines of business owing to maturity of existing business lines

—Desire for contracycle and contraseasonal lines of business to reduce variability of revenue and profit

—Desire for better use of capacity—to benefit from economies-of-scale effect

—Desire to develop synergy through related diversification

—Desire to capitalize on existing strengths—marketing or technologically driven

—Desire to exit original business and build a conglomerate

7. Acquisitions and mergers

—Desire to implement a diversification strategy

—Desire to pursue a market-share-building or market-share-holding strategy

—Desire to acquire competitors, if this is legal

—Desire to acquire new sources of capital: financial or human

—Desire to benefit from tax or other incentives

—Opportunity to make personal financial gains

—Opportunity to capitalize on a turnaround situation

—Opportunity to acquire one's own business via employee stock ownership or management ownership plan

—Desire to expand geographically

8. Vertical Integration

—Desire to acquire control over sources of supply: security of supply, denial of supply to others, control of cost and quality, possibility of improved earnings

—Opportunity to benefit from economies-of-scale effect

—Opportunity to gain greater share of technology

—Desire to gain better control over marketing of product

—Desire to acquire specialized knowledge

9. Horizontal integration

—Desire to expand geographically in non-competing trade areas

—Opportunity to acquire a failing competitor

—Desire to expand market share (antitrust considerations)

—Desire to gain economies of scale by serving larger market territory

---

portions of its business portfolio that lie outside the chosen field of concentration. Edgar Bronfman, Jr., when he was Chairman and CEO of Seagram Co., sought a leading role in the entertainment industry, as opposed to passive investment in that industry and others through stock ownership. The opportunity arose in 1995 to purchase for $5.7 billion a majority interest in MCA Inc. (Universal Studios, etc.) from Matsushita, which desired to refocus to consumer electronics. To pay for MCA and other expected acquisitions, Bronfman sold Seagram's 24 percent position in DuPont for $9 billion.

In 1998, Bronfman purchased Dutch-owned PolyGram Records, the world's leading recording label for $10 billion, to augment the music business that he acquired in the MCA deal. To help pay for this purchase and retire debt, Seagram sold Tropicana, the largest juice company in the United States, to PepsiCo for $3 billion, its G. H. Mumm and Perrier-Jouet sparkling wine brands for $310 million, and its Universal Concerts unit for $190 million.[74] Bronfman also invested in overseas pay-TV channels, digitized its music catalog, and began selling music through digital downloading on the Internet.[75] After a three-year realignment, Seagram Co. was focused as an "entertainment" company of the first rank. Whether it would be profitable remained to be seen.[76]

That will now be the problem of Vivendi, which purchased Seagram for $34 billion and named the newly combined entertainment, water treatment, and construction company Vivendi Universal, with headquarters in Paris.[77]

DuPont's Choice of Fundamental Strategies. E. I. du Pont de Nemours and Company provides an excellent example of a diversified, multiproduct firm that has chosen strategies to meet specific conditions in its key industry segments. In the late 1990s, DuPont was facing (a) major challenges in one industry area, oil, (b) steady-state conditions in many of its mature chemical businesses, and (c) opportunities for potentially explosive growth in another industry, life sciences.

In 1997 the company had sales of $24 billion and operating income of $1.4 billion, which was not particularly outstanding. Facing industry changes and sluggish growth in key business sectors, management developed a new objective: to make this nearly 200-year-old firm a faster-growing, more profitable, and less cyclical company.

To accomplish this objective, DuPont's top management selected five strategies, which they began executing in 1998:[78]

- Exit energy. In 1998 Conoco, DuPont's oil subsidiary, became publicly traded with the then-largest initial public offering in U.S. history, generating $4.4 billion in cash, followed by a second spin-off in 1999 of a 70 percent stake, which raised $11 billion. DuPont had acquired Conoco Oil Co. in 1981 for $7.6 billion.[79]

- Strengthen differentiated businesses. Management sought to strengthen those businesses where DuPont's products, technology, and brand power allow it to compete in a manner that differentiates them from others in the marketplace. Example: for $1.8 billion DuPont acquired Herberts, the coatings company of Hoechst, making DuPont the world's leading supplier of performance coatings.[80] Immediately following the acquisition, second-quarter 1999 income in this business sector jumped 39 percent.[81]

- Reshape mature businesses. With mature businesses in mature markets, DuPont planned to build a new business model to create more value with less capital. This typically involves partnering with an industry or geographic market leader. Example: strengthening Dacron polyester through a joint venture with Alfa.

- Position DuPont advantageously in life sciences. Management viewed the critical growth areas as pharmaceuticals, agriculture, and nutrition. Example: DuPont purchased Merck's half of the DuPont Merck Pharmaceutical Company, bringing DuPont's investment to $6 billion in life sciences during 1997–98. In its 1999 second-quarter results, DuPont's aftertax operating income in pharmaceuticals almost doubled.[82] Example: in 1999, DuPont completed its acquisition of the largest U.S. seed company, Pioneer Hi-Bred International Inc., for a total investment of $9.4 billion, a key element in its strategy to become a world leader in biotechnology.[83]

- Drive productivity through Six Sigma. As a tool to improve productivity, Six Sigma methodology (3.4 defects per million) has been adopted throughout the company. Also, every DuPont business unit is now including asset and cost productivity strategies in its business plans.

These five strategies are intended to invigorate America's largest chemical company, putting it on a long-term high-growth, high-productivity course.

DuPont's five strategies are examples of a large, diversified business employing portions of the nine fundamental business strategies for its business units (see Figure 2.3).

DuPont is also employing the Six Sigma methodology to stimulate and sustain productivity improvements throughout the company in all its busi-

Figure 2.3
Fundamental Business Strategies and DuPont

—Market share building is one strategy used to develop a position in life sciences.

  —DuPont sees growth opportunities in that sector and is focusing resources there to develop a position to advantageously exploit the opportunities.

—Market share holding is the strategy to strengthen differentiated businesses.

  —DuPont will hold its market position for mature products, like coatings, in mature industries by investing and acquiring where prudent to secure its already dominant position in this core business area.

—Divestiture is the strategy to exit energy.

  —DuPont redefined its business mission and the oil and gas industry no longer fits; plus, the sale of Conoco Oil Co. generated resources needed to grow the firm's position in the sector of new strategic focus: life sciences.

—Diversification is another strategy to position advantageously in life sciences.

  —DuPont seeks growth industries in growth markets to reduce its dependency on mature businesses in mature markets and to develop noncyclical businesses for business base stability.

—Acquisitions and mergers is a strategy for strengthening differentiated businesses and for positioning in life sciences.

  —DuPont acquired a coatings firm, Herberts, to strengthen its dominance in a core, differentiated business area; it acquired Merck's half of the joint venture in a biomedical business that had already shown great promise; and it acquired Pioneer Hi-Bred International seed company for its biotechnology business.

—Vertical integration is another strategy to position advantageously in life sciences.

  —DuPont bought out Merck's half of the biomedical joint venture and all of Pioneer Hi-Bred International to gain specialized knowledge in a new growth area of technology, gain economies of scale, have greater control over sources of supply, distribution channels, and markets—all to improve potential earnings.

—Horizontal integration is the strategy used to reshape mature businesses.

  —DuPont is employing new business models that require less capital, such as joint ventures, to expand geographically, to grow market share, and to gain still greater economies of scale for mature businesses and brands, such as the Dacron joint venture with Alfa.

nesses—a key part of management's drive to improve asset utilization, cut costs, and enhance earnings in every business unit.

So, DuPont is now a "global science company," having three main thrusts in its strategy to increase and sustain growth: integrated science to develop unique technology platforms, generating value through knowledge intensity, and productivity improvement through Six Sigma.

After two full years of implementation, how have these strategic trusts paid off? In 1999, DuPont's sales were $26.9 billion, up from $24.7 billion in 1998, and net income grew to $7.6 billion, up from $4.6 billion. Yet, earnings per share continued to be flat—for the fourth consecutive year—after allowing for nonrecurring items. Chad Holliday, Chairman and CEO, stated that he does "not consider this lack of growth acceptable."[84] He gave himself one or two more years to achieve double-digit earnings per share growth.

Strategies for Family Businesses

Family businesses often have unique strategy needs in attempting to determine what business they should be in and how to add value. In the quest for an appropriate strategy, family-owned firms often uncover fundamental issues of identity that, rather than being exceptions, can become models for any business. Recent research has identified three issues relevant to all family businesses:[85]

1. Strategic imperatives and family life cycle events are out of phase. Stages in family life cycle, such as the death of the business's founder or children entering the firm, may be events out of sync with the stages of the business, such as external threats or expansion needs. Henry Ford's son, Edsel, could not persuade his father to offer multiple car models to compete with General Motors. Edsel's son, Henry Ford II, was able to revitalize the firm by offering customers choices only after his grandfather died.

2. The tie to the founder. After the founder's death, heirs are psychologically tied to the patriarch and are often reluctant to make changes, fearing to violate his core business idea. After Walt Disney's death and his nonfamily, hand-picked successors were floundering, Walt's nephew, Roy Disney, brought in outside leadership, Michael Eisner and Frank Wells, to run the company. The rest is history.

3. Trust and leadership in the second and later generations. Later generations often seek to protect their personal wealth by diversifying assets away from the family business, not having confidence in the leadership of cousins or other peer-generation leaders they once had in the founder, who may have taken on mythical proportions as a leader. These actions can deprive the firm of needed capital and other support. A third-generation heiress to the Campbell Soup fortune, Dodo Hamilton, sold her stock when

the company's fortunes declined, feeling she had to protect her own family and not the company as a whole.

Simulation tools can help family businesses effectively deal with these issues and plan for their future by linking their thinking to their feelings, their strategic plans to their family relationships, and their issues of strategy and stewardship to ownership. Such techniques are useful for any company, but are especially helpful in the often emotionally charged atmosphere of a family firm.

McDonald's Global Strategy. As much as any company, McDonald's Corporation is global. At the end of 1998, there were almost exactly as many golden arches stores in the United States as there were outside, with a total of 24,800, generating systemwide sales of $35.9 billion and operating income of $2.7 billion and serving 40 million customers a day worldwide. The bulk of the company's growth in the second half of the 1990s was international, in terms of numbers of new stores opened, sales, income, and assets. This accomplishment is no accident. It resulted from a clear vision and strategic focus for fulfilling the company's mission.

Its CEO, Jack Greenberg, stated:

McDonald's vision is to be the world's best quick-service restaurant experience. Being the best means consistently satisfying customers better than anyone else through outstanding quality, service, cleanliness and value. Supporting this vision are five global strategies:

- develop our people at every level of the organization, beginning in our restaurants
- foster innovation in menu, facilities, marketing, operations and technology
- expand our global mindset by sharing best practices and leveraging our best people resources around the world
- continue the successful implementation of change underway in McDonald's USA
- long term, reinvent the category in which we compete and develop other businesses and growth opportunities.[86]

Outside the United States, McDonald's has 48 percent of globally branded quick-service restaurants and 63 percent of the sales. It plans to strengthen this leadership position: in 1999 it added nearly 1,800 restaurants, 90 percent outside the United States, for a grand total of 25,000 worldwide, and it added 1,800 to 1,900 restaurants in the year 2000—90 percent outside the United States.[87] The international strategy is highly focused, simply stated, well communicated, and clearly paying off.[88] However, there are major risks. With more than one-third of its revenues in Europe, the health risks from "mad-cow" disease have depressed hamburger sales there, and the company has cut back the number of restaurants it had planned to open in 2001 to 1,600 worldwide, with most of the reductions in Europe.[89]

Risks of Global Strategies; Example: Lincoln Electric. Going global is not always a virtue, particularly without a plan and substantial international experience to base it upon. As an unnamed CEO said to a partner at Deloitte & Touche, "I globalized this company out of necessity and because it was the right thing to do, and in the last couple of years it's bitten me in the ass."[90]

The example of Lincoln Electric is instructive.[91] This old-line, $853-million-in-sales, Cleveland-based manufacturer of arc-welding equipment and other industrial products had some international exposure, but in 1986 a newly installed CEO dreamed of becoming a global power. He embarked on an expensive acquisition program in Europe, Latin America, and Japan without experience in international business, without testing local work rules and customs, and made these purchases at the height of the market, which then tanked. Soon after, Lincoln Electric sustained its first-ever quarterly loss, which was repeated with sickening regularity.

A new CEO, Donald Hastings, took personal control over Lincoln's non-U.S. operations, moved to Europe, and discovered that for each newly acquired business "the size of its budget was based on the forecasted, rather than the actual, sales and profits of those businesses. To inflate the management company's own operating budget, its leaders had encouraged the businesses to submit optimistic—rather than realistic—forecasts. I was shocked."[92] The new CEO rationalized the international operations, liquidated nonperforming plants, installed a management team with international know-how, benefited from a market upturn, and expanded the Board of Directors to include new outside directors with substantial international industrial and financial experience.

By 1994 the company was saved: sales reached $1 billion, debt-to-equity ratio dropped from 63 percent to 12 percent, and the company had a successful IPO. Harsh lessons had been learned in a pressure cooker. The prior CEO had put the company at risk with no clear strategy, no international expansion plan, and no substantial international experience.

Transform Strategy into Action

How do you transform a big, hairy, audacious goal into action? Simply writing stimulating vision and goal statements is not enough. Some mechanism is needed by each firm to translate that big, bold goal into a practical, workable strategic process that gears the entire firm to the goal's achievement. Jim Collins has labeled this the "catalytic mechanism." Such mechanisms are "the crucial link between objectives and performance; they are a galvanizing, nonbureaucratic means to turn one into the other."[93]

They have five characteristics:[94]

- A catalytic mechanism produces desired results in unpredictable ways. For example, in 1956, 3M Company instituted a catalytic mechanism to stimulate a constant flow of new products by urging its scientists to spend 15 percent of their time experimenting and inventing in areas of their own choice. No one could predict the products that would result from this uncontrolled, liberating process. And the products did flow, producing a fortyfold increase in sales and earnings since the process was put in place. More recently, to better stimulate break-through product development, 3M set a bold objective: 30 percent of sales would result from products that had not existed four years earlier; the "lead user" development process is the principal mechanism being employed to achieve "non-incremental" product development growth.[95]

- A catalytic mechanism distributes power for the benefit of the overall system, not those who traditionally hold power. For example, Granite Rock, a company that sells crushed gravel, concrete, sand, and asphalt, instituted a transforming mechanism to achieve total customer satisfaction called "short pay." At the bottom of every invoice is this statement: "If you are not satisfied for any reason, don't pay us for it. Simply scratch out the line item, write a brief note about the problem, and return a copy of this invoice along with your check for the balance."[96] This mechanism provides the customer with complete discretion whether and how much to pay based on satisfaction level, without returning the material. It transformed the entire company into a customer-oriented enterprise because the customer holds the power. Granite Rock won the Malcolm Baldrige National Quality Award in 1992.

- A catalytic mechanism has teeth. For example, Nucor Corporation, a successful American steel company, established the goal of being the most efficient, high-quality steel company in the world. Bold words for a rust belt industry ravaged by foreign competition. By adding teeth, the goal is being fulfilled. Compensation at all levels is clearly linked to performance, driving productivity to levels where five people do the work of ten at other steel companies and get paid like eight.

- A catalytic mechanism ejects abuses. Hiring and retaining the right people in the first place, those who fit the productivity culture, is critical. For example, at Nucor good workers drive out lazy, nonproductive co-workers. The company sets up its mills in rural areas, hires farmers who have a work ethic, and instructs them in the steel trade. Nucor believes they cannot teach the work ethic but they can teach steel making. And the system disciplines itself every day.

- A catalytic mechanism produces an ongoing effect. The 3M 15 percent rule has stimulated product development for over forty years. Similarly, in 1971, Kimberly-Clark instituted a catalytic mechanism to sustain its transformation from a "so-so" forest-products company into a consumer-products company; they sold their paper-production mills and introduced a line of disposable diapers, directly challenging the world-class consumer-products leader, Procter & Gamble. There was no going back. The new Kimberly-Clark had to compete every quarter with P&G, forcing the company at all levels to perform or die. The transforming effect is still working today.

Linking goals and strategy to a catalytic mechanism will powerfully transform an organization—and it will sustain that transformation for years to come, if it is chosen well. These are not empty words or exhortations to the troops. These are processes that make the strategy real, make it happen, day after day.

The strategy statement should be crafted clearly to guide management in the achievement of its goals and to communicate to all stakeholders exactly how management intends to accomplish its goals and business mission. Linking the strategic goal, for example "total customer satisfaction," to a catalytic mechanism, like "short pay," will enliven and permeate the organization with the will to achieve its realization over a sustained period.

CONCLUSION

These three elements—goals, mission, and strategy—are included together in the same chapter of the plan because of their indispensable linkage with one another. The goal states what you will achieve and when, the mission states the nature and type of business you will be in, and the strategy states how the business will achieve these objectives. All three are the necessary and sufficient ingredients to successfully set your strategic focus.

Having completed this section of the plan, you now need to go back to your vision statement and reevaluate it in light of your goal, mission, and strategy statements. Does the vision statement still make sense? Is it still an accurate depiction of your ultimate dream for the enterprise? After you write the goal, mission, and strategy statements, the vision statement often needs some adjustment—sometimes a complete rewrite—because a fundamentally different business mission may have emerged, or it has become clear that a more viable, more likely-to-succeed strategic focus is simply a better way to proceed.

Remember, writing the business plan is a "messy" iterative process. After each chapter, you need to review prior work, testing it for viability and consistency with other portions of the plan.

NOTES

1. Peter F. Drucker, *Management: Tasks, Responsibilities, Practices* (New York: Harper & Row, 1973), p. 75. From *Management: Tasks, Responsibilities, Practices* by Peter F. Drucker. Reprinted by permission of Butterworth Heinemann.

2. The concept of this figure and an early version were suggested by Jack Blum, Jet Propulsion Laboratory, Pasadena, CA.

3. George A. Steiner, *Strategic Planning* (New York: Free Press, 1979), pp. 164–68.

4. John F. Kennedy, *Public Papers of the Presidents of the United States, 1961* (Washington, DC: GPO, 1962), p. 404.

5. The "inspiration" generated did not immediately show up in public opinion polling data of the day. In response to the question "Which country—the United States or Russia—do you think will be the first to send a man to the moon?" posed on June 4, 1961 (two weeks after Kennedy's moon speech), 34% said Russia, 33%

said the United States, and 33% had no opinion or believed no one would reach the moon. Hazel Gaudet Erskine, "The Polls: Defense, Peace, and Space," *The Public Opinion Quarterly*, XXV, no. 3 (Fall 1961), p. 487.

6. *Business Week*, August 24–31, 1998, p. 63.

7. John F. Kennedy, speech at Rice University, September 12, 1962, quoted in Allan Nevins, ed., *The Burden and the Glory* (New York: Harper & Row, 1964), p. 244.

8. For this discussion, see Derek Wesley Elliott, *Finding an Appropriate Commitment: Space Policy Development under Eisenhower and Kennedy*, George Washington University, Washington, DC, Ph.D. dissertation, 1992.

9. Kennedy, *Public Papers of the Presidents of the United States, 1961*, p. 404.

10. Ibid., p. 403.

11. Michael Dell, *Direct from Dell* (New York: HarperCollins, 1999), pp. 26–27, 33.

12. Ibid., p. 108.

13. Ibid., p. 108.

14. Ibid., pp. 107–8.

15. Thomas V. Jones, Chairman of the Board and CEO, Northrop Corporation, private conversation with the author, January 1982.

16. Drucker, *Management: Tasks, Responsibilities, Practices*, pp. 74–94. From *Management: Tasks, Responsibilities, Practices* by Peter F. Drucker. Reprinted by permission of Butterworth Heinemann.

17. Ibid., p. 61. From *Management: Tasks, Responsibilities, Practices* by Peter F. Drucker. Reprinted by permission of Butterworth Heinemann.

18. Ibid., pp. 80–86. From *Management: Tasks, Responsibilities, Practices* by Peter F. Drucker. Reprinted by permission of Butterworth Heinemann.

19. *Delphi Automotive Systems 1999 Annual Report*, March 27, 2000, p. 2.

20. Delphi Automotive Systems, *Investor Facts*, newsletter to shareholders, 1999.

21. *General Motors Corporation 1998 Annual Report*, January 20, 1999, p. 35 and *Delphi Automotive Systems 1999 Annual Report*, p. 3.

22. *General Motors Corporation 1998 Annual Report*, p. 35.

23. Joan Magretta, "Growth through Global Sustainability: An Interview with Monsanto's CEO, Robert B. Shapiro," *Harvard Business Review*, January–February 1997, p. 81. Monsanto was later acquired by Pharmacia Corporation.

24. Michael E. Porter, *On Competition* (Boston: Harvard Business School Publishing, 1998), p. 357, Chapter 10: "Green and Competitive." See also Jasbinder Singh, "Making Business Sense of Environmental Compliance," *Sloan Management Review*, spring 2000, pp. 91–100.

25. Susan A. Resetar, "Technology Forces at Work," RAND Science & Technology Policy Institute, Washington, DC, June 1999, reported in Jeff Johnson, "Environment and the Bottom Line," *Chemical & Engineering News*, June 21, 1999.

26. Bill Costello, "Make Money by Thinking the Unthinkable," *The Futurist* 33, no. 5 (May 1999), p. 31. Market size is from Nelson Schwartz; see below.

27. Nelson D. Schwartz, "Still Perking after All These Years," *Fortune*, May 24, 1999, pp. 203–10.

28. *Los Angeles Times*, August 18, 1999, pp. C1, C5, and December 2, 1999, p. C4.

29. Schwartz, "Still Perking after All These Years," p. 204.

30. Quoted in Costello, "Make Money by Thinking the Unthinkable," pp. 30, 31, respectively.

31. Resetar, "Technology Forces at Work."

32. Costello, "Make Money by Thinking the Unthinkable," p. 31. Examples in this paragraph are from Costello, "Make Money by Thinking the Unthinkable," pp. 32–33.

33. Andrew Campbell, "Mission Statements," *Long Range Planning* 30, no. 6 (December 1997).

34. Mark C. Baetz and Christopher K. Bart, "Developing Mission Statements which Work," *Long Range Planning* 29, no.4 (August 1996).

35. Andrew Campbell and Marcus Alexander, "What's Wrong with Strategy?" *Harvard Business Review*, (November–December 1997), p. 50.

36. Derek F. Abell, *Defining the Business*. (Englewood Cliffs, NJ: Prentice-Hall, 1980), p. 6. For a discussion of the three dimensions, see pp. 49–51.

37. *1999 America Online Annual Report*, June 1999, p. 2.

38. See James Brian Quinn, "Strategies for Change," in Henry Mintzberg and James Brian Quinn, *The Strategy Process: Concepts, Contexts, Cases*, 3d ed. (Upper Saddle River, NJ: Prentice-Hall, 1996), pp. 3–10.

39. For a discussion of generic strategy's relationship to strategic choices, see Henry Mintzberg, "Generic Business Strategies," in Mintzberg and Quinn, *The Strategy Process*, pp. 83–92.

40. For a discussion of strategy making, see Robert M. Grant, *Contemporary Strategy Analysis*, 3d ed. (Oxford, UK: Blackwell Publishers Ltd., 1998) and Henry Mintzberg, "Crafting Strategy," in Mintzberg and Quinn, *The Strategy Process*, pp. 101–10, where the potter's wheel analogy is presented.

41. John A. Pearce II and Richard B. Robinson, Jr., *Strategic Management* (Homewood, IL: Irwin, 1982), pp. 186–88.

42. Arthur Schlesinger, Jr., ed., *The Almanac of American History*, (New York: Barnes and Noble Books, 1993), p. 484.

43. Peter F. Drucker, *The New Realities* (New York: Harper & Row, 1989), pp. 125–26.

44. Christopher A. Bartlett and Meg Wozny, "GE's Two-Decade Transformation: Jack Welch's Leadership," Harvard Business School Case 9-399–150, rev. January 6, 2000, p. 5.

45. Robert Slater, *Jack Welch and the GE Way* (New York: McGraw-Hill, 1999), pp. 19–21; *1998 Annual Report of the General Electric Company*, February 12, 1999; and *Fortune*, April 26, 1999, pp. F–1, F–2. GE continued to hold first place as *Fortune*'s "Most Admired" company; see Nicholas Stein, "The World's Most Admired Companies," *Fortune*, October 2, 2000, pp. 183–84.

46. Thomas A. Stewart, "See Jack. See Jack Run Europe," *Fortune*, September 27, 1999, p. 124. For Asia, see also Jim Rohwer, "GE Digs into Asia," *Fortune*, September 27, 2000, pp. 165–78. Welch had announced he would step down as CEO in the spring of 2001, coinciding with his twentieth anniversary as CEO; *Wall Street Journal*, November 3, 1999, p. B12. However, the Honeywell International acquisition delayed his retirement by at least one year; meanwhile, Jeffrey Immelt has been named his successor; see "The Man who Would Be Welch," *Business Week*, December 11, 2000, pp. 94–97.

47. *1999 Annual Report of the General Electric Company*, February 11, 2000, p. 1.

48. Ibid., p. 4.

49. On June 14, 1999 Wal-Mart announced it will buy for $10.8 billion Britain's third-largest supermarket chain, the Asda Group, expanding in Europe beyond Germany for the first time; *Los Angeles Times*, June 15, 1999, p. C3, and *Wall Street Journal*, September 27, 1999, p. B1.

50. Jeremy Kahn, "Wal-Mart Goes Shopping in Europe," *Fortune*, June 7, 1999, p. 106.

51. *Los Angeles Times*, February 17, 1999, p. C3.

52. Ibid., June 15, 1999, p. C3.

53. *Fortune*, April 17, 2000, p. F1.

54. *General Motors Corporation 1999 Annual Report*, February 25, 2000, p. 10. GM's year 2000 results were $183 billion in sales and $5 billion in earnings. GM, *Stockholder News*, vol. 7, no. 1, March 2001, p. 2.

55. John F. Smith, Jr., Speech to Los Angeles World Affairs Council, Beverly Hills, CA, May 19, 2000.

56. John F. Smith, Jr., *General Motors 1996 Midyear Report*, September 10, 1996, p. 2.

57. *General Motors Corporation 1998 Annual Report*, January 20, 1999, p. 32.

58. *New York Times*, February 28, 2001, p. W1.

59. The emerging market discussion and the quotation is from General Motors, *Stockholder News*, vol. 3, no. 1, March 1997, pp. 2–3, and *General Motors Corporation 1998 Annual Report*, pp. 32–34. The value and domestic focus of the Buick assembly plant in Shanghai is from Smith, Speech to Los Angeles World Affairs Council.

60. This discussion of Coca-Cola is based primarily on *The Coca-Cola Company 1998 Annual Report*, February 18, 1999.

61. Ibid., p. 3.

62. *Beverage Digest*, reported in Patricia Sellers, "Crunch Time for Coke," *Fortune*, July 19, 1999, p. 76.

63. *Beverage Digest/Maxwell's*, reported in *Wall Street Journal*, February 22, 2000, p. B5.

64. *The Coca-Cola Company 1997 Annual Report*, February 19, 1998, p. 65.

65. *Wall Street Journal*, July 28, 1999, p. B10; Goldman, Sachs & Co. reports "rebuilding consumer confidence [after the health scare product recall] will probably require significant marketing investment." Recall data from *New York Times*, October 3, 1999, p. B–U10.

66. *Los Angeles Times*, December 18, 1999, p. C3.

67. Ibid., July 22, 1999, p. C2.

68. Sellers, "Crunch Time for Coke," pp. 72–78; M. Douglas Ivester, letter to share owners, July 1, 1999, discussing Coca-Cola recall in Belgium and France, and *The Coca-Cola Company 2000 Annual Report*, February 15, 2001, p. 4.

69. *Los Angeles Times*, July 16, 1999, p. C3; 1999 second-quarter earnings declined 21%; third-quarter 1999 earnings declined 11%—the fourth consecutive quarterly decline; also August 22, 1999, p. C3.

70. Ibid., December 7, 1999, p. C1.

71. *The Coca-Cola Company 1998 Annual Report*, p. 17.

72. James Flanigan, "Can Coke Avoid Mistakes and Reach Its Potential," *Los Angeles Times*, March 11, 2001, pp. C1, C12.

73. Based on Hale C. Bartlett, *Cases in Strategic Management for Business* (New York: Dryden Press, 1988), pp. 42–43.

74. *Los Angeles Times*, July 27, 1999, p. C9; Seagram's 1998 sales were $9.71 billion.

75. Ibid., August 20, 1999, p. C7.

76. Ibid., April 13, 1999, p. C7. Seagram, the world's sixth-largest entertainment company, reported continuing losses; the 1998 third-quarter loss of $199 million was greater than that a year earlier at $21 million despite increased revenue of 7.5 percent, and cash flow fell by 25 percent year to year. Bronfman stated it would be several quarters before the film division turns a profit, following a string of box-office failures. See also May 7, 1999, p. C4. Bronfman made the same remark after a fourth-quarter loss was reported, August 29, 1999, p. C7. The 1999 first quarter also saw a loss, which was reported over two months early on rumors the company was floundering; Ibid., August 22, 1999, p. C6.

77. *New York Times*, June 20, 2000, p. A1.

78. *1998 Annual Report of E. I. du Pont de Nemours and Company*, March 1, 1999.

79. *New York Times*, August 10, 1999, p. C4.

80. *Los Angeles Times*, July 8, 1999, p. C2; DuPont announced it would cut 1,300 jobs, or 8.7% of the workforce, at six Herberts plants outside the United States, as it integrated Herberts' paint business over the next nine months.

81. *Wall Street Journal*, July 29, 1999, p. B2.

82. Ibid.

83. Ibid., September 30, 1999, p. A8. Owing to public concerns of consuming genetically modified food, farmers are showing reluctance to plant biotech seeds; see also November 19, 1999, p. A1.

84. *1999 Annual Report of E. I. du Pont de Nemours and Co.*, March 1, 2000, p. 2.

85. This discussion based on Nancy Drozdow and Vincent P. Carroll, "Tools for Strategy Development in Family Firms," *Sloan Management Review*, Fall 1997. For further discussion, see J. L. Ward, *Keeping the Family Business Healthy: How to Plan for Continuity, Growth, Profitability, and Family Leadership* (San Francisco: Jossey-Bass, 1988).

86. *The Annual, McDonald's Corporation 1998 Annual Report*, March 15, 1999. Under the category "develop other businesses," McDonald's announced in December 1999 that it would buy bankrupt Boston Chicken, Inc. for $173.4 million and assume debt, giving it 751 Boston Market restaurants and rights to an additional 108 franchise locations; McDonald's had previously bought Chipotle Mexican Grill and Donato's Pizza chains; *Los Angeles Times*, December 2, 1999, p. C1.

87. *McDonald's Corporation 1999 Annual Report*, March 15, 2000, p. 1; *Los Angeles Times*, March 30, 2000, p. C4.

88. McDonald's 1999 systemwide sales were $38.4 billion and operating income was $3.3 billion; *McDonald's Corporation 1999 Annual Report*, p. 2.

89. *Los Angeles Times*, March 15, 2001, p. C3.

90. Thomas A. Stewart, "Getting Real about Going Global," *Fortune*, February 15, 1999, p. 170.

91. This discussion is based on Donald F. Hastings, "Lincoln Electric's Harsh Lessons from International Expansion," *Harvard Business Review*, May–June, 1999.

92. Ibid., p. 171.

93. Jim Collins, "Turning Goals into Results: The Power of Catalytic Mechanisms," *Harvard Business Review*, July–August, 1999, p. 72.

94. This discussion is based on Collins, "Turning Goals into Results: The Power of Catalytic Mechanisms." pp. 71–78. See also Jim Collins and Jerry I. Porras, *Built to Last: Successful Habits of Visionary Companies* (New York: HarperBusiness, 1994).

95. Eric von Hippel, Stefan Thomke, and Mary Sonnack, "Creating Breakthroughs at 3M," *Harvard Business Review*, September–October, 1999, pp. 47–57.

96. Jim Collins, "Turning Goals into Results," *Harvard Business Review*, July–August, 1999, pp. 71–82.

Resource Audit

The purpose of the resource audit is a self-evaluation to determine the firm's ability to fulfill its vision, perform its chosen business mission, and achieve its selected business goals. This self-analysis addresses the internal business environment of the firm; in the next chapter the external environment is discussed.

BE FAIR AND HONEST

A resource audit is useful only if it is fair, honest, and real. Self-deceit and grandiose exaggerations of one's abilities and strengths without a firm foundation of reality is a waste of time and may result in self-delusion as to the firm's true abilities to meet its stated goals. Similarly, overly cautious and understated assessments of the firm's underlying strengths and resources are also unwise, leading to unnecessarily pessimistic conclusions as to the company's true abilities and likelihood of success. A balanced assessment is required, taking the real strengths and weaknesses clearly into account.

To achieve the goals laid down in the previous chapter, the firm will require a certain roster of assets, resources, and capabilities. In this chapter managers evaluate the firm's capabilities to achieve their goals within their business mission. Sometimes this self-audit can be painfully uncomfortable, laying open the reality of weaknesses that previously had not been recognized or properly faced. Other times, the self-analysis reveals strengths and assets that had previously been hidden, overlooked, or not fully appreciated. The bottom-line result is typically a mixed bag of goods and bads. It is up to the managers to build on the strengths and remediate the identified weaknesses. Much of the rest of the business plan is based on this exercise, which must be conducted honestly.

Example: Northrop Grumman Corporation. How honest is honest? An example of a self-audit by a firm presented with the opportunity for a major expansion is illustrative. In 1966 Northrop Corporation (now Northrop Grumman) signed an agreement with The Boeing Company to build the center fuselage of a new airliner called the 747, the largest commercial aircraft ever built. Northrop's task was to finance its work, build a new facility, buy and install modern tooling in that facility, manage the fabrication activities for the gigantic pieces of aluminum that formed the entire body of the airplane from aft of the cockpit to just before the tail assembly—a total of 153 feet of structure—and ship it by rail to Everett, Washington for assembly by Boeing at their plant. This task was larger than anything Northrop had ever undertaken.

Approximately three years later, as the 747 work was well underway and running into every kind of difficulty imaginable, McDonnell Douglas approached Northrop with the proposition of building the same large piece of fuselage structure for its proposed new DC-10 wide-body jet liner, which would compete on some routes with Boeing's 747. McDonnell Douglas believed Northrop's 747 experience equipped it with the abilities needed to perform the DC-10 work, coupled with the geographic benefit of relative close proximity of the two factory sites (Douglas Aircraft in Long Beach and Northrop nearby in Hawthorne, California). Nothing in the Boeing contract barred Northrop from undertaking this work for Douglas, which would have virtually doubled Northrop's business in commercial aircraft subcontracting, carrying Northrop from a nonplayer in commercial work to the world's largest commercial aircraft subcontractor within a three-year period. The rewards were potentially great but so were the risks, so the company undertook a self-audit to determine its capability to undertake the DC-10 subcontract in the presence of the existing 747 work.

The Northrop self-audit was comprehensive. It was conducted by an internal team of division and corporate office personnel, supplemented by outside consultants. It lasted several months and covered every area of analysis the team could imagine: financial capacity, factory facilities and space, tooling and equipment, factory labor, logistics of inbound supplies and outbound deliveries, supporting management and technical (especially engineering) staff, management oversight, financial rates of return, etc. Everything everybody in the company could think of was included, evaluating the company's ability to perform the task or buy, lease, hire, or borrow that which was found to be lacking.

In every category the company's evaluation produced a positive answer—the task could be performed on the schedule required—with *one* exception:

management oversight. It was concluded, based on this searing self-analysis, that top management was not capable of managing the DC-10 program in the presence of the 747 program and the other military programs the company was then contractually obligated to perform. This new major program would simply be too much to handle from a management standpoint. As a result, Northrop turned down McDonnell Douglas, which then approached General Dynamics' Convair Division in San Diego to perform this work, which it undertook.

How honest is honest? Painfully so. An opportunity of a lifetime was handed to Northrop, which it rejected because of its own evaluation of its inability to manage the task at that time. A few years earlier or later, the answer would likely have been different. But at that time, Northrop simply could not accept the challenge, in fairness to its other obligations. The analysis revealed a serious flaw—the weakness of its own management team. Northrop learned that if it had real pretensions to achieve the top ranks in aerospace, it would have to strengthen its management team. What the company learned about itself in the DC-10 exercise was that it lacked a management "bench," and that needed immediate correction. The company undertook an urgent program of talent recruitment and internal management training to rectify this deficiency.[1]

SWOT ANALYSIS

There are a number of approaches to evaluating internal strengths and weaknesses. One is to use the value chain analysis: evaluate every link in the firm's value chain to determine the firm's capacities.[2] Another approach that is widely used is the SWOT analysis. Using this technique, you look at your firm's Strengths, Weaknesses, Opportunities, and Threats in an orderly and careful way.[3] This is an internal situation audit that should produce an accurate and comprehensive list of the organization's strengths and weaknesses, which should then be used to reevaluate the vision and goal-mission-strategy statements. Later, opportunities and threats are examined in the external environment and competitive assessment chapters. So significant is this strength/weakness step in the planning process that some firms begin their strategic planning with the SWOT analysis.[4]

Recent studies have criticized the SWOT approach as inadequate for a number of reasons. One study of United Kingdom companies in 1993–94 reports on the use of SWOT as a technique for improving corporate strategy. Of the 50 firms surveyed, 20 actively used SWOT analysis, employing 14 outside consulting companies in the process. All these companies showed similar characteristics: long lists of factors (over forty) evaluated, often meaningless descriptions of factors identified, failure to prioritize, and no attempt to verify any points that were raised. "[T]he most worrying general characteristic was that no-one subsequently used the outputs within the later stages of the strategy process."[5] It is pointless to undertake the analysis if the results are not used.

President Kennedy performed something of a SWOT analysis when he decided to pursue the moon shot. He and the country were still reeling from the Soviet Union's 1957 achievement with Sputnik of being first in space, and he was determined to recapture leadership in space for the United States. "Since early in my term, our efforts in space have been under review," he said in mid-1961. "[W]e have examined where we are strong and where we are not, where we may succeed and where we may not," which is a resource audit on a grand scale. "Now it is time to take longer strides—time for a great new American enterprise—time for this nation to take a clearly leading role in space achievement, which in many ways may hold the key to our future on earth."[6] Kennedy's goal statement was preceded by a resource audit to assess its feasibility, concluding: "I believe we possess all the resources and talents necessary."[7]

Functional Checklist for SWOT Assessment

Every organization, however small or large, whether manufacturing or service, has a number of functions that have to be performed. A useful way to evaluate the firm's capabilities is to review each function to assess whether current capabilities are adequate to meet the goals and mission of the business, and, if not, to develop remedial action plans. The key functions are as follows:[8]

Marketing. You start with selling something. The question is: are there customers who demand or will demand your product? How do you know—through market research, hunch, logical analysis of projected growth based on past sales trends, etc.? Validation of the market (i.e., customer demand) is critical before attempting to implement the plan by introducing a new product. "80% of all NEW products that come to market fail in a few short years."[9] Validation of the market by test marketing, surveying, or other techniques can dramatically reduce the probability of failure. Do you have or can you obtain a capable sales force, a dealer or distributor network, skill in promotion and advertising, and ability to keep in touch with changing customer needs?

Operations. You have to produce something. The question is: can the product/service be produced and delivered? Follow-up questions are: does the firm have enough facilities and factory space, equipment, and skilled workers; the proper location close to suppliers, market, and labor; enough managers and skilled technicians in the right specializations; flexibility of production capability to weather low-production periods and to surge in periods of high demand; and manufacturing cost control and learning curve experience?

R&D. You have to have a product/service that is different. The question is: do you have a product or service differential that is marketable and sustainable in the marketplace? Research and development can produce the initial product, but that product may be copied or obsolesced by others in time, so continuing product improvement or new product launches will be needed and can be achieved only with sustained R&D activity. What is your level and quality of technological sophistication; do you have patents and copyrights to protect your intellectual property; do you have the capability of developing new products over time?

Finance. You have to have financial resources to start and/or sustain the enterprise. The question is: do you have the necessary cash or credit or can you obtain it? Are you credit worthy? Many start-up firms are not, and to overcome this weakness the principals use credit-card credit for initial operations, accepting the high interest rate involved in this approach for at least a while. More mature companies have established lines of credit with major lending institutions, usually money-center banks, upon which they draw for operating capital and for expansion needs. Some firms are self-financing; i.e., cash flow from ongoing operations finances expansion requirements. Key questions: do you have good return on investment and other strong financial measures of performance, access to capital (internal and/or external), willingness and ability to borrow, financial management ability, and costs in proportion to competition?

Management. You have to run the business. The question is: can you and/or a team operate the business? Do you and the management team have the requisite leadership qualities of motivation, values and ethics, and style; the experience to organize, operate, and control a business; knowledge of strategic decision making; appropriate age, training, and functional experience; and flexibility and adaptability to sustain the business?

Organization. You have to organize the business. The question is: can you and a management team organize the human and physical resources needed to operate the enterprise? To succeed initially and to succeed in the long run, the business will need an organizational structure suitable to its size, operations, and market and be capable of expansion and contraction depending on changing conditions. Can the management team put together an organization that is effective, has a proper division of labor, hire and retain people having shared values and unity of purpose, and has a business structure consistent with the firm's strategy and mission?

Suppliers. You have to have suppliers. The question is: can you identify the best, most appropriate suppliers for the business, command their support, sustain it over time, and be able to depend on their quality and goodwill in good times and bad? For manufacturing firms, suppliers are critical to success, especially if a few key components in the product are outsourced. The days of "beating on the suppliers" to get cost down and improve schedule are largely over. More recently, long-term relationships have been established with key suppliers to integrate them semipermanently into the business's operation, sharing information, treating each other more like partners than buyer/seller. Stable, reliable relationships are sought today. This may include supplier financing of work in process ("wip"), as well as supplier financing of major expansions.

The SWOT analysis will not only evaluate the organization's critical capabilities and the opportunities they present in the presence of threats to them, but the analysis will also suggest strategic implications of your findings related to those factors. Figure 3.1 illustrates this with a summary of a few factors in the functional analysis.[10]

If the management team can satisfy itself that the firm can adequately exploit its strengths and opportunities and deal with its functional weaknesses, either today or after performing some remedial action, then the team will have gone a long way toward honestly assessing its underlying capabilities. This list is especially useful for mature, established organizations.

Checklist for Start-Ups

For start-up companies, the above functional approach may be useful, also. However, William A. Sahlman has developed a convenient checklist to evaluate start-ups' particular strengths and weaknesses.[11] This list identifies four key factors:

- The people. The principals who are starting the firm are the key personnel who will largely determine whether the firm will succeed or fail.[12] This category also includes outside parties who provide key services or resources for the business, such as lawyers, accountants, bankers, suppliers, etc. Venture capitalists look at this roster most closely in the belief that the founders of the firm must have the requisite skills and commitment to make it a success. Personal biographies attached to the plan and to proposals for financing are reviewed most carefully.
- The opportunity. This is a profile of the business: what it will sell, to whom, whether the business can grow and how fast, what its economics are, who and what stand in the way of success, including competition from existing suppliers or competing technologies.
- The context. This is a discussion of the big picture: the regulatory environment, interest rates, demographic trends, inflation, etc.—all the factors that inevitably change but cannot be controlled by the entrepreneur.
- Risk and reward. This is an assessment of everything that can go wrong and right, an analysis of the investment required and the rate and timing of return, and a discussion of how the entrepreneurial team will respond.

By filling out this checklist, the entrepreneur can maximize the potential success of the venture and minimize the prospects for failure. As Professor Sahlman says, "One of the great myths about entrepreneurs is that they are risk seekers. All sane people want to avoid risk."[13] A good way to do

Figure 3.1
SWOT Analysis/Implications Summary of Selected Factors

Factor	Strategic Implication
	Strengths

(1) Management
    (a) Strong R&D group
	(1) Management
	    (a) Rely on in-house product development, plus acquisitions for expansion

(2) Markets
    (a) Product C has a growing share in a growing market
	(2) Markets
	    (a) Invest in C to increase market share and increase return on investment

	Weaknesses

(1) Management
    (a) We have 6 different products and a centralized organization that is not working well
    (b) Too many middle managers have poor performance ratings
	(1) Management
	    (a) Decentralize
	
	    (b) Begin management development program
	    In acquiring companies insist on strong management

(2) Markets
    (a) Product A is losing market share because it is becoming obsolete
    (b) One customer buys 50% of product B
	(2) Markets
	    (a) Redesign product A
	
	    (b) Find new markets for product B to reduce reliance on one customer

	Opportunities

(1) Markets
    (a) Strong growth is forecast for product D in South America
	(1) Markets
	    (a) Prepare analysis whether we should build plants, export, or license in South America

(2) Finance
    (a) We have strong cash position, low debt/equity ratio, and a high price/earnings ratio
	(2) Finance
	    (a) Search for new acquisitions

	Threats

(1) Suppliers
    (a) New government safety standards are likely at key supplier's plant and they cannot meet them easily
	(1) Suppliers
	    (a) Begin now to devise methods to help supplier meet the new standards to avoid a shutdown

(2) Operations
    (a) Peru threatens to nationalize our plants
	(2) Operations
	    (a) Begin negotiations with U.S. State Department and government of Peru

this is to have a solid business plan. In the past twenty years, *Fortune* 500 companies have shed five million jobs, but the overall economy added nearly thirty million jobs. Many of those new jobs were created by entrepreneurial ventures, such as Microsoft, Genentech, and Cisco Systems. Each of those companies began with a business plan.[14]

Start-up companies often need help performing the resource audit. Self-appraisals are inherently difficult to do honestly. Most visionaries wear rose-colored glasses regarding their own strengths and capabilities, especially regarding the nature of the project they have conceived. Ego is clearly involved. Therefore, some outside assistance is useful for expertise and balance. Following are suggestions of where you can go and who you can get for help.

- Family and friends. Some family members or family friends may be experienced in business and can provide a useful sounding board for the entrepreneur's business plan and concept based on their own experiences and insights.

- Professionals. Your accountant, lawyer, banker, and other professional advisors are usually seasoned professionals who have "been there, done that" and can be expected to provide advice and counsel. Some caution is needed here because these professionals also hope to gain your future business.

- Delphi session. Call in an expert in each functional field germane to the business to provide critical commentary in a roundtable discussion of the business plan and/or fill out a previously provided questionnaire to get the experts' comments in writing.

- Red teams. Consultants and other experts experienced in the business area of the start-up can be called in to critique the plan and the business concept, typically from the perspective of the competition. This exercise unearths risks and weaknesses in the business concept, perhaps even in the product itself, that might otherwise go unnoticed.

- Facilitator. Hire a professional meeting facilitator to preside over a roundtable session of the entrepreneurial management team to discuss the draft business plan in an open atmosphere. Such sessions often clear the air, surface issues, and expose problems that previously were unstated or unappreciated. The facilitator provides a catalyst for discussion and provides a buffer between the managers to minimize ego involvement and intimidation from the owner.

- Consultant. Retain the services of an outside consultant who specializes in helping start-up businesses evaluate their strengths and weaknesses in the context of their business strategy. Consultants can often ask the probing, difficult questions that the entrepreneurs often do not realize are critical and can assist the management group by developing business plans that will supplement existing strengths and provide a road map for resolving the weaknesses.

Using any or all of these resources, the entrepreneurial management team can often expose risks and rewards that had not previously been appreciated. Fawning over an inventor's latest gadget is not a basis for starting a business. The project got where it is because someone believed in it, but blind faith is not enough to start or sustain a business. These mechanisms can help avoid some of the pitfalls from making it a success.

LEADERSHIP AS A RESOURCE

In the functional checklist presented above "leadership qualities" was identified as a critical skill of the firm. This is true of a start-up as well as a *Fortune* 500 company. Leadership qualities are essential in any organization, whether in business, government, not-for-profits, or civic and social groups. Leaders can be found in all echelons of an organization regardless of title and position, not just top management. Leaders are a vital resource throughout an organization, a major strength if the firm has them and a serious weakness if it lacks them. It is, after all, people who run a business, not charts and spreadsheets. And leaders come in all sizes, ages, colors, and shapes.

Change leaders are especially valuable to enable their organizations to be change leaders. "In a period of rapid structural change the only organizations that survive are the 'change leaders,' " writes Peter Drucker. "It is therefore a central 21st-century challenge for management that its organization become a change leader."[15]

Someone has to take the lead and make changes happen. Some people are better at managing "things" than "people." It is "people" leadership skills that are addressed here. Figure 3.2 is a roster of the "personal" skills a leader of people needs, regardless of formal title or position on an organization chart.

Figure 3.2 lists key qualities of leadership.[16] Few people have all of them full strength in their personal makeup, but most leaders have most of them in varying degrees. One individual may possess some and another others— that is why a management team is so useful, particularly if the individuals in the team supplement each others' weaknesses with their own strengths.[17] Therefore, in selecting a management team, in addition to the normal parameter of qualifications of functional specialty, the top leader should also focus on personal qualities of the individuals to build a well-rounded team.

It should never be forgotten that a leader needs followers. "Leadership," writes Warren Bennis, "is never exerted in a vacuum. It is always a transaction between the leader, his or her followers, and the goal or dream. A resonance exists between leaders and followers that makes them allies in support of a common cause."[18]

The Chief Executive Officer is by definition the leader of the organization. The role of the leader "is to provide strategic directives, to encourage learning, and to make sure there are mechanisms for transferring the lessons," says John Browne, CEO of BP Amoco. "The role of leaders at all levels is to demonstrate to people that they are capable of achieving more

Figure 3.2
Leadership Qualities

Personal Trait	Reason for This Quality's Importance in a Leader
Intelligence	To command respect of others, a reasonable level of native mental capacity or IQ is needed
Vision	A simple, powerful idea or "dream" is needed
Charisma	An intangible quality of charm, style, attractiveness, making others want to follow this person's lead
Savvy	Street-smart, clever, nobody's-fool qualities inspiring confidence
Communication	Able to articulate and define a message simply and powerfully
Ethics	Trustworthy, genuine, able to assure others of solid character
Inspiring	Lofty goals, strength of character, clear message all combine to uplift others, making them want to follow
Decisive	Can be counted on to make timely decisions and enforce them
Serious	Earnest, determined, focused, self-disciplined

than they think they can achieve and that they should never be satisfied with where they are now."[19]

It is a job like no other in the organization because it is ultimately responsible for every decision and action of the entire organization. Since there is no CEO school, CEOs gain on-the-job training, are closely scrutinized by every stakeholder, and are allowed few mistakes. Research indicates that between 35 and 50 percent of all CEOs are replaced within five years.[20]

Patterns of Leadership Styles

Is there a pattern to leadership styles or approaches? One consultant has concluded there are six leadership "styles": coercive, authoritative, affiliative, democratic, pacesetting, and coaching. Successful leaders learn to blend these styles in the right measure at the right time.[21]

Bain and Company has also examined this issue.[22] They studied 160 companies in different industries around the world and discovered that there are only five distinct approaches to leadership by CEOs. These five CEO leadership approaches are as follows:[23]

- The Strategy Approach. CEOs using this approach believe their main task is to create, test, and design the implementation of long-term strategy, spending approximately 80 percent of their time on matters external to the organization (customers, competitors, technological advancements, market trends) and leaving internal matters to others. They spend their day ascertaining the organization's point of departure (current situation) and point of arrival (most advantageous situation in the future). These CEOs value employees to whom they can delegate the day-to-day operational aspects of the business, as well as those having excellent analytical and planning skills. Michael Dell of Dell Computers is an example of a CEO using this approach.

- The Human-Assets Approach. CEOs using this approach see their primary job as imparting to the organization certain values, behaviors, and attitudes; thus they closely manage the growth and development of individuals. These CEOs travel extensively, spending their time in personnel-related activities like recruiting, performance reviews, and career mapping. They like "company way" behavior and dislike "mavericks." Herb Kelleher of Southwest Airlines and Al Zeien of Gillette use this approach.

- The Expertise Approach. These CEOs believe their most important duty is selecting and disseminating within the organization an area of expertise that will be a source of competitive advantage—technological research, process improvements, new systems and procedures, promotion policies, training programs, etc. They hire people who are trained in that expertise and also seek others who are open minded and willing to be indoctrinated in it. They spend the majority of their time cultivating and improving the expertise—with customers, engineers, and those who analyze competitors. Julian O. Thompson of Anglo American South African mining company and Charlotte Beers of Ogilvy & Mather advertising use this approach.

- The Box Approach. CEOs using this approach believe they add most value to the organization by creating, communicating, and monitoring explicit sets of controls—financial, cultural, or both—to assure uniform, predictable performance by the firm. Their objective is to provide the customer with a risk-free experience. Outside hires are rare, and promotion is from within to proven performers. John Bond of HSBC Holdings (formerly Hong Kong Shanghai Banking Company), Richard Rosenberg, former Chairman and CEO of Bank of America, and Colin Marshall of British Airways employ this "no surprises" approach.

- The Change Approach. These CEOs believe their critical role is to create an environment of continual reinvention, even if this produces anxiety and confusion and leads to some strategic mistakes, temporarily hurting financial performance. These executives spend 75 percent of their time communicating (speeches, meetings, etc.) to motivate personnel to embrace the "gestalt of change." They spend their days in the field meeting stakeholders and developing the processes of change, not being concerned about the end point. They value not seniority and past performance but the maverick—aggressive, passionate, independent people who view their jobs as opportunities that must be seized every day, and not an entitlement. Stephen Friedman, former managing partner of Goldman, Sachs, and Dana Mead of Tenneco adopted this approach.

Whatever approach the CEO adopts, it must be used with clarity, consistency, and commitment. The stakes are too high for the leader to permit confused, misguided, or unguided organizations. Any successful leadership approach requires "conscious intent."[24]

Personal Strengths of Leaders

Leaders have a special obligation to evaluate their personal strengths and weaknesses because the entire organization is depending on them to direct and inspire and because the leader's skills may require sharpening as well as supplementing. "Most people think they know what they are good at," says Peter Drucker. "They are usually wrong. More often, people know what they are not good at—and even then more people are wrong than right. And yet, a person can perform only from strength. One cannot build performance on weaknesses, let alone on something one cannot do at all."[25] Some learn by doing, some by hearing, some by reading, some through feedback analysis. Some are better as commanders, others as subordinates. Some are best at analysis, others at making decisions. Some relate well to technical people, others to generalists. Some are loners, others are best working with others.

Self-discipline, especially control of ego, is essential for success—for hitting the target. "If you want to hit a bird on the wing," said Supreme Court Justice Oliver Wendell Holmes, "you must have all your will in a focus. You must not be thinking about yourself, and, equally, you must not be thinking about your neighbor; you must be living in your eye on that bird. Every achievement is a bird on the wing."[26]

Each person is unique in the way he/she learns, behaves, manages, and performs. Each person needs to understand his/her personal characteristics and then guide himself/herself accordingly. Drucker's advice is: "Work to improve the way *you* perform."[27]

CONCLUSION

Having completed the self-audit of the firm's strengths and weaknesses, including its leadership's capabilities, you must now return to the beginning of your plan and review the Vision Statement and the Goal, Mission, and Strategy Statements to insure that these previously written chapters are fully consistent with the ability of the firm to achieve them.

After all, if the vision and goals of the enterprise have turned out to be only a pipe dream without underlying reality of their attainment because of serious deficiencies of resources or leadership, the planning process either can stop here or it can restart with the help of the strong dose of reality that this internal resource audit chapter has provided.

For those areas of deficiency that have been identified during the self-audit, the chapter on Specific Objectives and Operating Plans should address them and provide for their amelioration—adding resources where deficiencies have been found and building on strengths where they have been found. This later chapter contains the detailed operating plans that provide for resources that have been identified as needed, in the quantities needed, when needed. It is in this chapter that those weaknesses are provided for.

Following the review of the prior work for consistency based on this chapter's "reality check," and taking note of the weaknesses that have been unearthed for later amelioration, you can now proceed to assess the external business environment within which the enterprise will operate.

NOTES

1. This discussion is based on the author's personal experience and management interviews at Northrop Corporation.

2. See Chapter 8 for a discussion of Michael Porter's value chain analysis.

3. Jay B. Barney, *Gaining and Sustaining Competitive Advantage* (Reading, MA: Addison-Wesley Publishing Co., 1997), Chapter 5: "Evaluating Firm Strengths and Weaknesses: Resources and Capabilities."

4. George A. Steiner, *Strategic Planning* (New York: Free Press, 1979), p. 143; Steiner refers to SWOT as the WOTS UP Analysis.

5. Terry Hill and Roy Westbrook, "SWOT Analysis: It's Time for a Product Recall," *Long Range Planning* 30, no. 1 (February 1997).

6. John F. Kennedy, *Public Papers of the Presidents of the United States, 1961* (Washington, DC: GPO, 1962), p. 403.

7. Ibid., p. 403.

8. Based on ideas presented in David A. Aaker, *Developing Business Strategies* (New York: Wiley, 1984), p. 145, and Michael E. Porter, *Competitive Strategy* (New York: Free Press, 1980), pp. 64–65.

9. Laura David, "Consumer Product Survey of America," Consumer Research Center, Buffalo, NY, February 1999.

10. Chart in Figure 3.1 is adapted with the permission of The Free Press, a Division of Simon & Schuster, Inc. from *Strategic Planning: What Every Manager Must Know* by George A. Steiner. Copyright © 1979 by The Free Press.

11. William A. Sahlman, "How to Write a Great Business Plan," *Harvard Business Review*, July–August 1997, pp. 98–105.

12. Ibid., p. 101, provides a useful checklist of fourteen "personal" questions regarding the principals' skills and qualifications for success.

13. Ibid., p. 105.

14. Ibid., p. 108.

15. Peter F. Drucker, "Change Leaders," *Inc.*, June 1999; excerpts from Peter F. Drucker, *Management Challenges for the 21st Century* (New York: Harper Business, 1999).

16. For a discussion of leadership, see: Warren Bennis, *On Becoming a Leader* (Reading, MA: Addison-Wesley, 1989), Howard Gardner, *Leading Minds: An Anatomy of Leadership* (New York: Basic Books, 1995); and James MacGregor Burns, *Leadership* (New York: Harper & Row, 1978).

17. Jon R. Katzenbach, "The Myth of the Top Management Team," *Harvard Business Review*, November–December 1997, warns that a so-called top management "team" seldom functions as a real team; yet, there are situations where a team is needed to accomplish more than its members could working on their own.

18. Warren Bennis, "The Leader as Storyteller," *Harvard Business Review*, January–February 1996, pp. 157, 160.

19. Steven E. Prokesch, "Unleashing the Power of Learning: An Interview with British Petroleum's John Browne," *Harvard Business Review*, September–October 1997, p. 148.

20. Charles M. Farkas and Suzy Wetlaufer, "The Ways Chief Executive Officers Lead," *Harvard Business Review*, May–June 1996, p. 110.

21. Daniel Goleman, "Leadership that Gets Results," *Harvard Business Review*, March–April 2000, pp. 78–90.

22. See Charles M. Farkas and Philippe De Backer, *Maximum Leadership: The World's Leading CEOs Share Their Five Strategies for Success* (New York: Holt, 1996).

23. The research is summarized in Charles M. Farkas and Suzy Wetlaufer, "The Ways Chief Executive Officers Lead," *Harvard Business Review*, May–June 1996, pp. 110–22, from which this discussion is drawn.

24. Ibid., p. 122.

25. Peter F. Drucker, "Managing Oneself," *Harvard Business Review*, March–April 1999, p. 66.

26. Quoted in Dean Acheson, *Sketches from Life of Men I Have Known* (New York: Harper & Brothers, 1959), pp. 147–48. Secretary of State Acheson used Justice Holmes' quotation to describe this trait in General George C. Marshall, an inspiring leader with a commanding presence grounded in self-discipline producing laser-like focus.

27. Drucker, "Managing Oneself," p. 68, emphasis added.

Chapter 4

Business Environment Assessment

To be successful, the business plan must addresses the overall context, the external environment, in which the firm will be operating during the planning period—and beyond, for sustained success. Whether the plan is a two-year or a ten-year plan, the planner is obligated to make an assessment over at least that time horizon to determine whether the goals and mission of the firm can realistically be achieved in that environment, examining the risks and opportunities that will confront the business. It is at this point, performing the environmental assessment, that the planner becomes a forecaster.[1]

The critical questions to keep in mind are these: what is the market for the firm's products or services and how will the firm satisfy that demand over time in this environment? Examination of competitive factors in the external environment is also required; this is addressed in the next chapter.

FOCUS THE ANALYSIS

To avoid endless analysis of every conceivable factor imaginable, the examination of the external environment should be focused. The focus is essentially on two elements of your firm's present and future products and services: market analysis and customer analysis.[2]

Market analysis provides a lens through which the analyst looks to understand the overall market in which your firm's products, both present and future, will be presented. Market analysis includes such factors as size, segment, projected growth, profitability, entry barriers, cost structure, distribution system, trends, and key success factors.

Customer analysis provides a second lens to help focus the external analysis. This area of analysis includes identification of customer segments, which helps in turn to define alternative product markets and strategic investment decisions. Customer motivation is examined to provide information to management to decide whether it can or should make the attempt to gain or hold a sustainable competitive advantage. Finally, this analysis should identify and evaluate unmet customer needs—to help management find ways to compete successfully in a marketplace where there are entrenched competitors.

Examining the External Business Context

The task of answering the questions—what is the market and how will it be satisfied?—is not as daunting as it sounds. There is plenty of help to aid in this undertaking. There are professional forecasting services to which one can subscribe, "free" advice from the larger banks and other financial institutions that have economic forecasting publications, and the U.S. government has everything from industry sector forecasts provided by the Commerce Department to the macroeconomic model used by the Federal Reserve. Each of these will provide the analyst planner with useful information.[3]

The business "environment" is a summation of the overall external climate where the future operations of your firm will be conducted—its markets and its means of satisfying demand in them. This assessment is performed on the macrolevel as well as the microlevel for your particular industry and product environment. On the macrolevel, for example, it may be widely believed that the overall business climate will be hostile in the immediate future, i.e., that an economic depression is just over the horizon; under such conditions it would be a major act of courage for the entrepreneur to attempt to start up a new business in that negative climate. Yet, that is exactly what Crowell, Weedon and Co. did in 1932—a stock brokerage firm initiating business in the depth of the Great Depression. And they are still in business today.

On the microlevel, the firm needs to evaluate the future from a company-specific and product-specific standpoint. What is the anticipated business climate for your company's product likely to be? For example, if taste in fashion among teenagers and young adults were to change away from snug-fitting blue jeans to a baggy, slouchy look and other trendier cuts of denim, then you would be in trouble in the marketplace if you were Levi Strauss & Co. and had no product for the new-look fashion. That is exactly what happened in the 1990s when Levi's sales slumped and its market share for jeans dropped from 50 percent to 25 percent in nine years, sales skidded

Figure 4.1
External Environment: Factors of Analysis

Factor	What the Factor Addresses
Physical	Where things are done; who will do them
Technological	How things are done
Legal/regulatory	The rules of the game in the legal and political system
Economic	Macrotrend factors in the economy
Sociocultural	Social structure and cultural conditions

from $7.1 billion in 1996 to $5.1 billion in 1999, and profits plunged to a mere $5.4 million in 1999 from $411 million two years earlier. These poor results happened despite the company's 50 percent cut in U.S.-based manufacturing plants and the layoff of 18,500 employees.[4] Cost of domestic production was a major contributing factor, causing the firm to refocus to designing and marketing products, rather than production.[5]

Another example of "change in taste" affecting its market is the cigar industry. In 1993 cigar sales in the United States soared, stimulated by a backlash against health consciousness that had branded cigarette smoking as dangerous. Baby boomers and Gen-Xers rediscovered (or discovered) the joy of cigar smoking. It became fashionable to be seen with a large stogie, partly because some highly visible celebrities were seen cigar smoking—Arnold Schwarzenegger, Bruce Willis, even Demi Moore. Cigar sales surged. By 1996, sales had grown 17.7 percent over 1995, and in 1997 they gained another 16.4 percent. The record year in the decade was 1998 when 3.33 billion cigars were sold, but sales growth in 1998 slowed significantly to just .4 percent over the prior year. "The bloom is off the rose. The craze is over," said Norman Sharp, head of the Cigar Association of America.[6] Was this just a five-year fad? The answer to that question is vital if you are in the cigar industry or operate a cigar bar.

There are factors in the business environment that affect all businesses to one degree or another. The business plan needs to address each of these. The degree of importance of each of these factors to your markets is your evaluation of each's impact on your business. Some may be more important to your ability to supply changing demand than others, and you should put greater emphasis on those in your business plan's environmental assessment. Figure 4.1 lists factors of analysis in the external environment that are germane to all business.[7]

These factors in the environment need to be analyzed and evaluated to ascertain the prospects for your firm and its products in its marketplace for the near term and longer-term future. The assessment needs to be general for the overall business climate affecting your particular industry; it also needs to be specific for the products and services that your firm will present to the marketplace during that time horizon. Use the lens of customer analysis and market analysis for your business to aid in this evaluation. Each of the five factors will be discussed in turn below.

Two other elements of the external environment are important to consider: the domains of the firm and the change drivers that affect the firm.

DOMAINS OF THE FIRM

Today, most firms operate in at least two domains and many operate simultaneously in all four domains: domestic, regional, international, and global.

- Domestic: Every company operates within its own domestic setting—its country of origin. If your firm is located in Los Angeles, its domestic domain has at least three parts—the city of Los Angeles, the state of California, and the United States of America. If it is located in Montreal, its domestic domain is the city of Montreal, the province of Quebec, and the federation of Canada. Laws, regulations, and rules emanating from any of the jurisdictions in the domestic setting of the firm will influence its business operations.

- Regional: Many countries are now part of a regional economic group. The United States is a party to the North American Free Trade Agreement (NAFTA), which impacts firms located in the United States, Canada, and Mexico in numerous ways—factory location decisions, investment decisions, labor decisions, decisions to export and import, etc. Similarly, firms operating in the fifteen member nations of the European Union are even more significantly impacted by that organization than U.S. companies are impacted by NAFTA because of the more comprehensive nature of that regional entity. Regional economic groupings can also be found throughout Latin America, southeast Asia, and eastern Europe.

- International: The international domain refers to transnational activities of a firm—exporting and importing, making foreign direct investments, repatriating profits from foreign operations, recruiting foreign-based labor, etc. Firms conducting international business need to be mindful of the differing legal, regulatory, economic, social, and other factors present in those other domestic settings.

- Global: The global environment refers to activities conducted transnationally on a large-scale basis, usually by multinational corporations having multiple product lines and production operations in several countries, and having its top management drawn from a variety of countries where it has operations. Such companies need to organize their activities to gain maximum advantage from their global reach and minimize negative impacts from any one domestic situation. The complexities of the tasks of currency hedging, transnational employee relations, coordination of multinational R&D activities, multiple brand coordination, meeting a variety of local regulatory standards, etc. are a major management challenge.

CHANGE DRIVERS

The external environment is not static, but dynamic. It is constantly evolving, and the rate of change appears to be accelerating. To identify emerging trends to enable your firm to deal with them, it is essential to identify the forces causing the changes in the external environment that affect your company. These causal factors, or change drivers, can be grouped into seven categories:

- Customer: This is the firm's main change agent. Identifying and satisfying changing customer demand is the major purpose of the firm. Keeping up with changing demands with respect to new tastes, new products, new modes of access, new forms of promotion, new channels of delivery, new supporting services, etc. are all drivers for change within your firm.

- Technology: The invention and application of new technologies is a constant factor in the external environment. Performing technology scanning, discussed below, to identify emerging technologies and to evaluate their significance and importance to the firm is a vital undertaking in the planning process. The emergence of the Internet as a change agent itself is a tribute to the powerful impact of information technology in the early 21st century.

- Capital: The ready availability of capital is a change driver. Conversely, its limited availability is a change inhibitor. For entrepreneurial firms to get started, for small businesses to grow, for established corporations to expand all require a ready supply of capital. Companies that have access to capital can accomplish these goals; firms that do not cannot. If a country has a readily available capital market, firms within that domain have these opportunities, while others are limited or dependent on governmental largesse or foreign investment. Having venture capital markets or a Nasdaq exchange is a dream in many parts of the world. The restrictions on the use of capital and the returns required by investors or lenders are also factors in the usefulness and flexibility of capital.

- Talent: Having people with talent to invent new products, to write the software needed to operate new systems, to design next year's model of an existing product line, to reorganize the business model of a firm in changing times is necessary for growth or sustained growth. Talent is a precious commodity that is perennially in short supply. The firm may have to venture beyond its domestic domain to find it, and once it is found the firm will have to find ways to keep it. In a free-agent economy, talent is perhaps the most valuable and perishable asset of all.

- Suppliers: Companies supplying vital inputs to your firm are often among your most valuable change agents. These firms often see, before you do, new and better ways of doing things to improve your end product or to make prices more competitive.

- Competitors: Your competitors will drive you to change or to extinction if you fail to change. Other than your customer, an aggressive competitor is your most motivating change agent. The competitor will stimulate you to develop new products, lower costs and prices, find new distribution channels, scour the world for talent, and motivate your entire organization like nothing else can. Every quarter will provide you with a report card on how well you are running the race against your opponents. Gaining the lead and/or keeping the lead is the true challenge for first-rate organizations.

- Leadership: A critical internal change agent is leadership. If the firm needs a change-agent leader, it can recruit one from within or outside the company. Such a leader can either lead the charge for change or foster an atmosphere within the firm for revolutionaries from below to take and hold ground for change. Or a change-agent leader can do both: lead it and stimulate the conditions for it. Firms, like countries, needing fundamental change rarely are able to accomplish it without a change-agent leader at the top directing the effort.

Having identified the domains of the firm, the factors of analysis, and the change drivers, it remains to identify the principal focus of the entire analysis: the customer. If, as Peter Drucker wrote, the purpose of the firm is to find and keep a customer, it can be added that without the customer the firm cannot accomplish its fundamental task: building wealth. The customer is both the focus of the firm and its main change agent.

Successful firms establish and maintain a two-way relationship with the customer, sending and receiving—providing goods or services that the customer demands or accepts, and registering the implied input from the customer when he or she sends signals that demand is changing for what you are supplying. That change signal can be based on changing taste, changing technology, changing economic conditions, changing demographics, changing competitive conditions, etc. Being ever alert to the two-way nature of the firm-to-customer relationship is imperative for sustained success.

In the early 21st century it is clear that the external environment is not only highly dynamic, it is also interactive. Technological innovations made by your firm are quickly copied by competitors, a rival can hire away your talented people at a moment's notice, suppliers may sign exclusive relationships with others offering greater reward or stability, and domestic or foreign conditions may help or harm your standing with key customers. The old analogy that the environment is like the chessboard on which companies move their pieces is far too static to express today's true conditions—which more resemble a three-dimensional interactive video game.

Figure 4.2 summarizes the above analysis.

Let us turn now to a discussion of the five factors of analysis.

PHYSICAL ENVIRONMENT

This is the factor that addresses where things are done and who will do them. In the broadest terms this factor in the environment can fundamentally alter the way business is done, or in a narrower sense it can marginally change the nature of business, such as providing a process improvement. In this category and the next the planner is scanning for "megatrends."[8]

Figure 4.2
Today's Interactive Business Environment

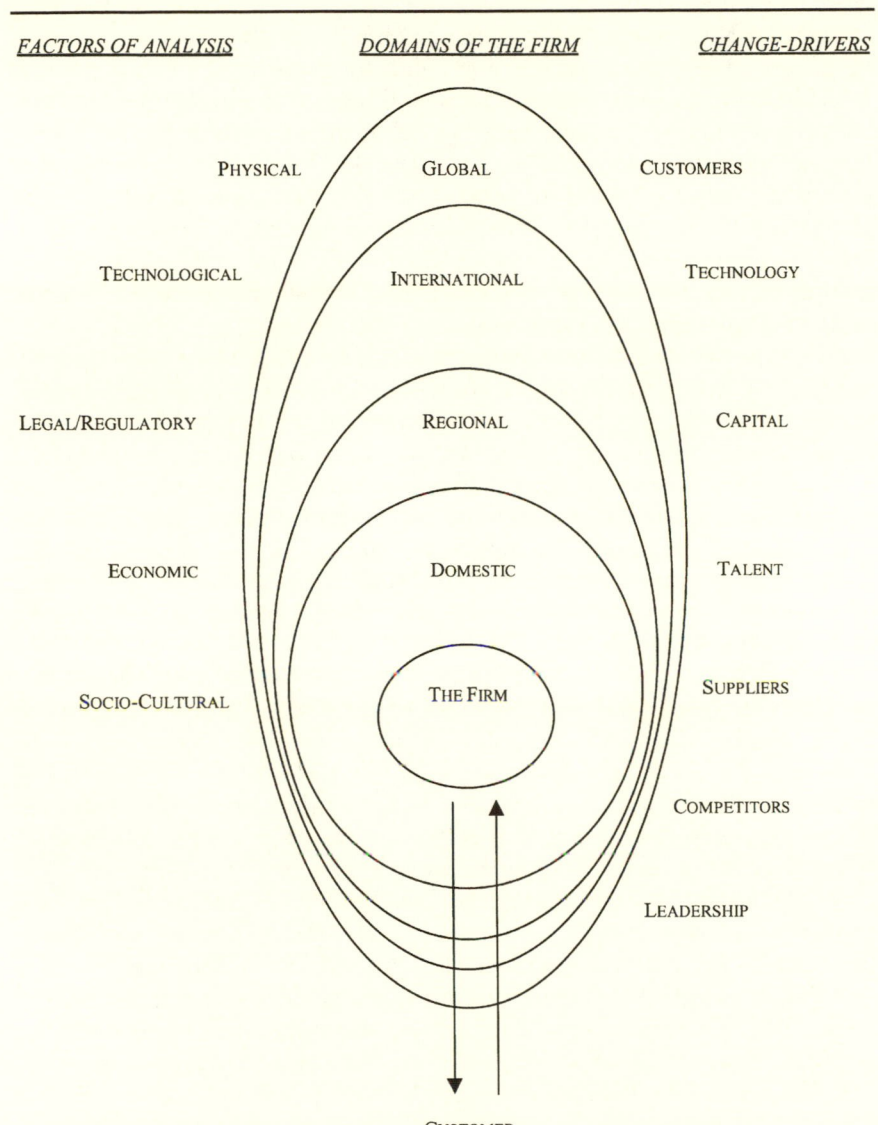

FACTORS OF ANALYSIS   DOMAINS OF THE FIRM   CHANGE-DRIVERS

PHYSICAL   GLOBAL   CUSTOMERS

TECHNOLOGICAL   INTERNATIONAL   TECHNOLOGY

LEGAL/REGULATORY   REGIONAL   CAPITAL

ECONOMIC   DOMESTIC   TALENT

SOCIO-CULTURAL   THE FIRM   SUPPLIERS

                                      COMPETITORS

                                      LEADERSHIP

CUSTOMER

Fundamental Changes in Industry: Where Things Are Done

One such megatrend change in the physical environment was initiated by Sir Richard Arkwright in England in 1767 when he began what came to be called the "factory system."[9] Arkwright was in the textile industry and sought a better way to make cloth. He invented a spinning frame powered by water, and later he and others mechanized more of the spinning processes. These machines were too large for the small homes in which workers then labored.

Arkwright had the vision that the production process of the day could be improved by taking the spinners and weavers of cotton out of their individual homes, then called cottages, and bringing them together into one place to perform these tasks together using the large, efficient machinery he and others of the day had invented. The skill levels of some people were such that they were better at spinning the flax into thread, and the skills of others were superior in weaving the thread into cloth. Arkwright set up a factory floor where the raw material entered at one end, was spun into thread, which was then carried forward to the weavers, and the finished bolts of cloth exited the factory out the other door.

Example: Richard Arkwright's Factory System. What had Arkwright accomplished with this simple dream? He had invented the factory system, which was fundamental to the establishment of the Industrial Revolution. He also institutionalized division of labor based on skill specialization. In so doing he changed the physical environment. No longer did workers work at home. Now they "commuted" to work in a factory setting together with others, leaving home for the entire day every day to work outside the home. This was fundamentally new. All the issues of human resources now began—interaction of people in the workplace, compensation structure, rank, rest breaks, promotion, etc.

Another level of physical factors also emerged. Arkwright believed that by centralizing the process, the quality of the final product would be improved by skill specialization, quality inspection, and improved overall performance. He also found that costs were lowered through bulk buying of raw materials and reduced cycle time in production, and larger quantities of throughput were achieved both at lower unit cost and at higher quality.[10] While production capacity grew, generating greater returns for managers, real earnings for manual workers essentially did not. Recent studies have shown the average working-class family's standard of living improved by less than 15 percent between the 1780s and the 1850s in Britain.[11]

What Arkwright also "invented" was management—organizing and directing complex activities involving people and things on a large scale. The physical environment of where things are done and by whom was fundamentally altered by Richard Arkwright's factory system. Only in the late 20th century did we see the beginnings of a partial return to the "cottage" industry through the "electronic cottage"—telecommuting by stay-at-home workers made possible by advancements in technology.

Example: Henry Ford. Henry Ford's invention of the moving assembly line is another example of a fundamental change in the physical environment. Prior to Ford, autos and other large items were manufactured using craft techniques that were as much 18th century as they were 19th. In 1913, five years after he introduced the Model T, Ford brought production into the 20th century with the introduction of the assembly line—moving the vehicle (at first by pulling a rope attached to the chassis and winching it) from one workstation to another, each station performing a specialized function (putting on doors, inserting the engine, mounting wheels, etc.), until the auto was fully assembled and driven out of the factory.

This new manufacturing process increased productivity and improved efficiency, reduced cycle time, dramatically lowered cost, and "automated" large-scale production operations. Ford's production time on the Model T was cut more than 75 percent[12] and the price was reduced from $850 to $260 per car, making it affordable even for his own workers when, in 1914, he introduced the $5, eight-hour workday, more than doubling wages and reducing the workday by 90 minutes. In the next twenty years Ford sold seventeen million Model Ts, about half of all the cars produced in the world at that time.[13]

"Most people had never been more than 20 miles from their homes prior to the introduction of the Model T," said his great-grandson, William Clay Ford, Jr., currently Chairman of the company. "It was a staggering change in the history of mankind. It changed where people lived, where they worked."[14] The basic idea of a "moving" assembly line has since been replicated in virtually every industry, from washing machines to airplanes, for the same reasons Henry Ford envisioned. Ford changed the physical environment forever with his "process improvement."[15]

The linkage between the physical and technological environments is of course quite close. Technological improvements in how things are done impact who does them, which also affects where things are done. Just as Arkwright's workers 200 years ago left their cottages to go to a factory because of the new spinning manufacturing technology, so too many of today's workers remain in their "electronic cottages" telecommuting because new communications technologies have enabled them to work there. Changes in either the physical or technical environments will impact the other, providing synergies and complementarity.

Fundamental Changes in Industry: Who Does Things

Who is going to do the work? The physical environment addresses this question along with the where issue. Unskilled labor in large quantities was needed to transform the North American continent in the 19th century by binding together the east and west coasts of the United States and Canada with railroads. Untrained laborers were imported largely from Ireland and China for this mammoth task. Later, many of these immigrants' sons became the semiskilled labor in the growing coal and steel industries in the Allegheny Mountains area. Owing to the rise in technology and its requirement for more educated labor, the 20th century's requirements for unskilled labor declined with virtually each passing decade, except for service jobs at the minimum wage level and below. The 21st century's need for highly skilled labor will intensify, putting a premium on well-trained and well-educated "knowledge workers."[16]

Temporary workers have become endemic in American manufacturing. This approach enables employers to reduce production costs, expand or shrink payrolls as needed, and replace underperformers quickly. Nearly one of every twenty manufacturing jobs in the United States is filled by a temporary worker, according to the Chicago Federal Reserve Bank, and the U.S. Labor Department projects a continued explosion of blue-collar temporary jobs well into the next decade, while white-collar assignments stagnate or decline. Moreover, temporary assignments are now typically used as an "audition" for the industrial worker—testing him/her out on the job to determine whether or not to hire that person permanently. In 1998, approximately 2.75 million temporary workers were employed in the United States daily, with over 40 percent of all clerical jobs and 34.5 percent of all industrial jobs held by "temps."[17]

Another long-term secular trend is an increase in the female component of the workforce. In 1968 women represented 37 percent of the U.S. labor force of 78.7 million people; thirty years later women composed 46 percent of the 137.6-million labor force. The number of women in the labor force with children under age six nearly doubled between 1978 and 1998 to 10.6 million.[18] In 1998, 62 percent of mothers of children under school age worked.[19] The reasons for these trends result from both supply and demand: women are well educated and are motivated to work because they either desire to work or decide to do so for economic reasons, and the labor market needs well-educated workers whose brains are today more important than muscle.

The supply of certain critical skills is periodically short, and firms have developed techniques for overcoming such shortages. These range from aggressive recruitment for permanent employment, hiring temporary workers to meet surges, contracting out the task to other specialty firms or to suppliers who have the requisite capabilities, sending the task offshore to countries where there is an adequate labor supply in the critical skill area (software development to India), importing labor from countries having high supply and low demand for the key skills (Filipino software programmers coming to the United States), and overcoming the skill deficit by "workarounds" involving schedule changes or employing alternative processes or technologies.

To illustrate the last point, secretaries are a vanishing breed except for certain high-level executives because they are expensive (salary and fringe package) to employ and the task they traditionally performed can be done by the boss (typing his/her own correspondence on a word processor and e-mailing it to the addressee) or by technology (automatic answering machines and pagers). Between 1987 and 1994, homes and offices added 10 million fax machines, e-mail addresses increased by over 26 million, and the number of secretaries declined by 521,000.[20]

Example: Ireland. Some countries have become economically developed by specializing in key "job descriptions." For example, in the 1990s Ireland began a highly successful effort, centered on free university education, to educate and train its young people to become "service" providers—performing high-skill tasks in record-keeping, claims management, and account-processing services especially for the financial and insurance industries, the so-called "backroom" tasks. These are services that American, British, and German companies require but had an insufficient labor pool to draw from at the salary level desired.

This "services" strategy was conceived after years of failing to develop "heavy" industries such as manufacturing to develop Ireland's economy. It, along with reduced government debt and an infusion of foreign investment attracted by their low 10 percent corporate tax rate, has transformed Ireland's economy from its chronic characteristics visible as recently as the 1980s, when it was the poor cousin of the European Union with 17 percent unemployment and a young population with no prospects, into a super-charged economy with net immigration and unemployment in 1999 at less than 6 percent. Ireland's GDP per capita is about to surpass Britain's, and its population is expected to reach four million by 2006.[21]

Indeed, Ireland, which missed the Industrial Revolution, is "in mid-leap from the Agricultural Age to the Information Age—literally."[22] Ireland is the European headquarters for Microsoft and numerous other multinational companies taking advantage of its highly educated, English-speaking workforce. Intel's $2.5 billion wafer-fabrication plant sits in County Kildare; it is the largest building project in Irish history, and Intel's largest non-U.S. facility, manufacturing the Pentium III chip; it employs 4,000 people. Technology advancements in instantaneous global telecommunications and the Internet have enabled this "service industry" economic development strategy to work for Ireland.[23]

Example: Gateway Computers. An example of linking the where and who elements of the physical environment is Gateway Inc., the computer company. Though now headquartered in San Diego, Gateway initially located their operations in South Dakota, a low-cost, low-wage, yet high-skill area of the United States where there is little competition in the labor market. Gateway's strategic approach is "direct" selling of their computers over the telephone and Internet to mostly small business and consumer end users, not retail outlets other than their own Gateway Country stores. The strategy is working: in the second quarter of 1999, Gateway shipped over one million PCs, up 36 percent from the comparable quarter a year earlier, generating revenue of $1.9 billion, up 18 percent, and gross margins of 22 percent, the highest ever for a quarter.[24] Thus, a host of telecommunications advancements enable this strategy to work—in South Dakota or anywhere else the labor market and cost structure fit the company's needs.

Where People Work

Where people work used to relate to the industry they work in. Until approximately 1900, 85 percent of America's workers were in agriculture. That meant most people lived and worked in the country, not the city. With increased industrialization and the mechanization of agriculture, labor needs in agriculture declined just when labor needs in manufacturing increased. People left the country and moved to the city. By 1950, 73 percent of U.S. employees worked in production or manufacturing in an urban setting. Automation changed the way work was performed and the types of work needed changed, so that, by the end of 1990s, less than 2 percent of the U.S. workforce was in agriculture and only 17 percent worked in manufacturing.[25]

Today, the great majority of Americans (probably over two-thirds) work in the "services" sector, and the majority of them live and work neither in the city nor the country, but in a phenomenon that began at mid-20th century called the suburbs. And growing numbers of well-educated, middle-class professionals are working at home, wherever that is located.[26]

What is happening in America's suburbs? "Between 1970 and 1990, U.S. central cities lost 1.3 million two-parent families to the suburbs. Thirty years ago, the suburbs had 25% more families than the city; today, they have 75% more," wrote Joel Kotkin, a Senior Fellow at Pepperdine's Institute of Public Policy.[27] The San Fernando Valley of Los Angeles is typical. Between 1950 and 1970, 90 percent of the Valley's suburbanites were white. As they left or died off, they were replaced by nonwhites; by 1997, according to L.A. County estimates, Latinos accounted for 41 percent and Asians 9 percent of the Valley's population.

At the end of the 20th century, nearly 51 percent of Asians, 43 percent of Latinos, and 32 percent of African-Americans live in U.S. suburbs. New York City's borough of Queens twenty years ago was the city's largest middle- and working-class white bastion; today it is the city's most diverse borough with more than 40 percent of its businesses minority-owned, twice as many as Manhattan, the immigrant's former main point of entry.[28] What is happening in Los Angeles and New York is typical of Houston, Miami, San Francisco, and Washington, DC, cities where immigration is heaviest; these cities' suburbs now mirror the cities they surround.

The traditional coupling of where people work and what type of work they perform is dissolving. Farming and being in the country, auto making and being in Detroit still hold, but what is the reason for being in the suburbs? Unless you have to be in your suburban or urban office or factory there is no need to live nearby. Today, you can telecommute from very great distances. The implication of this physical trend based on technological innovation is that the attractive power of the suburbs may weaken in favor of more rural, less expensive home sites for many "knowledge" workers.

This change would be provoked for the same reasons the suburbs were attractive in their day—a less congested, less dangerous location to provide a nice home and better schools for your family. Today, a knowledge worker can buy a small farm in Vermont and telecommute to Boston, and the farm is less expensive than a suburban house near Boston. The schools and crime rate are probably better, too. The geographic redistribution of the American laborforce is in the early stage of change—once again. The long-term secular trend for America's population is and always has been change.

TECHNOLOGICAL ENVIRONMENT

How things are done and the technologies involved in doing them is the subject of the technological environment. Richard Arkwright's factory system would not have come about except for his invention of the water-powered spinning wheel. Technological inventions and their applications in the production process power innovation and change.

Fundamental Changes in Industry: How Things Are Done

Eli Whitney's cotton gin was a marvelous invention in 1793 for replacing the human hand with a machine to perform the drudgery job of separating cotton from the cottonseed faster and more efficiently. The more fundamental invention that Whitney's cotton gin, and later a musket for the U.S. Army, represented was the way it was made—by assembling standardized, interchangeable parts.

Whitney had the idea that his machines and guns should be made not as every machine and musket had been made up to that time—one at a time, each a separate creation by a craftsman—but by making the individual parts that went into the machine exactly alike, making them in bulk quantities, and then assembling the individual parts into the final machine. Thus, how the cotton gin and firearms were made, more than the products themselves, was the triumph of Whitney's invention. All production operations since have employed Whitney's fundamental concept of mass-produced, identical, interchangeable parts.[29]

Social Changes

Changes in technology produce social changes as well as process changes. Henry Ford's mass production of affordable automobiles—produced and priced low enough to be able to be purchased even by his own workers because he paid them a wage high enough to make them customers for the product—produced far-reaching economic and social consequences still felt today. Americans became mobile like never before, able to travel freely over what used to be considered vast distances, with relative ease and comfort. This spawned industries that became dependent on the car—auto dealers, service stations, motels, shopping malls, freeway systems, the petroleum industry, and all the services that support suburban life—to name just a few. Indeed, as early as the midpoint of the 20th century, one observer declared that one-sixth of the U.S. economy was already auto-dependent, making the automobile "the industry of industries."[30]

Invention of the computer chip along with advancements in telecommunications is enabling average citizens to have the ability to perform complex tasks in their homes or offices with relative ease that previously only large teams of people could perform, if at all. Computing power increases on an ever-rising scale over time.

ENIAC, the first digital, general-purpose electronic computer, invented by Mauchley and Eckert during World War II, filled a very large open-bay area in the Engineering Building at the University of Pennsylvania. It performed many of the large-scale computations needed to calculate trajectories for artillery guns.[31] Since these early times, the cost of computing power has dropped roughly 30 percent every year, and microchips double in performance power every 18 months.[32] In the 1980s, the computing power of any kid's arcade computer game had more power than ENIAC. Today, the average person can wear on his or her wrist more computing power than existed in the entire world before 1961.[33]

This power is a great enabler, permitting vast mobility, independence, and convenience for individuals at low cost. Automated, computer-controlled machinery, linked to telecommunications equipment, enables the motorist to stop at a gas station, fill up, pay for the purchase at the pump, and have the ATM card or credit card information uplinked through a satellite, and record the transaction with 100 percent accuracy at a computer server anywhere in the world—and all of this is done in a shorter time span that it would have taken a gas pump attendant to handle the change in times gone by.

Home-based securities trading is becoming a major force in the financial industry—enabling the individual to access the New York Stock Exchange trading floor via an e-trader instantaneously, taking advantage of moment-to-moment changes in stock prices. Home-based banking spares the individual the need to travel to a branch bank in bad weather, through traffic, over some distance, and wait in a line—to perform routine functions more quickly and efficiently than ever imagined. The consequences for the gas station attendant, the stockbroker, and the branch bank teller are clear.

What has been described illustrates the process of "creative destruction." Joseph A. Schumpeter developed this concept to explain the change process inherent in capitalism. Schumpeter wrote that capitalism is a process that "incessantly revolutionizes the economic structure from within, incessantly destroying the old one, incessantly creating a new one. This process of Creative Destruction is the essential fact about capitalism. It is what capitalism consist in and what every capitalist concern has got to live in."[34] This is an economic system that is never stationary; the "fundamental impulse that sets and keeps the capitalist engine in motion comes from the new consumers' goods, the new methods of production or transportation, the new markets, the new forms of industrial organization that capitalist enterprise creates."[35]

Technology Forecasting

Forecasting changes in technology and their applications to business and their impacts on society is a major task.[36] In the early 1990s the George Washington University Forecast of Emerging Technologies project began making such forecasts every two years. The project utilizes a number of methods to make the projections—environmental scanning, trend analysis, Delphi surveys, and scenario building—for at least the next fifty years to determine which technologies are likely to emerge as important and when. The project's 1997 report evaluated eighty-five technologies and reported twelve of these would "emerge" as important during the next three decades: energy, environment, farming and food, computer hardware, computer software, communications, information services, manufacturing and robotics, materials, medicine, space, and transportation. The study concludes, "The Technology Revolution seems destined to transform modern civilization."[37]

Example: Communications. Communications was identified as one of the twelve most important technologies. It is an industry where technology has already changed in the 1980s and 1990s to create vast new markets without destroying existing ones. Wireless telephones linked to computers enable subscribers to have telephone communication to and from remote, moving locations almost anywhere in the industrial world. In the United States alone the number of wireless telephone subscribers in the ten-year period from 1988 to 1998 increased from 1.6 million to 60.8 million, and the average monthly bill declined by more than half, from $95 to $39.88, over the same period. A new class of phones linked by computers through the Internet will combine the features of mobile phones and portable computers to enable subscribers to have wireless data connections as conveniently as cell phone conversations.[38] This is technology creating markets that never existed before.

Example: Stealth Technology. Another example of innovation resulting in "technology push" is stealth. During the 1970s two U.S. aerospace companies independently began development of a new technology called stealth—an aircraft that would be "invisible" to radar. Lockheed and Nor-throp each had its own technological approach, and each was funded by the U.S. Air Force to pursue that approach to determine whether radar invisibility was possible. Each company proved its design worked in com-puter simulations and/or test flights of prototype aircraft. Once the tech-nology was proven, the demand was created.

This is classic technology push—an invention that instantly generates market demand for itself. The Air Force awarded production contracts to both companies: to Lockheed for the F-117A stealth fighter/attack aircraft and to Northrop for the B-2 stealth bomber. Eventually both firms com-peted for the Advanced Tactical Fighter, a stealth fighter intended to replace the F-15, which Lockheed won in a prototype fly-off competition, putting its version of stealth into preproduction in the late 1990s as the USAF's F-22 Raptor.[39]

"Networked Companies"

The emergence of powerful new technologies, like communications, and their widespread availability at low cost have not only enabled new prod-ucts and markets to be created, they also have enabled a new paradigm of company to emerge. Kenichi Ohmae has named these "Networked Com-panies." This new type of company depends on global real-time telecom-munications, global logistical and distribution systems, global financial services capabilities, and management that is globally focused. This type of company keeps only its core skills in-house and outsources everything else to the most competent, lowest-cost suppliers wherever in the world they may be.

Example: Nike. Nike is a good example of such a firm.[40] This firm's specialization is sports marketing of sports products and supplier manage-ment. Nike managers and creative people design athletic footwear and other sports products at their headquarters in Oregon, transmit the designs electronically to mills, cutters, and assemblers in low-cost locations mostly in East and South Asia where this work is outsourced at over forty facto-ries, have United Parcel Service transfer piece parts from one supplier to another in the work process, and have UPS deliver the finished products to retailers' warehouse and distribution centers around the globe. Payments are made electronically using VISA International. The entire process is man-aged from Oregon, where none of the work is performed except design and management oversight.

The individual components of this entire process are "networked" with one another electronically, with management control from the top. Nike owns nothing. They lease their Oregon office campus, and they outsource *all* the manufacturing and distribution. Nike's core skill is sports market-ing—designing athletic products, managing their creation, and selling them

Figure 4.3
Problem/Solution Paradigm

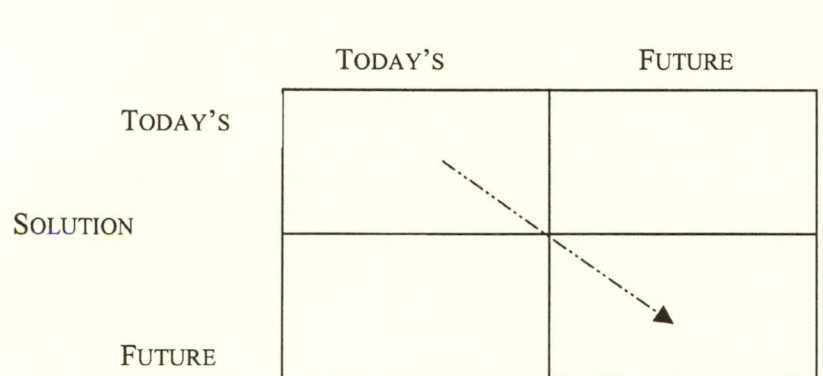

to customers around the globe. There is nothing traditional in the way Philip Knight, Nike's CEO, designed and operates this new type of business system. Through the late 1990s, Nike experienced 49 percent growth per year.

Nike searches the globe for the lowest-cost operators and locations for its manufacturing operations. In the 1990s Vietnam, Asia's poorest country, was selected for its shoe and apparel assembly operations. Nike has five South Korean and Taiwanese subcontractors in Vietnam who employ 43,000 people, making Nike's suppliers Vietnam's largest private employer, and its footwear and apparel account for 7 percent of Vietnam's exports. Average monthly wage is $65, versus national per capita income of $1 per day, more than twice what a teacher or young doctor earns at a state-owned hospital. These jobs are scarce and much coveted, despite the nine-hour day, six-day week on the assembly line.[41]

Problem/Solution Paradigm

Fundamentally, there are two types of problems and two types of solutions: today's problems solved by today's solutions, and future problems solved by future solutions. Technological innovation can assist the firm in making a quantum jump over its competition by attempting to find tomorrow's solution to today's problem—which of course could also be the solution to future problems. This concept is illustrated in Figure 4.3, which outlines a useful way to evaluate a problem that will be illustrated by air pollution and its causes and possible remedies.

Example: Air Pollution and the Auto Industry. A "problem" "today" is environmental pollution resulting from the internal combustion engine in today's motor vehicles. That engine and the motor vehicles that use it solved an earlier problem—horse-drawn vehicles 100 years ago were also "polluting" the city streets and provided low-speed, high-maintenance transportation. Daimler's invention of the internal combustion engine and his and Benz's Mercedes auto provided the technology to solve it. One hundred years later the air pollution resulting from yesterday's "solution" is today's "problem."

How to solve it? "Today's" solution is environmental control devices on these vehicles, restrictions on their use on certain days of the week, such as odd/even license plate restrictions on use, no use in some inner-city areas, carpooling requirements, and, where possible, different fuels (e.g., natural gas) than gasoline. These solutions all employ today's technologies and techniques against today's problem.

A "future" solution to "today's" problem is a propulsion technology different from the gasoline-powered engine.[42] One such approach gaining wide attention is called "fuel-cell" technology. Fuel-cell power plants are attractive alternatives to traditional gasoline-powered internal combustion engines because they are 50 percent more fuel-efficient, yet are as much as 90 percent less polluting. Most use methanol, not gasoline, because it can easily be converted into hydrogen by means of an onboard reformer. Ford Motor Company, General Motors, DaimlerChrysler, Toyota, and Honda are all working on fuel-cell autos.[43]

A Ford/DaimlerChrysler alliance claims to be in the lead, having unveiled a fuel-cell passenger vehicle in March 1999 that is more powerful and has greater range than previous prototypes, accelerating the team's plans to bring this type of vehicle to market in five years. DaimlerChrysler alone has spent $1 billion on research and development and will spend $400 million more before the first fuel-cell vehicles are sold in 2004.[44]

General Motors and Toyota have agreed to a five-year research-and-development effort to jointly develop alternative-powered vehicles, hoping through their sheer size to set the standard for the future of environmentally friendly vehicles. Much of the effort of this joint activity will be to produce a viable fuel-cell-powered vehicle.[45] Separately, GM has been developing "hybrid-electric" propulsion technology to reduce emissions and overcome the limitations of pure electric vehicles; GM is the first to announce testing of this technology in pickup trucks.[46]

Putting Technological Solutions to Work

The implications of this use of "tomorrow's" technology to solve "today's" problem are immense. They will impact virtually every sector of the automobile industry, the petroleum industry, and even geopolitical relationships, such as reducing the importance of certain countries' influence in world affairs because they are key oil-producing states. If this new technology is proven feasible and practical, ripple effects will flow throughout the industrial world, and importantly, the atmosphere will also improve. One can only wonder what the next hundred years will see with respect to this "solution" to "today's" problem.

Technological innovation can of course be more than a cutting-edge differential in any future competitive environment. It can also be a clear-cut differential in the current business environment, if employed properly. There are examples of firms that develop technological innovation with immediate product applicability but then are reluctant to proceed to the next step to put the product into production.[47] Investing in the invention of technology solutions is only half the equation; putting those technologies to work is a management decision of equal importance. Finally, a warning from an advanced-technology company which exited a disastrous high-technology joint venture at great loss: "We must not be seduced by technology. We must soberly evaluate potential markets. The moral is not to avoid all risks, but to take sensible risks."[48]

The planner's job is to scan the external technological environment, identify critical trends, and evaluate them to determine their applicability to your firm and its competitors. Then decide which technologies are maturing, which are becoming obsolesced, and which new technologies would provide your firm with a future competitive advantage at manageable cost and risk. This analysis is a key component in determining the firm's "scope"—the very definition of the business activity the firm intends to undertake and the strategic choices it will make to pursue them.[49] No more fundamentally important technological trend has emerged than e-business, whose impacts are altering the scope of virtually every business.

e-Business

The "new economy" has emerged as a transforming power throughout global industry. Its implications are as far-reaching as any in modern economic history. At its heart are technological advancements in computing, communications, and information management. All this is predicated on enormous investments in technology-rich activities, both hardware and software, and, as importantly, investments in new ways of thinking. The spine of this new structure is the Internet, and its nerve endings have global reach.

In 1999, the Internet economy in the United States alone added 650,000 jobs and generated more than $500 billion in revenue, according to Cisco Systems' CEO John Chambers, a major Internet product provider. The Internet's workforce has grown quickly and now exceeds the U.S.'s active military, insurance, communications, and public utilities industries. It is twice the size of the airline, chemical, legal, and real estate industries. "Over the next two decades, the Internet economy will bring about more dramatic changes in the way we work, live, play, and learn than we witnessed during the last 200 years of the Industrial Revolution," according to Chambers.[50]

In 1997 IBM coined the term "e-business" to define "an enormous new industry category to describe the broad implications of the Internet as a medium for real business and institutional transformation."[51] Louis Gerstner, Chairman and CEO of IBM, has written that "1999 was the year e-business and the global Internet economy came of age. It was a tidal wave, sweeping everything before it, driving new levels of megamerger activity, carrying thousands of entirely new businesses to unprecedented levels of wealth . . . , submerging almost as many others, and rearranging the landscape of commerce."[52]

Gerstner has identified six trends in the brief evolution of e-business:[53]

1. The Internet is creating not just new businesses but new business models. New types of companies performing tasks that were never before performed have burst forth, almost immediately generating great wealth and with it great power. One of the largest of these is America Online. AOL's spectacular growth as the world's largest Internet service provider has enabled it to amass immense wealth at previously unimaginable speed, empowering it to acquire rivals, CompuServe and Netscape, and a provider of both content and delivery, Time Warner, the world's largest entertainment company and one of America's largest cable operators.

2. Competitive advantage in the information technology industry is moving from creating technology to helping customers use it. In business-to-business relationships, there are numerous examples of companies using the Internet for component purchasing. Ford Motor Company buys $80 billion in goods a year from its main suppliers and has transactions worth $300 billion a year through its extended supply chain.[54] Ford established an online parts procurement system called AutoXchange using software from Oracle Corporation in a joint venture with that firm.

In its first use, Ford bought $78 million worth of auto parts in one online auction. The experiment worked, and in the next month alone Ford expected to procure $300 million worth of parts. AutoXchange will be spun off as a separate company, with Cisco Systems buying a stake. Through its online auction system, AutoXchange is expected to save Ford "billions and billions" of dollars, said Ray Lane, Oracle's president.[55]

Enabling companies to transform themselves is another example of the new technology's power and application. General Motors has established its own e-commerce activity within the company, called e-GM. This entity is expected to "fundamentally change the way" GM does business by coordinating GM's various Internet sites, GM BuyPower and gm.com. "The goal is to transform GM's traditional automotive operations into a global e-business enterprise, thereby enhancing the customer experience, improving efficiency, and cutting costs."[56]

At GM, one of the most anticipated benefits is a major reduction in the time needed from design freeze to customer product delivery. The "old" process took 48 months, in May 2000 it took 24 months, and the hope is that the Internet process will bring it down to 18 months. Improved speed from design to delivery will reduce GM's cost, reduce dealer inventory (eighty-day average in 2000) and cost, and bring "fresher" products to the customer.[57]

GM's ultimate goal is to transform one of the world's largest corporations into a true e-business, moving it from a build-to-stock operation to a build-to-order company, delivering a tailor-made vehicle to a customer within eight days. To achieve this monumental goal, GM concluded that "everything" at GM will have to change—from vehicle design, to parts-ordering processes, to manufacturing systems, to customer interface, to delivery system, to administrative structure—"everything."[58] The new system will be entirely Web-based.

Like GM, General Electric is using the Internet to dramatically reduce cost, speed decisions, and transform itself. The pilot project was a $5,000 computer program to centralize employee business travel approval at the division manager level. The savings in travel costs in the second month of operation, August 2000, was $40 million, compared with the same month a year earlier. Based on this experience, the CEO, Mr. Welch, is expanding Internet-based decision making throughout the management structure. His goal is to save $12 billion from corporate-wide operating costs within the next eighteen months.[59]

Four of the world's leading aerospace and defense companies are forming a massive Web-based marketplace for aerospace parts and services. This new company will be an independent entity in which the four will have an equity interest. The four are Boeing, Lockheed Martin, Raytheon, and BAE Systems (formerly British Aerospace). They are partnering with Commerce One, Inc. These four companies spend approximately $71 billion per year for parts and services, which will now be online. They have 37,000 suppliers and customers, all of which will be invited to join the marketplace.[60]

Another example is GlobalNetXchange, a new joint venture company between Oracle, on the one hand, and, on the other, Sears, Roebuck, and Carrefour, France's largest retailer. Using the AutoXchange model, this new company will provide Web-based purchasing for the two big retailers in what is essentially a purchasing cooperative, holding "live" auctions with suppliers on a global basis. This is business-to-business Internet activity on a grand scale, creating a "revolution in retail," said Arthur C. Martinez, Sears' CEO. "It will forever redefine supply-chain processes, increase collaboration with suppliers and reduce supply-chain costs."[61]

3. With the rise of the networked world, the PC era is over. The world

has evolved from the personal computer era, which began in the late 1970s with Apple and 1981 with IBM's PC, where the desktop device was the beginning and the end of the technology's impact. Today, PCs are linked via networks and computer servers within companies and with other PCs throughout the world via the Internet. The "networks" are provided by hardware and software companies, such as Cisco Systems and Oracle, which were not in existence when the PC era began, but which now have greater market capitalization values than almost any company in America. This networked world enables individuals and businesses not only to communicate with others, but also to perform numerous tasks, such as purchase goods and services that previously they could obtain only through traditional bid/award processes and through "brick and mortar" stores.

New companies have emerged, like Amazon.com, to provide shopping through the PC on the Internet. Jeff Bezos, Amazon.com's CEO, forecasts sales on the Internet may capture 15 percent of the world's $5 trillion retail market.[62] A Commerce Department study estimated Internet retail sales in the fourth quarter of 1999 at $5.3 billion; private research groups cite figures as high as $10 billion for the same period.[63] Along with Internet companies like Amazon.com are a new breed of companies that are being created by joint ventures between software manufacturers and existing retailers to satisfy their own in-bound logistics needs. In time, people and businesses will be freed from dependency on the PC and will be able to make purchases from cell phones and palm-held devices, which is an illustration of how the "wireless world" is diminishing dependence on the PC.

4. The Internet is reinventing entire markets—the very idea of a market. Entirely new business forms are being created: they do not make anything, they do not sell anything. They *are* the market. These are "e-marketplaces" and "e-exchanges." EBay is an example of a company fitting this description. It is an auction house online, facilitating sellers of items to find buyers for those items and providing a medium of exchange. The business-to-business examples cited above, AutoXchange and GlobalNetXchange, are also examples fitting this category.

Business-to-business transactions are already transforming supply-chain activities in autos, aerospace, chemicals, retail, steel, pharmaceuticals, and industrial goods of all kinds, plus capital and labor. The ramifications are far-reaching.

In business-to-customer marketing relationships, the Internet is also a transforming force. The last major innovation in marketing was the advent of brand management and the introduction of network television after World War II. Under this half-century-old model, manufacturers depend principally on an intermediary—retailers—as the medium and mechanism for product delivery to the customer.

Now, with the Internet, there is an alternative: customer-driven marketing. "The Internet permits companies to put separate channels of customer communication into a single, focused, coherent response mechanism."[64] The Internet "gives customers an unprecedented degree of control over the entire marketing process."[65] It enables customers to directly obtain a great deal of information about prices and benefits of competing products and to dialogue directly with their marketers as coequals, actively soliciting product information and eagerly buying the product when they find the right match of product and need. This is a marketing sea change.

5. Market control is no longer sensible or achievable as a business goal. Customers, not technology providers, are in the Internet driver's seat. The era defined by proprietary technology and computing architectures is over. Customers used to be dependent on providers of pieces of technology. No longer. Now e-business requires organization from the customer in, not from the provider out. Technology does not confer control. This changes everything. In the auction environment on eBay, the customer—the buyer— is in control: he can bid or not, raise the bid or not, and stop bidding when he wants. The technology does not control; it enables, facilitates.

6. The intersection of societal issues and the Internet will force the industry to grow up fast and assume a new level of public responsibility. Responsible leadership for using the Web, and not abusing the Web, is imperative. If industry itself fails to perform this function, government will. Issues of propriety, privacy, equal access, data security, national security, protection of children, and education are in the forefront. Health care is an example: six large managed-care companies are developing a jointly operated Internet venture to reduce administrative costs and reduce administrative hassles for doctors and patients by shifting to the Web as many of the transactions involved in health care as possible.[66] Sensitivity of the data involved, involving patient and health care professional information— doctors, hospitals, and insurers—requires the utmost protection. Today, technology has become both a threat and a solution to privacy and security.

The transforming power of e-business is revolutionizing the value chains of old-economy firms as well as establishing those in the new economy. These far-reaching effects are as profound as any in modern economic history.

LEGAL/REGULATORY ENVIRONMENT

The legal and regulatory environment portion of the plan addresses the rules of the game in the domains, the society or societies, where the business operates. This section addresses the political and legal system of the nation(s) where the firm has factory operations, major markets, distribution systems, research-and-development centers, test facilities, and/or significant investments or other holdings.

Therefore, the system of laws, the dispute resolution system, the civil order and justice system, rights of redress of grievance, sanctity of contract, and law-making and law enforcement systems are all part of this evaluation. Outcomes of these processes are also evaluated, such as laws governing competition, regulation of certain industries, environmental regulations, price setting by governmental agencies in certain industries, extent of deregulation, governmental ownership of certain industries or policies leading to privatization, administrative rulings, and executive policies governing industry sectors.

Evaluate Changes in the Rules of the Game: System versus Policy Changes

The method of analysis the planner should employ is first to look for normative behavior in the legal/regulatory environment and then to search for and identify change. Normative behavior is what is typical and usual—the normal way the society operates. Change of course refers to alterations in the usual pattern. Change can occur gradually or it can happen suddenly; typically the planner cannot forecast sudden changes in this environment (unless the situation was unstable at the outset of the evaluation), but the planner should scan for trends in the environment indicating likely changes that will affect the business to enable the firm to best plan for and manage the risks inherent in such changes.

Example: France. An example of a "sudden" policy change produced by a stable system occurred in France.[67] This is a law enacted in 1998 without much prior discussion by the French National Assembly reducing the nation's work week on a voluntary basis from 39 hours to 35 hours in an effort to reduce unemployment (then running at 11.4 percent) by sharing work among more workers. Within a year approximately 1.7 million workers, mostly blue-collar workers in state-owned companies, were affected. The Socialist-led government later proposed more sweeping legislation expanding the concept to white-collar workers. On February 1, 2000 a further expansion of the law took effect, reducing the work week to 35 hours for all French companies with 20 or more employees, and providing a procedure for implementation that had been agreed to by management and labor.

Such governmental manipulation of the "rules of the game" by making a major policy change to deal with a political and economic problem illustrates the need for forward-thinking risk analysis of the legal/regulatory environment. This French law produced labor unrest, including roadblocks by truckers causing colossal traffic tie-ups all across the country, and a demand by workers for pay increases to offset their loss of hours worked.[68]

Example: United Kingdom. If you were in business in the United Kingdom in the 1970s, you would have been deeply familiar with that nation's legal and regulatory environment, which had been set in its broadest terms for centuries with respect to its parliamentary system of government, a system of common law based on legislation and precedent, and a code of "fair play" throughout the entire society. More recently, following World War II, a pattern of state ownership of principal industries (coal, steel, railroads, telecommunications, electric utilities, etc.) had developed under several Labor governments. This was the legal/regulatory environment you confronted in the 1970s. Some of this was about to change.

With the election of a Conservative majority in 1979, the House of Commons, led by the new Prime Minister, Margaret Thatcher, began to enact legislation that had been promised by the Conservatives in their campaigning to bring about a reversal of the socialist policies of the past thirty-four years and a partial return to a free-enterprise economy. These measures included overhauling the economy by privatization of state-owned industries (gas, electricity, telephones, railroads, etc.), reducing taxes on businesses, freeing up regulations on investment and profits, and cracking the hold trade unions had on the wage-price structure in key industries.[69] Over a few years' time these conservative measures were enacted into law and dramatically altered the rules of the game in Britain. And they did stimulate the economy into a growth mode.[70]

Were these changes predictable? Yes, because the trend of change had been announced by political leaders, and once those leaders were elected in the majority and were able to effect the change, they did so over a period of time. It was the British system that changed the "rules of the road" in the British economy. The system was not changed; policy governing the business environment over which the system presided was the thing that changed.

Example: Russia. Examples of whole systems that change are abundant in the 20th century. After the Bolsheviks came to power in Russia in October 1917, Lenin and his fellow Communists fundamentally changed the way the former Czarist civil/political order had ruled the country. Lenin threw out the parliament, the system of laws, the administrative and judicial structure in the country, and all the apparatus of the old rule. These were replaced with a new model based on Marxist-Leninist theories of state control under a dictatorship of the proletariat emphasizing egalitarian rule among the working class, led by the vanguard of the proletariat, the Communist Party.[71]

This structure of totalitarian rule held an iron grip on what became known as the Soviet Union for sixty-four years, until 1991 when the Union of Soviet Socialist Republics was dissolved, broken up into fifteen separate ethnically based countries, each ruled by a popularly elected parliamentary system. Thus, the rules of the game changed again, quite dramatically, in the early 1990s, as fundamentally as they had at the beginning of the Communist rule, this time opening the economy to private enterprise as much as the previous change had closed it.[72] Could these changes be forecast?

Probably not in either case because the extent and degree of change in the entire system was more fundamental and far-reaching than anyone would have believed possible.

Example: Cuba. In 1959, Fidel Castro led a revolutionary group that came to power in Cuba, defeating a dictatorial regime led by Fulgencio Batista. Almost since Cuba had gained independence following the Spanish-American War in 1898, it had been governed by dictators. These regimes were openly friendly to foreign investors, especially American, and presided over a laissez-faire economic system and a corrupt, repressive political system. Did business understand the rules of the road in Cuba during the sixty-years before Castro? Clearly it did, and many investors in such industries as sugar, tobacco, hotels and resorts, and gaming prospered under this system. A senior State Department official expressed the prevailing view at the time: "I know Batista is considered by many as a sonofabitch . . . but American interests come first . . . at least he is our sonofabitch."[73]

Castro changed the system with great suddenness beginning in 1959, announcing shortly after coming to power that he was a communist and instituting nationalization and state ownership of the principal means of production in Cuba. He threw out the vestiges of a parliamentary system, ruling by decree.[74] Forty years after coming to power, Castro still has not fully resolved claims against his government from the nationalization or confiscation of valuable foreign-owned assets in pre-Castro Cuba. The rules of the game under Castro have been relatively stable, but adjustments at the margins began in the 1990s with some loosening of state control once economic and financial support from former communist Russia was no longer provided.

These changes in the rules of the game in Russia and Cuba are examples of fundamental changes in the entire political/economic/social *system*, altering the rules of the road dramatically throughout the entire political and economic structure. The examples in France and Britain are those of *policy* change by intact, stable political systems, altering the economic structure to achieve policy ends.

Example: China. Another example of a policy change comes from the People's Republic of China. In the late 1970s, the political leadership of China, the Politbureau of the Central Committee of the Chinese Communist Party, decided to permit a modified form of free-market economy to develop in certain coastal regions of South China in an effort to stimulate economic growth and employment. Deng Xao Ping made his famous trip to South China and announced these reforms upon his return to Beijing.

The reforms have been spectacularly successful, raising the Chinese GDP dramatically and providing a revenue stream to the Chinese government for many purposes, including military modernization and expansion. The political system that produced this policy change was the same: the communist-led central government. Unlike the changes that occurred in

Figure 4.4
Input/Output Model

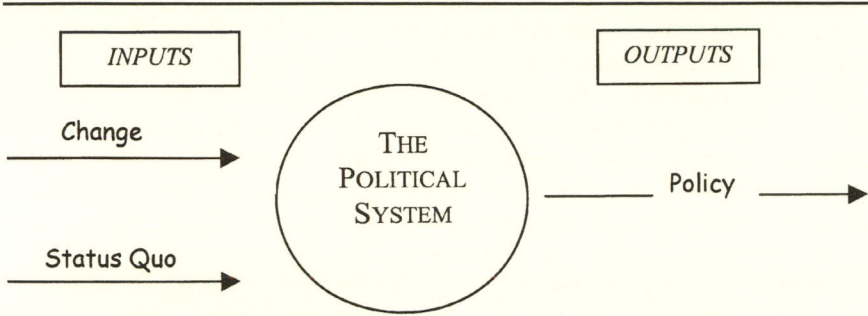

Russia in 1917 and 1991, which were system changes producing policy changes, China preserved its system by making policy changes. The changes are purely economic, not political; the totalitarian/authoritarian regime is still intact.[75]

Example: United States. Systemic changes are rare, but when they occur they are overwhelming, fundamentally altering the rules of the game in that society. France before the Revolution of 1789 was fundamentally different from the French Republic, which followed from a system standpoint. Before 1776 the thirteen British colonies in North America were significantly different from the United States of America, which was established by the Constitution in 1789, when a new system was introduced.

Over the 200-plus years of the United States, policy changes have abounded, but the system is stable. The United States has had laissez-faire capitalism in the 19th century, emergence of a regulatory environment in the late-19th and early-20th centuries, dramatic governmental intervention in the economy during the 1930s and 1940s, and deregulation of portions of the economy beginning in the late 1970s. These are all policy changes produced by a stable system.

Input/Output Model

The job of the planner is to anticipate, analyze, and evaluate both systemic and policy stability and change. You are always looking for trends to alert you to change because what business seeks is no surprises—to operate in a familiar or "anticipatable" environment. A useful model for identifying and evaluating change is the "Input/Output Model" of David Easton[76] (see Figure 4.4).

In this model there are two types of inputs: those demanding change and those supporting the maintenance of the current status quo, i.e., no change. These inputs can be pressure on either policy or on the entire system—for change or status quo of either. Inevitably, demands for change in the entire system are motivated by the desire for change in both the system and policy. The decision-making arena is called the political system. This is the entire governmental system that makes political decisions affecting any and all aspects of daily life in a society governed by that system.

In the United States "the political system" is the federal government (executive, legislative, judicial branches), the fifty state governments, and the nation's county and city administrate structure. It is these arenas that produce outputs, called policies, which can be decisions and actions. Policies are in the form of laws, administrative decisions, and judicial rulings. Each policy output influences the next input through a feedback mechanism, either by strengthening the current status quo or by exciting the forces of change to redouble their efforts. The entire process is dynamic.

Occasionally the political system itself changes. The locus of decision making can be altered from one location, one center, to another. This is what happened when the Soviet Union was broken up in the early 1990s; at the time if you were living in Kiev, suddenly the capital of your country had become your own city, not Moscow, when the Ukraine became an independent country. Similarly, on January 1, 1999 eleven countries of the European Union faced a change in the decision-making arena for their money and monetary policy when the European Monetary Union went into effect, introducing the Euro as the common currency for member countries, with Frankfurt as the headquarters of the European Central Bank, not their own country's central bank.[77]

Stability versus Risk Analysis

Easton's model can be used to evaluate the stability of any decision-making system. Use the model to evaluate a corporation's, for example. Substitute "the political system" with the term "the decision-making system," meaning the Board of Directors, CEO, and top management team. Pressures for "policy" changes constantly arise from the corporate structure below and from outside the company, and pressures for the maintenance of current policies tend to balance and usually overwhelm the forces of change.

The decision-makers' job is to evaluate the virtues and strengths of those pressures, adjust their policies accordingly, using as a touchstone for decision the future best interests of the firm. The result of that decision-making process is a policy output, to either make the change recommended, stay put, or adopt a middle course of some type. The outcome of this process will provide feedback to the next set of inputs.

A principal reason for undertaking this analysis of the rules of the road is to assess risk. Often the critical risk in international business is political risk.[78] Political risk exists when discontinuities occur in the business environment, reducing your ability to predict behavior and circumstances. Political instability is one form of risk; it usually produces sudden policy changes, difficult to anticipate in terms of timing and degree.[79]

There are a number of services one can purchase to help evaluate political risk in specific foreign locations.[80] Rarely, however, do such firms evaluate political risk of their home country, except in some statistical aggregate. Evaluating the stability/instability of the home country objectively is more important than any other evaluation because the implications for the firm are usually the greatest at its domestic base.

How to Forecast Political Risk

To evaluate and forecast political risk in any country, there are five basic elements of the analysis:

- Try to determine the sources and degrees of potential risk and their probability:
  - —Chances of a major party candidate contesting a presidential election, destabilizing the orderly succession of power (e.g., Al Gore or George W. Bush in U.S. 2000 election)
  - —Chances of a fiscally conservative group winning an election and radically altering tax and other fiscal policies (e.g., Steve Forbes with his flat tax)
  - —Chances of another political party having a different economic program gaining power (e.g., Margaret Thatcher coming to power in Great Britain)
  - —Chances of an antiestablishment group gaining power and radically changing economic policy (e.g., the Green Party gaining a majority in Germany)
  - —Chances of civil insurrection succeeding, destroying current systems (e.g., Castro beating Batista in Cuba)
  - —Chances of wholesale revolution bringing in anticapitalist economic policies (e.g., Lenin in Russia and Mao in China)
- Understand the present government in power thoroughly, its behavior and norms:
  - —Does the government have a solid consensus of support among the citizenry?
  - —Does it have the means and will to coerce acceptance over time, if necessary?
  - —Does it provide payoffs to the majority of the citizenry, securing their support?
  - —Does it utilize means and behaviors that are onerous to a significant portion of the population?
  - —Does it ignore or flaunt the will and needs of significant portions of the population?
- Evaluate the government's success or failure in managing the economy:
  - —What is the government's scorecard in GDP growth, inflation rate, unemployment rate, currency exchange rate stability, etc.?
  - —What is the government's record in investment in infrastructure, education, debt retirement, foreign debt repayment, etc.?

—Do government policies promote the development of a middle class, or do they weaken it?

- Project into the future the probability of political risk on a time line:

—Are there labor disputes? General strikes? Revolts by key interest groups?

—Is there growing civil disobedience in the country? Armed insurrection? Is it gaining strength or being contained/defeated by the government?

—Is the military likely to remain obedient to the government? Is there a tradition of military coups?

—Are present trends of instability likely to continue? Accelerate? Over what issues? Time frame?

- Make an analysis of the company's operations in an attempt to identify the degree of political risk it might face and determine whether it is a system or policy problem:

—System-based risks are nearly impossible to guard against or manage; the best strategy is withdrawal, eliminating risk.

—Policy-based risks can be managed through reduction of exposure (sell a percentage of the business), insurance, change in location of incorporation to offshore, improved public relations, and the like.

Deregulation Changed the Rules of the Game in the United States

A set of clear-cut policy changes in the legal/regulatory environment in the United States began in the late 1970s during the Carter administration and continued through the Reagan, Bush, and Clinton administrations. The motivation has been to increase competition and lower cost to the consumer through the deregulation of specific industries: airline, trucking, railroads, telecommunications, and banking.

Example: Trucking Industry. Following the Carter administration's partial deregulation of the airline industry in 1978,[81] the trucking industry was the next to begin deregulation.[82] The day that act went into effect, July 1, 1980, beginning the deregulation of the American trucking industry, the basic ground rule in that $108-billion industry changed from being highly regulated by the Interstate Commerce Commission, where companies applied for licenses to service particular city pairs and accepted ICC-determined tariffs, to one of limited regulation, allowing anyone "fit, willing, and able" to gain an operating permit to haul freight anywhere and, after a transition period, at any price. The ICC itself later disappeared.

Deregulation ended the dominance of a few large long-distance carriers and opened the door to independent haulers to compete for any job. The book value of a number of the large trucking companies diminished to near zero when they had to write off the asset value of their licenses, leaving their rolling stock as their principal asset.

Figure 4.5
Largest U.S. Mergers Announced in 1996

---

1. British Telecom to buy MCI for $25.3 billion (this deal fell through later).

2. Bell Atlantic bought NYNEX for $23.6 billion.

3. SBC Communications bought Pacific Telesis for $16.6 billion.

4. Boeing bought McDonnell Douglas for $14.6 billion (the amount later reduced).

5. WorldCom bought MFS Communications for $13.4 billion.

Similar open competition occurred in the airline and railroad[83] industries, with a shakeout period lasting more than a decade in each industry with mergers, bankruptcies, and consolidations occurring regularly. Similar shakeouts and consolidations are occurring in telecommunications and banking. The rules of the road in all these critical industries certainly are different today compared with the mid-1970s because of these policy changes. Whether more competition and lower prices have resulted is debatable.

Example: Telecommunications Industry. Changes in the regulatory environment of the telecommunications industry have had a dramatic impact. In the year the Telecommunications Act of 1996 went into effect, there was a total of 10,000 mergers in the United States, and $660 billion changed hands; the prior record year was 1989 with 5,000 mergers. The five largest mergers of all types announced in 1996 are listed in Figure 4.5.[84]

Note that four of the five largest announced mergers involved telecommunications companies in the very first year of telecommunications deregulation. It appears the players in this industry were well prepared for the moment of deregulation and had their plans laid for immediate action. Mergers and acquisitions in the industry continue with announcements and mergers in subsequent years including SBC Communications buying Ameritech, WorldCom buying MCI, AT&T buying Tele-Communications, Inc., and Bell Atlantic buying GTE, becoming Verizon. Three of the top five U.S. mergers announced in 1998 involved telecommunication companies.[85] The then-largest acquisition of all time was announced in October 1999: MCI Worldcom buying Sprint for $108 billion.[86]

International telecommunications mergers and acquisitions are a major factor in this process.[87] In early 1999 alone three major deals were announced:

(1) Vodafone Group of Britain announced its purchase of the largest U.S. wireless phone company, AirTouch Communications, for $65 billion, a $19-per-share premium, to create the world's largest wireless phone com-

pany with 23 million mobile customers, compared to number two, Japan's NTT DoCoMo with 22 million mobile customers.[88]

(2) Chicago-based Ameritech agreed to buy a 20 percent stake in Bell Canada, Canada's leading carrier, for $3.4 billion, taking advantage of Canada's recently deregulated telephone market. This deal filled a key gap in SBC/Ameritech's North American market, given that SBC already owned a 10 percent stake in Mexico's largest phone company, Telefonos de Mexico. This Canadian deal enables SBC/Ameritech to provide almost seamless service throughout much of NAFTA.[89]

(3) AT&T and British Telecommunications announced they would each buy a 15 percent stake in Japan Telecom for a total of $1.85 billion, making this the first large investment by foreign majors in Japan's deregulating telecommunications industry.[90]

Example: Industry Consolidations. Consolidations in a number of other industries continue as well, with abundant examples in:

- Banking and financial services: Travelers Insurance bought Citicorp, Deutsche Bank bought Bankers Trust of New York, Solomon Brothers brought Smith-Barney, and an accounting firm named PricewaterhouseCoopers was formed, speaking volumes.
- Airlines: Who remembers the names Eastern, Western, North Central, PSA, National, Piedmont—all absorbed by United, Delta, American, Northwest, and USAir, with USAir absorbed by United Airlines?
- Railroads: In 1995 Burlington Northern bought Santa Fe Pacific to become Burlington Northern Sante Fe, and in 1999 this company proposed to merge with Canadian National Railway Co. In 1998 Union Pacific bought Southern Pacific. None of these mergers has been without massive absorption problems and rail traffic congestion.[91]
- Broadcasting: Walt Disney bought CapCities/ABC. Westinghouse bought CBS, spun off Westinghouse, bought TV stations in key markets, and was bought by Viacom.
- Defense: Boeing bought McDonnell Douglas and parts of Rockwell; Lockheed bought Martin Marietta, part of General Dynamics, and most of Loral, and tried to buy Northrop Grumman; and Raytheon bought part of General Dynamics, part of Texas Instruments, and most of Hughes Aircraft.
- Utilities: PG&E bought Texas Utility, Duke Power bought PanEnergy, Sempra Energy (parent of San Diego Gas & Electric and Southern California Gas Co.) and Public Service Enterprise Group of New Jersey announced the purchase by their joint venture of 90 percent of Chilquinta Energia of Chile.[92] Edison International bought two British power plants from PowerGen of London.[93]

Risks are very high in the United States for firms in these industries. Companies expect to acquire or be acquired in the free-for-all of a deregulated business environment. Only occasionally does the government inter-

Figure 4.6
Largest Mergers Announced in 1998

Acquiring Company	Acquired Company	$ Value in Billions
Exxon	Mobil	81.2
Travelers	Citicorp	70.2
Bell Atlantic	GTE	66.9
SBC Communications	Ameritech	64.4
AT&T	TCI	62.7
NationsBank	BankAmerica	62
British Petroleum	Amoco	53.6
Daimler-Benz	Chrysler	42.4

vene to deny an acquisition[94] or to modify it requiring a partial divestiture on competitive grounds.

Pressures for Mergers and Consolidations

Pressures for mergers and consolidations stem from a variety of sources:

(a) Deregulation, privatization, and other changes in law and policy permitting or encouraging mergers.

(b) Changes in market conditions: the procurement portion of the U.S. defense budget declined by 50 percent in ten years beginning in FY-88, forcing elimination of excess capacity, Defense Department policy encouraged company consolidations, and synergies were sought wherever possible by industry management.

(c) Technological changes: wireless communications became feasible and widely used, threatening carriers like AT&T using wires and fiberoptic cable, stimulating them to buy McCaw Cellular for $12 billion in 1994.[95]

(d) Globalization of industry: consolidations at home were used to secure domestic markets against incursions by foreign competitors as well as to establish footholds or economies of scale in other countries, such as Deutsche Bank buying Bankers Trust of New York, British Vodafone buying American AirTouch, Edison International buying two British power plants and a 40 percent stake in Contact Energy Ltd., owned by the New Zealand government,[96] and British Petroleum buying Amoco and Atlantic Richfield.[97]

In the United States the number of merger deals in 1998 was 11,486, valued at $1.62 trillion, up 78 percent from the previous year.[98] The largest of these deals announced or concluded that year are shown in Figure 4.6.

It is critical to evaluate the political and legal/regulatory environment carefully, anticipate likely changes, and position your firm to take advantage of the upside opportunities and hedge against the downside risks. This is equally true of the economic environment.

ECONOMIC ENVIRONMENT

In this portion of the external environment evaluation the planner is charged with identifying and evaluating conditions and trends in the economy that will impact the firm during the planning period, which is typically five years. This evaluation begins with the current, basic conditions and then makes a forecast of future economic conditions in which the firm will operate. From that forecast the planner makes assumptions about the environment that will form a critical base for the plan. "Economics, not politics," wrote Kenichi Ohmae, "defines the landscape on which all else must operate."[99]

Analysis of Basic Trends

These assumptions include GDP growth rates, inflation rates, interest rates, employment rates, consumer income rates, consumer confidence, and the like. For firms involved in international commerce, the planner also must make similar forecasts and assumptions regarding the economies of the countries in which the firm is deeply committed or is intending to become committed, plus make forecasts and assumptions regarding transnational factors such as currency exchange rates, trade growth and trade restrictions (such as import quotas, tariffs, etc.), and transferability of capital, conversion of currency, and repatriation of profit. All these assumptions will form a basis for the firm's strategic decisions regarding capital investment, marketing strategies, risk exposure, and overall opportunity evaluation.

The basic economic conditions need to be evaluated and presented.[100] These basic conditions include market size, which is derived from per capita national income and population size, and the overall economic environment expressed in such data as GDP growth rate, inflation rate, savings rate, investment rate, factory utilization rate, trade balance, foreign debt, foreign currency reserves, and any other economic factors that bear on the firm's operations.

Productivity Growth

Productivity improvement rates are a key component of the analysis. This is one of the major drivers behind the sustained U.S. economic expansion in the decade of the 1990s.[101] Defined as GDP divided by the civilian workforce, productivity has kept output rising without generating inflationary pressures. Indeed, output per worker has generally risen in the United States since the 1960s, except for two periods of recession, and during the later years of the 1990s it accelerated. "Technology innovation, and in particular the spread of information technology, has revolutionized the conduct of business over the past decade and resulted in rising rates of productivity growth," declared Fed Chairman Alan Greenspan in December 2000.[102]

In 1999, U.S. productivity growth was the best in seven years, growing by 2.9 percent, and the manufacturing sector's productivity gained 6.4 percent (the largest increase since 1971). Coupling these gains with thirty-year low unemployment of 4 percent, declining unit labor costs, and the implicit price deflator gaining at a minuscule 0.8 percent annual rate in the 4th quarter, "this is the best of all worlds," said Bank of America's chief economist.[103]

What is causing this productivity growth? Gross private domestic investment is a principal driver, fueled by purchases of computers. The percentage contribution of investment to GDP rose from less than 12 percent in the early 1990s to almost 18 percent by the late 1990s. Spending growth on computers and peripherals averaged more than 40 percent annually during the later 1990s, enabling output per worker to climb 20 percent faster than growth in the workforce during the same period. These productivity gains allowed companies to maintain profit growth without price increases, keeping inflation in check and perpetuating a positive investment climate. From an economic standpoint, 1999 was almost "picture-perfect."

U.S. Economic Performance

Looking at the U.S. economy over the past several years, the data support this conclusion. According to the Commerce Department, U.S. GDP growth in 1999 was 4.2 percent, following gains in 1998 of 4.3 percent and in 1997 of 4.2 percent. The GDP grew in the fourth quarter of 1999 at a sizzling rate of 7.3 percent, the fastest rate in 16 years, and certainly the fastest quarterly growth rate since the economic expansion began in March 1991. After-tax corporate profits rose 2.7 percent in 1999's fourth quarter, up 15 percent from the same period a year earlier, and the best year-over-year performance since 1995.

Despite these remarkable growth rates, inflation remained in check. An inflation gauge tied to the GDP was up at an annual rate of only 2 percent in the fourth quarter, showing little increase from 1.7 percent in the third quarter of 1999. The Federal Reserve had increased interest rates three times in 1999 and several more in 2000 to dampen inflation. Consumer and government spending fueled 1999's fourth quarter's growth; consumer spending rose 5.9 percent, reflecting record-high consumer confidence and low unemployment, and government purchases jumped 14.7 percent.[104] The year 1999 was about as good as it gets.

Fear of Recession

If yours is a small, capital-intensive business that produces capital goods, your greatest fear is that once you have committed to a major plant expansion to facilitate production expansion, the economy will go into recession. Why such fear? Because industry cuts capital goods spending instantly at the slightest whiff of a recession. And you would be left hanging out to dry with debt and an expanded facility if the economy were to turn sour with no one wanting your capital goods.

Example: Japanese-Owned Real Estate. Similar recession fears abound in the real estate industry. In the 1980s, the Japanese economy was riding high, and Japanese companies were prospering, exporting their goods and services globally in a seemingly unbeatable, relentless procession toward world dominance. They were amassing great fortunes, which in the late 1980s many invested in American hotels, golf courses, and landmark commercial properties including New York's Rockefeller Center and Los Angeles' twin-tower fifty-two story ARCO Plaza, paying top dollar. Soon after these deals closed, the real estate bubble began to burst in both countries, and the value of these investments declined as both economies entered recession.[105] By the late 1990s, these properties had declined in value, some to more than 50 percent of the price paid by Japanese investors, and were being repurchased by American investors at a fraction of the price paid by the Japanese.[106] What happened? In short, the American economy recovered and Japan's didn't.[107]

For nearly the entire decade of the 1990s, Japan was in near-depression, with its domestic real estate declining in value each year relative to the prior year. In 1998 commercial real estate prices fell 8.1 percent below the 1997 level, which had seen a 6.1 percent drop over 1996. From its peak in 1993, commercial property in Japan fell 51 percent by year-end 1998, while residential property prices were down 26.5 percent over the same period. In the late 1990s foreign investors bought Japanese property at bargain prices, taking advantage of Japan's continuing deflationary spiral.[108]

Foreign investors also bought "nonperforming assets" (defaulted and foreclosed loans estimated at $1 trillion) from Japanese banks, typically at three cents to fifteen cents on the dollar. In 1998 foreign investors bought $44 billion in such assets, and in the first quarter of 1999, in the rush to meet the March 31 deadline to qualify for tens of billions in government bailout funds for banks to clear their books, the amount of these purchases soared by another $20 billion.[109]

Japan's "bubble economy" of the 1980s, which was based on soaring Japanese real estate and stock prices stimulated by a booming export-driven economy, high liquidity, and low interest rates, burst—enabling foreign investors to repurchase Japanese-owned real estate in their own countries, to buy real estate in Japan, and to buy at rock-bottom prices Japanese "nonperforming assets," changing the ownership of vast holdings to foreign hands at a revolutionary rate. Should the planner have fear of recession? Just recall the 1990s in the world's second largest economy for your answer.

Example: Nissan Motor Company. Individual Japanese companies suffered along with this general economic decline. Few companies dramatically illustrate the rise-and-fall syndrome as well as Nissan Motor Company. During its rise in the 1970s and 1980s, Nissan was customer focused, designed sporty cars with high quality and competitive prices, and made solid profit margins.[110] "Nissan [then] lost touch with the market," said George Peterson, president of AutoPacific, Inc., a former Nissan executive. "It became very conservative. Instead of being entrepreneurial, Nissan went into a shell."[111]

While in that shell, it lost market share, had reduced revenue, lost money year after year, and amassed a debt of $37.7 billion. In the 1990s, Nissan faced a worldwide glut of production capacity, forcing automakers to reduce costs and achieve economies of scale as never before, which Nissan did not do. It also failed to keep up in styling, cost control, and marketing, causing it to lose ground globally to Toyota Motor Corporation and Honda Motor Company, its largest Japanese competitors, as well as to U.S. and European automakers in Nissan's largest markets outside Japan. While Nissan was losing ground, auto sales in the United States were growing, from the recession trough in 1991 of twelve million units to the high in 1998 of 15.5 million vehicle sales, the second-best year ever.[112] "This company was hit with a big 'stupid stick,' " said Jason Vines, Nissan North America spokesman.[113]

By 1999, this once-mighty icon of Japanese industrial power was humbled into seeking a foreign investor to invigorate its worldwide production capacity of 2.5 million vehicles. DaimlerChrysler courted Nissan but gave up because it believed it lacked the management resources, was too occupied with the Chrysler merger, and concluded the investment was too risky.[114]

In March 1999 Renault, needing to expand its markets, purchased 36.8 percent of Nissan for $5.4 billion. Soon after this deal closed, Nissan announced fiscal year-end financial forecasts, citing an anticipated loss three times larger than previously projected on continuing lower domestic sales and reduced production. By April 1999 Nissan had more than 30 percent excess capacity and was considering idling still more. For the first time in a half-century, Nissan eliminated its shareholder dividend.[115] Soon after, Carlos Ghosen, a former Renault executive known as Le Cost Killer, was named Chief Operating Officer of Nissan. "Our priority," he stated, "is putting Nissan on a profitable track."[116]

Scenario Forecasting

Forecasts are developed by academic and business economists, governmental institutions, and forecasting services. Scenario planning involves testing strategies and business decisions against a series of alternative futures and has been practiced in one form or another since the early 1960s when it was first employed at Royal/Dutch Shell. Using this technique, Shell Oil foresaw the energy crises of 1973 and 1979, the global environmental movement, the trend toward energy conservation, and the breakup of the Soviet Union.[117]

Typically, a "scenario" analysis is developed based on relevant trends and events.[118] These scenarios are hypotheses of a set of possible futures, ranging from pessimistic to optimistic, and a most likely. The "most likely" scenario usually has a greater than 50 percent rate of probability of actually occurring.[119] Projections into the future help managers and planners gain a broader perspective of future trends, seeing variables that might normally be overlooked, and helping to identify interrelationships among variables that are not normally evaluated.

For example, in working with a large oil company that had developed an econometric model in an effort to predict the future price per barrel of oil in 1999, an outside team using computer simulation techniques was able to see the dynamic interplay of such variables as (a) increased oil output from the former Soviet Union, (b) reduced demand for oil in Asia owing to its recession, (c) increased capacity in Latin America, and (d) holding other supply-and-demand factors constant. The resulting scenario forecast a dramatic short-term drop in the price of oil, which actually happened, but not exactly for the reasons cited. Often, such models produce "likely outcomes" that can be so dramatic they are not believed even by their own designers, much less by the decision makers they work for, even though they later turn out to be accurate.[120]

Forecasting Services

U.S. government analysts publish baseline data on the economy's performance and regularly produce forecasts of economic conditions. The Departments of Commerce and Labor are the source of much economic data, as well as the Council of Economic Advisors, which also provides forecasts. The Humphrey-Hawkins Act requires the Federal Reserve Chairman to appear twice a year to present to Congress the Fed's views on the U.S. economy. This presentation is eagerly awaited every six months to hear what the Chairman will say. His presentation is accompanied by the release of the Fed's forecast, called the Beige Book, of the country's economic conditions, because the action of the Fed to raise, lower, or leave alone interest rates is critical to all business planning.[121]

Important international data is available through the United Nations and various international organizations, such as the Organization for Economic Cooperation and Development, and important regional groups, such as the European Union.

Commercial forecast services are available from a number of sources. WEFA Group, which used to be affiliated with the Wharton School and later merged with Chase Econometrics, is one such service, and Economic & Policy Resources, Inc. is another. Forecasts from these and others can be purchased individually or on a subscription basis.[122] Some universities perform regular forecasts of the national economy and for the state in which they are located; UCLA's Anderson Graduate School of Management's Forecasting Project is particularly well known and respected for its track record forecasting the U.S. and California economies.

The New Economy

So much has been said about the "new economy" that it has almost become trite to mention the term. However, there is ample evidence that truly fundamental changes abound within the Internet-based new economy that make it difficult to forecast the logical future outcome of these revolutionary changes around us, except to say that they are far-reaching. Federal Reserve Chairman Alan Greenspan has said, "What differentiates this period from other periods in our history is the extraordinary role played by information and communication technologies. The effect of these technologies could rival and arguably even surpass the impact the telegraph had prior to and just after the Civil War."[123] IBM's CEO Louis Gerstner identified six trends regarding this phenomenon (presented above in the e-business section).

It remains to mention some of the companies that are participating actively in it today. The core traits that characterize "new economy" companies are these:

- they are Internet-related or Internet-dependent;
- they have the capacity to dramatically enhance corporate productivity and profitability by generating new revenue, reducing cost, empowering their employees, enhancing market reach, and/or improving efficiency through Internet application;
- they can significantly improve competitive posture by an appropriate Internet strategy;
- their products and/or services will remain relevant and in strong demand; and
- they are globally relevant, either today or potentially.

Figure 4.7
Argus Research's "New Economy" Companies

America Online	Merck
American Intl. Group	Microsoft
Amgen	Motorola
Cisco Systems	Nortel Networks
Citigroup	Oracle
Comcast	Solectron
FactSet Research	Source Info Mgnt
General Electric	Sun Microsystems
i2 Technologies	Verizon
IBM	Wal-Mart Stores
Intel	WorldCom
Jupiter Networks	Yahoo!

A number of companies qualify for the "new economy" based on these criteria. Any number of analysts and stock mutual funds have their favorite lists of such companies. One such list is provided by Argus Research. Their list of "new economy" companies is as follows, covering companies in nine different industries: communications, health care, technology software, technology semiconductor, technology networking, technology hardware, financial services, business services, and consumer[124] (see Figure 4.7).

Again, the characteristics that distinguish these companies from others are their Internet relationship and their potential to deliver substantially improved efficiency, through either increased sales or reduced costs or both, because of that Internet relationship. Hardly a company anywhere does not try to advertise or position itself as a "new economy" company. According to Argus Research, the two dozen companies listed in Figure 4.7 meet the criteria.

SOCIOCULTURAL ENVIRONMENT

Finally, the sociocultural environment needs to be evaluated to understand the social structure and social conditions that the enterprise will confront. The social structure refers to the type of government the country has and how effective it is at maintaining civil order in the society, protecting the country, and living up to the stated philosophy of governance. It also refers to the social order in the society—whether it is a class society, class-less, or hierarchical. Social conditions refer to such macroissues as social stability, policies toward immigration, the society's demography, culture, and the like, all of which need evaluation to determine the risks and opportunities that will be faced. Some of these items were discussed above under the Legal/Regulatory Environment.

Demographic Projections

Demographic projections are critical to most businesses. There is abundant information on the U.S. population, age structure, geographic dispersal, income, education levels, health, etc. The Census Bureau tracks these data carefully, and information is readily obtainable, down to a local community's profile of age, sex, income, and racial patterns. Before starting or expanding a business, the entrepreneur needs to understand the "demographics" of the customer base, whether opening a florist shop or buying a script for a TV series.

Cultural-Behavioral Factors

Similarly, cultural-behavioral factors are also important. Factors need to be identified and their importance to your firm evaluated, such as drug use among certain age groups, education levels among job applicants, language differences in particular communities, increased tendency to litigate, increased health consciousness, smoking attitudes, urban gang activity, numbers of women working and two-income families, increased day-care requirement for preschool children, etc. What these and other cultural trends mean to your firm, its products, its customer base, its employees, and the legislation affecting it all need to be considered.

The importance of these factors to your firm may be straightforward or it may be subtle, relating to market conditions, customer base, labor pool, competitive trends, etc. For example, gang violence statistics contained in monthly police reports for particular neighborhoods would indicate which areas to avoid for opening a new retail business. High school dropout rates by ethnic group could affect your customer base as well as your labor pool for certain types of companies. Trend data from the U.S. Education Department indicate that the overall national dropout rate in 1995 (most recent available data) was 12 percent, down slightly from 14.6 percent in 1972. Looking more closely at the numbers, however, reveals declining dropout rates for white (8.6%) and black (12.1%) students, while the dropout rate for Latino students remained largely unchanged for the past twenty-five years at 30 percent.[125]

Household formations significantly affect market conditions for numerous industries: furniture and appliance manufacturers, utilities, housing, etc. U.S. Census Bureau reports indicate a decline in the number of adults living together as a married couple from 68 percent in 1970 to 56 percent in 1998, with a concomitant increase in "single, never married," divorced, and widowed people. Singles today are buying homes like never before: from 1997 to 1998 singles made 28.9 percent of U.S. home purchases, with single women representing 18 percent of that number.[126] "Married couple," however, is still the majority category of the total U.S. population of 281 million in 2000,[127] with 110.6 million Americans over age 18 married and living as a couple. The median age of first marriage for men declined in 1998 to 26.7 years from 27.1 in 1976, while the median age for females held steady at 25 for the same period.[128]

For the workforce, marriage has little impact. After marriage, both spouses typically continue working, and their average work time increased by seven hours a week between 1972 and 1994.[129] In 1994 there were 6.2 million married couple families with preschoolers and employed mothers; in those families, 27 percent of the fathers cared for their children during the mother's working hours. Interestingly, the number of single fathers grew from 1.7 million in 1995 to 2.1 million in 1998.[130]

Looking at the period between 1980 and 1996, the percentage of working mothers of school-age children grew from 60 percent to 75 percent, according to the U.S. Bureau of Labor Statistics. The percentage of mothers with children under age five who work increased from 50 percent to 62 percent over the same sixteen-year period. The state of Minnesota began a first-of-its-kind program in 1997, called At-Home Infant Care, to provide financial help averaging $250 per month for stay-at-home mothers in lower-income families during a child's first year.[131]

Futures Modeling

Forecasting and futures modeling of social phenomena are now routine. Forecasts are available for such issues as what postindustrial cities will look like and how to model them,[132] to lifestyles in the new millennium,[133] to the impacts of science and technology on the North American workforce and society.[134] Specific market forecasts, such as linking demographic trends (aging of baby boomers) to social issues (protected sex and birth control), can influence market plans based on projections of increased sales of less expensive contraceptive devices producing reduced revenue growth.[135] Depending on the importance of the forecast to the firm's overall business, one would be wise to obtain a second and even third opinion before making critical decisions based on any one forecast.

Example: Johns-Manville. Social consciousness and new information on such issues as health risks of products can have far-ranging impacts on companies. In the 1960s conclusive information became available showing a link between asbestos and cancer. Homes, offices, factories, ships, and aircraft had regularly used asbestos as an insulator in their construction. Now that very product had been proved to be harmful and, for its workers, fatal. The company that was the world's largest producer and distributor of asbestos was Johns-Manville.

What happened to that 140-plus-year-old company? In the 1920s, when it was taken over by J. P. Morgan & Co., it was to be the core component of a building materials empire that Morgan planned to become the world's leader.[136] But by the 1970s it was on the ropes. It was sued in virtually every court in the country, devastated by liability litigation. In 1982 Johns-Manville filed for Chapter 11 protection and descended to the top of the "least admired" list of companies.[137] Its major shareholder became Manville Personal Injury Settlement Trust. The company had been for sale off and on for nearly two years, but no buyer made an acceptable offer until December 2000.[138]

What happened to the town where a large asbestos mine was located, a town named Asbestos, Quebec? It went from boom to bust as the health hazards of its namesake mineral came to light. After a twenty-year slump, the town is reviving with the discovery that asbestos waste rock is rich in magnesium, and the demand for that metal is growing.[139]

Another example: in the 1960s General Motors' Chevrolet Division produced a car called the Corvair, which became the principal subject of Ralph Nader's book *Unsafe at Any Speed*. Sales of Corvairs virtually died, and the car was withdrawn from production soon after Nader's book was published.[140] Auto safety had become a "social" issue, and the Corvair was its first target. Seat belts, shoulder straps, air bags, side-impact air bags, etc. have become standard or options on vehicles as a result.

Example: Smoking and the Tobacco Industry. Smoking is another "social" issue. Following the release in 1964 of the U.S. Surgeon-General's report announcing findings that linked cigarette smoking with lung disease, the percentage of Americans who smoke cigarettes began to decline.[141] By the late 1990s that percentage became the lowest in the United States in the 20th century. What has been the impact on cigarette companies? Dramatic, in a word.

The industry's two-pronged strategic reaction to this altered U.S. market condition was (a) to use their substantial profits to accumulate other consumer products companies that had no health risks associated with their products and to grow those businesses, and (b) to expand their tobacco business internationally, where the health risk is viewed as less significant or not at all and where smoking is socially acceptable. For example, R. J. Reynolds became RJR-Nabisco, after buying the food products business, which in 1999 it spun off as a separate company, RJR Nabisco Holdings Corp.[142] Philip Morris and Co. purchased General Foods, Kraft Foods, and Miller Beer. Other major companies in the industry include Brown & Williamson, Lorillard, the Liggett Group, and Brooke Group, which acquired Liggett.

Not only are health risks impacting cigarette sales in the United States, but also individuals, groups, state governments, and the federal government virtually waged war on the major tobacco companies by litigating against them to recover the cost of health care for cancer patients whose conditions were allegedly caused by cigarette smoking. In forty years of litigation, juries awarded damages in smoking cases only five times: three were later overturned on appeal and two others were still in appellate courts awaiting decision as of 1999.

Until 1997 the industry had never paid a cent in damages, but in that year things changed. The tobacco industry settled for $300 million a class action law suit brought by U.S. flight attendants for second-hand smoke-related illness. It settled massive claims for $41 billion from four states (Mississippi, Florida, Texas, and Minnesota) seeking to recover costs from treating sick smokers. And for $206 billion it settled similar claims from the forty-six other states.

These settlements did not indemnify the industry against individuals' class action claims for smoking-related illness. Hundreds of those cases are still active, representing potentially enormous liability for the industry.[143] The first of these "individual" cases to reach a jury occurred in April 2000; a Florida jury awarded $145 billion against the tobacco industry.[144] The industry appealed to Federal court, which has consistently been favorable to the industry, but in this case the Federal District Court sent the case back to the original Florida state court, where the state judge will rule on the record-shattering punitive damages.[145]

Adding to the industry's worries, in September 1999 the U.S. Attorney General filed suit against the tobacco companies to recover the federal government's costs for smoking-related illness.[146]

Cigarette prices increased substantially in the United States owing to the industry's litigation and settlement costs, prompting new competition for the cigarette industry from the "homemade" smoking industry. Rolling your own is now far cheaper than buying ready-made smokes.[147]

Despite these events in the United States, international tobacco sales continue to grow. Philip Morris Companies, Inc. is the world's largest tobacco company with corporate-wide operating revenue in 1998 of $74.3 billion and operating income of $11.3 billion. Of those totals, $42.7 billion in revenue and $6.5 billion in operating income was derived from tobacco, after deducting $3.7 billion in pretax charges mostly for litigation expense; the balance came from food, beer, and financial services. In the tobacco category, $15.3 billion in revenue and $1.4 billion in operating income was derived from "domestic" tobacco, while $27.3 billion and $5 billion, respectively, were generated from "international" tobacco. In 1998, domestic tobacco operating income was down by 54.7 percent from the prior year, while international tobacco operating revenue was up 10 percent.[148]

Results in 1999 were similar, except that total Philip Morris Company reported revenue grew to $78.5 billion and operating income grew to $14.8 billion. Strikingly, the largest increases were in domestic tobacco, which rose to $19.5 billion in revenue and $4.8 billion in operating income. International tobacco in 1999 held steady at $27.5 and $4.9 billion, respectively. Despite the litigation, tobacco is still profitable at Philip Morris, accounting in 1999 for approximately two-thirds of the company's total income—$9.8 billion out of $14.8 billion. As Geoffrey Bible, the company's Chairman and CEO, put it, "Our domestic tobacco business was far more resilient than we might have expected at the beginning of 1999."[149]

Thus, the "international" strategy is working for Philip Morris, showing excellent growth in both sales and earnings, with room to grow—given that Philip Morris products account for only one out of six cigarettes smoked in the world.[150]

The campaign against the tobacco industry is being emulated in other industries, which are now targeted as "social issues." Supporters of gun control are seeking ways in more than two dozen U.S. cities and counties to hold gun manufacturers responsible for deaths and injuries stemming from their products' use and to seek reimbursement of the public costs of gun violence.[151] Families of three victims of school shootings in 1997 in Kentucky have filed suit against makers and distributors of violent movies and video games that the alleged gunman had watched. And Mothers Against Drunk Driving are seeking ways to rein in alcohol companies, whose products they estimate take 100,000 American lives each year.[152] Which industry will become the next "social issue" target?

Postmerger Culture Issues

Next, let us examine the sociocultural issues in another environment, the one created by a merger, by looking at three examples of companies having different approaches to postmerger consolidation. Two of the examples are multinational, and one is domestic.

Example: DaimlerChrysler. Social issues affect another company with an international strategy—DaimlerChrysler. The merger of Daimler-Benz with Chrysler in November 1998 created a new corporate entity with extensive operations in Europe and North America, combined revenue of $148 billion, and 434,000 employees. "In many ways, DaimlerChrysler A. G. may be the world's first truly global company. . . . Its stock is uniquely global as well. It is listed on stock exchanges in New York, Frankfurt, Paris, Tokyo, Toronto, Vienna and Zurich, making it so easily accessible to so many investors that it may be the most liquid stock in the world."[153]

Despite the merger at the top, the integration of research, and coordination of component manufacturing, the company has no intention of merging engineering or production operations.[154] Why? The products do not overlap in terms of market focus and customer base, the operations are geographically separate, and "cultural" differences between the former companies are viewed as nearly insurmountable. This approach appeared to be working; DaimlerChrysler profit rose 16 percent in 1999, the first full year of operation of the merged company, on stronger vehicle sales and cost cutting.[155]

Daimler-Benz conducted extensive research before the merger and found that 70 percent of all cross-border joint ventures and mergers were failures, within three years, primarily owing to cultural differences between the firms. Those differences include divergent compensation and benefit packages, different work rules, and dissimilar "corporate cultures."

In the case of these two companies, German workers have regular beer breaks, the *vesper*, throughout the workday beginning at 9:00 A.M., they smoke on the production line, and sexual harassment is a nonissue. Alcohol and tobacco are forbidden inside a North American plant, but women workers are not, and to protect them there is a phalanx of sexual harassment policies and procedures. American workers have a higher base wage than German workers, but the latter have a more substantial fringe benefit package including longer vacations, more sick days, and better insurance.

"We are not trying to bring two worlds together to create a new one," said Dirk Simmons, a Daimler-Benz corporate strategist. "The ideal merged company will still have noticeable differences, like a choir that needs different voices to achieve the perfect sound." The guiding principle is to preserve each working environment's unique qualities, not to blend cultures.[156]

If DaimlerChrysler bends to recent Wall Street pressure to fully integrate the two former companies to cut costs, Daimler will likely lose one of the chief benefits it acquired in Chrysler—its processes for designing products and integrating the activities of its subsystem suppliers. Daimler-Benz did not have these processes, and today's German management of the combined firm, if it does fully integrate the companies, could compromise the very processes that made Chrysler such an attractive acquisition.[157]

Example: Citigroup. Postmerger culture wars between the two previous companies' employees are well known. An explosive recent example is Citigroup, the name given to the 1998 marriage of Citicorp, previously headed by John Reed, and Travelers, headed by Sanford Weill, who became Co-CEOs of the merged Citigroup. Not quite two years after the merger, Reed quit; Weill won. Despite initial public protest to the contrary, the two cultures had not blended, and the two leaders had a "shootout" at an eight-hour Sunday board of directors meeting.[158]

Prior to Reed's exit, several former Citicorp executives had left Citigroup. These included Jamie Dimon, a possible future CEO, who left shortly after the merger. Robert Lipp, head of Citi's consumer banking business, was known to be considering leaving. And Heidi Miller, the CFO, quit to become CFO at priceline.com.

In a speech to the Academy of Management six months before quitting Citigroup, John Reed revealed the lack of coalescence, indeed the high state of tension, within the merged company. Reed made the following points:

- "We are talking about putting two cultures together that are quite different, quite distinct. I am trying hard to understand how to make this work. I will tell you that it is not simple and it is not easy, and it is not clear to me that it will necessarily be successful."

- "Just as the body can sometimes reject an organ that it needs, business systems can sometimes reject behaviors that are required for the system's success. As you put two cultures together, you get all sorts of strange, aberrant behavior, and it is not clear whether each side getting to know the other side helps, or whether having common objectives helps, or whether it is just the passage of time."

- "I will tell you that the literature on putting together two families speaks volumes to me. The problems of stepparents, the descriptions of some children rejecting one parent, and other children rejecting other parents . . . is all meaningful. . . . Sandy and I both have the problem that our 'children' look up to us as they never did before, and reject the other parent with equal vigor."

- "What you really have to do is change. . . . [T]he willingness of people to change is limited, and what you pay them seems to be inversely correlated with their willingness to change. I used to believe that once you paid people these astronomical salaries that we currently pay, you would have mature, self-sufficient, self-confident individuals on your team. Let me assure you, it is not the case."[159]

What John Reed is describing is a corporate torture chamber where the former Citibank and former Travelers people openly resisted the concept of teamwork. With Reed's departure and no clear successor to Weill in sight, it appears the Travelers side will likely prevail in this executive suite guerrilla war.

Example: Pharmacia Corporation. In 1995 Pharmacia AB of Sweden and The Upjohn Company of Kalamazoo, Michigan merged to form a promising multinational drug company called Pharmacia & Upjohn.[160] The combined company then acquired an Italian drug company, Farmaitalia. However, hemorrhaging began almost immediately: sales dropped 8 percent and earnings plunged 53 percent in a market experiencing double-digit growth. Two years later the CEO who engineered the mergers abruptly resigned.

In 1997 Fred Hassan, a Pakistani from American Home Products, took over as CEO. He immediately diagnosed the problem as low worker morale complicated by cultural wars between the former companies' employees, mostly the Europeans versus the Americans. The company was in complete disarray. Strong medicine was needed.

Hassan immediately held one-on-one meetings with key executives, not group sessions. Personal, eye-to-eye discussions were crucial, he felt, to reassure each person. Next, he boldly consolidated corporate operations from Europe to the United States, which is the center of gravity for the drug industry and its largest market. Finally, realizing that each of the warring cultures needed a unifying symbol around which to rally, Hassan focused the entire company on "five engines of growth"—five key products with high-revenue and unifying potential. People were now refocused on the business, not on nationalities and career anxieties.

Positive results were almost immediate. The culture wars ended, products entered the pipeline, and sales and earnings turned around. Net income more than doubled from 1997 to 1998 and surged another 14 percent in 1999, to $799 million. The stock rose 40 percent over two years.

In late 1999, with Pharmacia & Upjohn fully consolidated as one company and with a strong balance sheet, Monsanto Company opened discussions to form a "druggernaut" in the prescription and consumer drug market. After Monsanto spun off unrelated product lines, the merger was completed in early 2000 with Fred Hassan as CEO of the new company called Pharmacia Corporation, with headquarters in New Jersey, P&U's location. Robert Shapiro, Monsanto's CEO, planned to remain one year as nonexecutive chairman and then retire. Immediately after the merger was announced, Hassan began one-on-one meetings with key Monsanto executives, having developed hate-to-lose lists of key employees.

"*Behavior* is a better term than *culture*," Hassan states, "because it is active and has expectations." He aggressively fights against negativity: "We have very low tolerance for the energy absorbers, the loners, politicians, silo operators, and malcontents. They must be weeded out of the organization," he said.[161]

These were mergers of equals: an attempt by management to combine the best of separate companies to create a new and more exciting and innovative company with stronger positioning for the long run. In the pharmaceutical industry combining firms need to keep (not downsize) the talent and know-how that is essential to create and transition new products from the laboratory to the production (and profit) pipeline. It takes all the energy, skill, and diplomacy of a Fred Hassan to accomplish that—keeping the talent, keeping it motivated, and keeping it focused on the business.

Understanding behavioral, social, and cultural issues, then, is critical to the success of any merged enterprise. Acting on those differences by adjusting the combined firm to them is equally critical. The resultant, combined company may be a fully merged company with a harmonious culture, a merged company where open cultural warfare is regularly conducted at all levels at and below the Executive Office, or it may be a merged company with clearly separate, distinct operating styles for each of the previously independent entities. Realistic and pragmatic solutions to this issue largely make the difference in achieving long-term success or failure of the merger.

CONCLUSION

A thorough assessment of the business environments the firm faces is essential to underpin the vision and the goals, mission, and strategies that management has chosen for the business, to test their reality and their achievability in the real world around them, and to evaluate risks and opportunities.

Once again, you need to return to the beginning of the plan and review your prior work to ensure that it is consistent with your conclusions in the business environment analysis. Adjustments in the vision, goal-mission-strategy, and resource audit may be required, depending on your findings and the implications of the external business climate.

For example, you may have found that the business environment is far more open and hospitable to your vision of a new enterprise or for the prospects of a major new product launch than you had previously imagined, and therefore your goals may need to be elevated. The attainment of your vision may be closer than you had previously dreamed. The reverse, of course, may have been discovered, requiring appropriate downward adjustments of earlier portions of the plan or significant remedial action to correct areas of discovered weakness.

Each chapter in the planning process provides a "reality check" for the prior work, resulting in a business plan which is thoroughly tested and internally consistent.

NOTES

1. For environmental assessment methodology see C. W. Roney, *Assessing the Business Environment: Guidelines for Strategists* (Westport, CT: Quorum Books, 1999).

2. This discussion is based on David A. Aaker, *Developing Business Strategies*, 4th ed. (New York: Wiley, 1995), pp. 22–28. For customer analysis see Chapter 3; for market analysis see Chapter 5.

3. See also Michael A. Hitt, R. Duane Ireland, and Robert E. Hoskisson, *Strategic Management: Competitiveness and Globalization*, 3d ed. (Cincinnati, OH: South-Western College Publishing, 1999), especially Chapter 2, "External Environment."

4. *Los Angeles Times*, February 23, 1999, p. A1; March 1, 1999, p. E1; and May 5, 2000, p. C1.

5. Ibid., September 8, 1999, pp. C1, C15.

6. Ibid., March 11, 1999, p. C1.

7. Aaker, *Developing Business Strategies*, pp. 110–17. Aaker identifies five

components of environmental analysis: technological, economic, demographic, cultural, and governmental components. George A. Steiner, *Strategic Planning* (New York: Free Press, 1979), pp. 133–34, identifies six significant categories of environmental forces: economic, demographic, social, political, technological, and legal.

8. A term invented by John Naisbitt, *Megatrends* (New York: Warner Books, 1984).

9. In addition to Richard Arkwright, James Hargreaves, Samuel Crompton, and other inventor/industrialists contributed to the British Industrial Revolution. For a discussion see Robert Ergang, *Europe from the Renaissance to Waterloo* (Boston: D. C. Heath, 1954), pp. 558–61.

10. See James E. McClellan III and Harold Dorn, *Science and Technology in World History* (Baltimore: Johns Hopkins University Press, 1999), pp. 285–86. Arkwright also exploited child labor, provoking legislation limiting this abuse.

11. Charles H. Feinstein, "Pessimism Perpetuated: Real Wages and the Standard of Living in Britain during and after the Industrial Revolution," *Journal of Economic History*, 58, no. 3 (September 1998), p. 625ff.

12. Alex Taylor III, "Kings of the Road," *Fortune*, June 7, 1999, p. 151.

13. Henry Fuhrmann, "Ford Offered the Masses Freedom of Movement," *Los Angeles Times*, October 25, 1999, p. U4.

14. Ibid., p. U4.

15. P. Collier and D. Horowitz, *The Fords: An American Epic* (New York: Summit Books, 1987). See also David Halberstam, *The Reckoning* (New York: Morrow, 1986), Chapter 4.

16. A term coined by Peter F. Drucker; see his "Beyond the Information Revolution," *Atlantic Monthly*, October 1999, pp. 47–57.

17. *Los Angeles Times*, May 29, 1999, pp. A1, A20–21. Additional data from National Association of Temporary and Staffing Services.

18. U.S. Bureau of Labor Statistics, Howard Hayghe, Telecon, September 23, 1999.

19. *Los Angeles Times*, August 22, 1999, p. A3.

20. Rich Tetzeli, "Surviving Information Overload," *Fortune*, July 11, 1994.

21. Mary McAleese, President of Ireland, speech to the Los Angeles World Affairs Council, November 1999, cited in Los Angeles World Affairs Council, *World Affairs Journal*, November 1999.

22. Rob Norton, "Luck of the Irish," *Fortune*, October 25, 1999, p. 200.

23. James Flanigan, "Ireland on Web Points Way for Global Business," *Los Angeles Times*, July 25, 1999, pp. C1, C4, and October 5, 1999, pp. A1, A6. See also Frank Barry, ed., *Understanding Ireland's Economic Growth* (New York: St. Martin's Press, 1999).

24. *Wall Street Journal*, July 23, 1999, p. B2.

25. U.S. Bureau of Economic Analysis, *Survey of Current Business*, August 1999. See also "Western Economic Developments," Federal Reserve Bank of San Francisco, August 1999, p. 5 for national data.

26. *Wall Street Journal*, May 18, 1999, p. B2.

27. Joel Kotkin, "The Valley Unmasked," *Los Angeles Times*, July 18, 1999, p. M1.

28. Ibid., pp. M1, M6.

29. Dirk J. Struik, *Yankee Science in the Making* (New York: Dover Publications, 1991), pp. 182–88.

30. Peter F. Drucker, *The Concept of the Corporation* (New York: John Day, 1946), quoted in James P. Womack, Daniel T. Jones, and Daniel Roos, *The Machine that Changed the World* (New York: Rawson Associates, 1990), p. 11.

31. Scott McCartney, *ENIAC* (New York: Walker, 1999), p. 5. "They [Mauchley and Eckert] had vision but lacked the acumen to profit from their technological accomplishments," p. 7. Bill Gates refers to ENIAC as the first general-purpose computer; see Bill Gates, *Business @ the Speed of Thought* (New York: Warner Books, 1999), p. 13.

32. For implications, see "The 21st Century Economy," *Business Week*, August 24–31, 1998, p. 58ff.

33. For a discussion see Ian Morrison and Greg Schmid, *Future Tense: The Business Realities of the Next Ten Years* (New York: Morrow, 1994).

34. Joseph A. Schumpeter, *Capitalism, Socialism, and Democracy* (New York: Harper & Brother Publishers, 1950), p. 83.

35. Ibid., p. 83.

36. See Steven W. Popper, Caroline S. Wagner, and Eric V. Larsen, *Industry Views Critical Technologies* (Santa Monica, CA: RAND Corporation, MR-1008-OSTP, 1998).

37. William E. Halal, Michael D. Kull, and Ann Leffmann, "Emerging Technologies: What's Ahead for 2001–2030," *Futurist*, November–December 1997.

38. *Los Angeles Times*, March 15, 1999, p. C1.

39. The F-22 Raptor production program's future is continually uncertain, being subject to annual congressional budget infighting; see David A. Fulghum, "F-22 Headed for Reprieve from Congressional Ax," *Aviation Week & Space Technology*, August 9, 1999, pp. 28–29.

40. This discussion is based on Kenichi Ohmae, lecture to faculty at Anderson Graduate School of Management, UCLA, February 11, 1997. See also Kenneth Labich, "Nike vs. Reebok, a Battle for Hearts, Minds & Feet," *Fortune*, September 18, 1965, p. 90ff.

41. *Los Angeles Times*, April 18, 1999, pp. C1, C8. Vietnam has since mandated a forty-hour work week.

42. One informed commentator takes exception: "the most plausible scenario appears to be continued growth in U.S. consumption of gasoline during the first half of the next century." See Thomas F. Hogarty, "Gasoline: Still Powering Cars in 2050?" *Futurist*, 33, no. 3, March, 1999, p. 51ff.

43. See "A Clean Technology Powers Up," *Business Week*, May 8, 2000, pp. 102–5.

44. *Los Angeles Times*, March 18, 1999, p. C1.

45. *Wall Street Journal*, April 20, 1999, p. B4.

46. *Los Angeles Times*, March 31, 1999, p. C2.

47. For example, Northrop Grumman Corporation developed an innovative transit bus using fuel-cell and advanced technologies developed for aircraft and then was unwilling to put it into production; see José de la Torre and Wesley B. Truitt, "Northrop Grumman and the Advanced Technology Transit Bus Program," in José de la Torre, Yves Doz, and Timothy Devinney, *Managing the Global Corporation:*

Case Studies in Strategy and Management, 2d ed. (New York: Irwin/McGraw-Hill, 2001), pp. 259–71.

48. *Raytheon Company 1998 Annual Report*, February 24, 1999, p. 7.

49. For a discussion of "scope," see Ron McTavish, "One More Time: What Business Are You In?" *Long Range Planning*, 28, no. 2 (April 1995), pp. 49–60.

50. *Cisco Systems, 2000 Annual Report*, August, 2000, p. 3.

51. *IBM 1999 Annual Report*, p. 97. Reprinted by permission from the *IBM 1999 Annual Report* copyright 1999 by International Business Machines Corporation.

52. Ibid., p. 3. Reprinted by permission from the *IBM 1999 Annual Report* copyright 1999 by International Business Machines Corporation.

53. Ibid., pp. 6–9. Reprinted by permission from the *IBM 1999 Annual Report* copyright 1999 by International Business Machines Corporation.

54. *New York Times*, December 16, 1999, p. C28.

55. *Los Angeles Times*, February 10, 2000, p. C6.

56. General Motors, *Stockholder News*, 5, no. 3 (September 1999), p. 1. See also *General Motors Corporation 1999 Annual Report*, pp. 12, 14.

57. John F. Smith, Jr., speech to Los Angeles World Affairs Council, Beverly Hills, CA, May 19, 2000.

58. *Wall Street Journal*, February 22, 2000, p. B23.

59. *Los Angeles Times*, October 9, 2000, pp. C1, C5.

60. Ibid., March 29, 2000, p. C3.

61. *New York Times*, February 29, 2000, p. C2.

62. *Los Angeles Times*, December 24, 1999, p. C1.

63. Ibid., March 3, 2000, p. C3.

64. Peter Sealey, "How E-Commerce Will Trump Brand Management," *Harvard Business Review* (July–August 1999), p. 176.

65. Ibid., p. 176.

66. *Los Angeles Times*, March 31, 2000, p. C3.

67. Ibid., July 11, 1999, pp. C1, C16.

68. Ibid., February 2, 2000, p. A10.

69. Ibid., May 8, 1999, p. A2.

70. John Moore, "British Privatization—Taking Capitalism to the People," *Harvard Business Review*, January–February 1992.

71. See Richard Pipes, *The Formation of the Soviet Union*, rev. ed. (Cambridge, MA: Harvard University Press, 1997).

72. See Gregory L. Freeze, *Russia, a History* (New York: Oxford University Press, 1997). See also Maxim Boycko, Andrei Shleifer, and Robert Vishny, *Privatizing Russia* (Cambridge, MA: MIT Press, 1995).

73. Hugh Thomas, *Cuba, or the Pursuit of Freedom* (New York: Da Capo Press, 1998), p. 639, quoted in Paul Johnson, *Modern Times: The World from the Twenties to the Eighties* (New York: Harper & Row, 1983), p. 621. For a discussion of Cuba, see Johnson, pp. 618–25.

74. Robert J. Alexander, "Castro, Latin America and United States Policy," in Robert A. Goldwin, ed., *Beyond the Cold War* (Chicago: Rand McNally, 1963), pp. 174–85.

75. Michel C. Oksenberg, Michael D. Swaine, and Daniel C. Lynch, "The Chi-

nese Future" (Los Angeles: Pacific Council on International Policy and RAND Center for Asia/Pacific Policy, 1997). The author participated in this study.

76. Adapted from David Easton, "An Approach to Political Systems," *World Politics*, 9 (1957), pp. 383–400. See also David Easton, *The Political System* (New York: Knopf, 1960), pp. 125–41.

77. *Los Angeles Times*, January, 1, 1999, p. A1. Before the Euro went into effect, Chase Manhattan Corp. had already decided to adopt it for internal operations in Europe previously conducted in the currencies of the eleven countries joining the European Monetary Union; *Wall Street Journal*, August 26, 1998, p. B3.

78. For a discussion of political analysis for business, see David P. Baron, *Business and Its Environment*, 2d ed. (Upper Saddle River, NJ: Prentice-Hall, 1996), Chapter 6.

79. For a checklist of political risk indicators, see James C. Leontiades, *Multinational Corporate Strategy: Planning for World Markets* (New York: Lexington Books, 1985), p. 161. Also, Stefan H. Robock, "Political Risk: Identification and Assessment," *Columbia Journal of World Business* (July/August 1971).

80. See Franklin Root, *International Trade and Investment*, 7th ed. (Cincinnati, OH: International Thompson Publishing, 1994). Also, Stephen J. Kobrin, "Assessing Political Risk Overseas," in P. Grub and D. Khambata, *The Multinational Enterprise in Transition: Strategies for Global Competitiveness*, 4th ed. (Princeton, NJ: Darwin Press, 1993).

81. For a discussion of PL95–504, see *Congressional Quarterly Almanac, 1978*, p. 496.

82. For a discussion of PL96–296, see *Congressional Quarterly Almanac, 1980*, pp. 242–43. The quotation is on p. 242.

83. For a discussion of railroad deregulation, beginning in September 1980, see *Congressional Quarterly Almanac, 1980*, pp. 248–49.

84. Data in this paragraph and Figure 4.5 are from Shaifali Puri, "Deals of the Year," *Fortune*, February 17, 1997, p. 102.

85. *Fortune*, January 11, 1999, p. 72.

86. *New York Times*, October 5, 1999, p. A1. This deal later fell through.

87. See *Los Angeles Times*, April 4, 1999, pp. C1, C13 for numerous examples of European firms buying U.S. companies.

88. *Los Angeles Times*, March 11, 1999, p. C1 and *Fortune*, February 15, 1999, pp. 28, 30.

89. *Los Angeles Times*, March 25, 1999, p. C3.

90. Ibid., April 26, 1999, p. C2.

91. Ibid., December 21, 1999, p. C1.

92. Ibid., April 14, 1999, p. C2. The joint venture will later make a tender offer for the remaining 10 percent owned by shareholders. The 90 percent deal is valued at $830 million.

93. Ibid., May 1, 1999, p. C2. The purchase was valued at $2.03 billion.

94. An example is Lockheed Martin's failed attempt to acquire Northrop Grumman for $10.5 billion; U.S. Justice and Defense Departments objected on antitrust and competitive grounds. *Los Angeles Times*, July 17, 1998, p. C1.

95. *Fortune*, December 12, 1994, p. 100ff.

96. *Los Angeles Times*, March 23, 1999, p. C2.

97. Ibid., March 31, 1999, p. C3.

98. Ibid., January 2, 1999, p. C1 and *Argus Update*, February 1999, p. 1, reporting Securities Data Corporation data.

99. Kenichi Ohmae, "Putting Global Logic First," *Harvard Business Review*, January–February 1995, p. 119.

100. Useful print sources for these data include:

CIA, *The World Factbook* (Central Intelligence Agency, Washington, DC: GPO, annual editions).

The World Competitiveness Yearbook (Lausanne, Switz.: IMD, annual editions).

The World Bank, *The World Bank Atlas* (Washington, DC: The World Bank Group, annual editions).

International Monetary Fund, *World Economic Outlook* (Washington, DC: annual editions beginning in 1999).

Useful Web sites for economic data are listed in the Bibliography under Web Sites.

101. The following productivity discussion is based on John M. Eade, "A Productive Population," *Argus Update*, March 1999, p. 1.

102. Quoted in Edward E. Leamer, "Cyclically, We're Back to the Past," *Los Angeles Times*, December 6, 2000, p. B9.

103. *Los Angeles Times*, February 9, 2000, pp. A1, A22.

104. This section is based on ibid., March 31, 2000, p. C3.

105. Pebble Beach Golf Resort was bought by a Japanese investor in 1990 from a group headed by Marvin Davis for $850 million and sold in 1992 for $500 million to other Japanese investors. In 1989 Mitsubishi Estate Co. paid $846 million for Rockefeller Center, and defaulted in 1995. Hotel Bel-Air in Los Angeles was sold for $110 million in 1989 to Sazale Group of Tokyo, and when they defaulted in 1995 it was sold for $60 million. *Los Angeles Times*, May 27, 1999, pp. A1, A28.

106. Ibid., April 6, 1999, pp. C1, C14. By 1999 the commercial real estate market in Los Angeles had not yet recovered to its peak value in 1989; top-tier office buildings throughout the region sold in 1999 for $50 to $100 per square foot less than they had a decade earlier. *Los Angeles Times*, April 13, 1999, p. C1.

107. In 1999 Japan was in recession (two consecutive quarters of negative growth) and GDP grew in 2000 at an annual rate of 1 percent. Ibid., December 4, 2000, p. C9.

108. Ibid., March 26, 1999, p. C1.

109. Ibid., April 2, 1999, pp. C1, C6.

110. For this period see David Halberstam, *The Reckoning* (New York: Morrow, 1986), and Peter Wickens, *The Road to Nissan* (London: Macmillan, 1987).

111. *Los Angeles Times*, January 31, 1999, pp. C1, C14.

112. Ibid., January 6, 1999, p. C1.

113. Ibid., January 31, 1999, p. C14.

114. "Is the World Big Enough for Jurgen Schrempp?" *Fortune*, March 6, 2000, p. 141.

115. *New York Times*, April 17, 1999, p. B2. Renault will build Renault-brand cars at Nissan's Mexico plant for that market, cutting costs by improving factory utilization at that plant. *Los Angeles Times*, March 31, 1999, p. C5.

116. Ibid., July 16, 1999, pp. C3, C5.

117. Stuart Crainer, "The Days of Futurists Past," *Strategy + Business*, issue 20, 3rd quarter 2000, pp. 104–5.

118. See, for example, Pierre Wack, "Scenarios: Uncharted Waters Ahead," *Harvard Business Review*, September–October 1985, and Pierre Wack, "Scenarios: Shooting the Rapids," *Harvard Business Review*, November–December 1985.

119. In a study by the Conference Board, probabilities of 50 percent to 70 percent were found. See Rochelle O'Connor, *Planning under Uncertainty: Multiple Scenarios and Contingency Planning* (New York: The Conference Board, Inc., 1978), p. 10.

120. The author participated in this study.

121. Federal Reserve System, *Bulletin* (Washington, DC: GPO, monthly publication).

122. For example: World Future Society publishes *The Futurist*, a monthly journal; *Futures*, a multidisciplinary publication, based in the United Kingdom, of international forecasting for decision and policy making; and a private firm, Coates & Jarrott, Inc., Washington, DC.

123. Quoted in Edward E. Leamer, "Cyclically, We're Back to the Past," *Los Angeles Times*, December 6, 2000, p. B9.

124. "New Economy," Argus Research, *On Investing* (Fall 2000), p. 67.

125. Center for Education Statistics, U.S. Department of Education, reported in *Los Angeles Times*, August 1, 1997, p. A16.

126. Ibid., January 9, 2000, p. K5.

127. *New York Times*, March 13, 2001, p. A14.

128. *Los Angeles Times*, January 17, 1999, p. A9.

129. Marian Clarkberg, report to the American Association for the Advancement of Science, reported in ibid., January 24, 1999, p. C6.

130. Ibid., July 11, 1999, p. A3.

131. Ibid., August 22, 1999, p. A3.

132. Peter Hall, "Modeling the Post-Industrial City," *Futures* 29, no. 4/5 (May/June 1997), p. 311ff.

133. Marian Salzman and Ira Matathia, "Lifestyles of the Next Millennium: 65 Forecasts," *Futurist*, June–July 1998.

134. Joseph Coates, Jennifer Jarratt, and John Mahaffie, *Future Work: Seven Critical Forces Reshaping Work and the Workforce in North America* (San Francisco: Jossey-Bass, 1990).

135. Frost and Sullivan, "World Contraceptive and Infertility Drug Markets," reported in *Los Angeles Times*, April 15, 1999, p. C1.

136. "Management by Morgan," *Fortune*, March 1934, p. 82ff.

137. Bill Sells, "What Asbestos Taught Me about Managing Risk," *Harvard Business Review*, March–April 1994.

138. *New York Times*, April 21, 1999, p. C3; *Wall Street Journal*, December 21, 2000, p. A3.

139. Ibid., July 22, 1999, p. B1.

140. Ralph Nader, *Unsafe at Any Speed* (New York: Grossman, 1965).

141. Arthur M. Schlesinger, Jr., ed., *The Almanac of American History* (New York: Barnes and Noble Books, 1993), p. 566.

142. *Los Angeles Times*, August 22, 1999, p. C3.

143. Ibid., July 8, 1999, pp. A1, A11. See Michael Orey, *Assuming the Risk: The Mavericks, the Lawyers, and the Whistle-Blowers who Beat Big Tobacco* (Bos-

ton: Little, Brown, 1999) for a discussion focused on the Mississippi case—the lead state seeking recovery of health care costs from the tobacco industry.

144. *Los Angeles Times*, April 8, 2000, p. A1.

145. Ibid., November 6, 2000, p. C1.

146. Ibid., September 23, 1999, p. A1 and September 25, 1999, p. A13.

147. *Wall Street Journal*, May 11, 1999, pp. B1, B4.

148. *1998 Annual Report of the Philip Morris Companies, Inc.*, February 24, 1999.

149. *1999 Annual Report of the Philip Morris Companies, Inc.*, February 22, 2000.

150. *1998 Annual Report of the Philip Morris Companies, Inc.*

151. *Wall Street Journal*, October 28, 1999, p. B21.

152. Michael Massing, "Taking on Big Tobacco," *Washington Monthly*, October 1999, p. 42.

153. *New York Times*, September 19, 1999, p. BU9.

154. "Is the World Big Enough for Jurgen Schrempp?" p. 142.

155. *New York Times*, February 29, 2000, p. C2.

156. The DaimlerChrysler discussion is largely based on *Los Angeles Times*, January 17, 1999, pp. C1, C8.

157. Clayton M. Christensen and Michael Overdorf, "Meeting the Challenge of Disruptive Change," *Harvard Business Review*, March–April 2000, p. 76.

158. This discussion is based on Patricia Sellers, "Behind the Shootout at Citigroup," *Fortune*, March 20, 2000, p. 27, and Timothy L. O'Brien, "Reed Announces Plans to Step Down as Co-Chief of Citigroup, *New York Times*, February, 29, 2000, p. C1.

159. John Reed, *Journal of the Academy of Management*, summarized in Sellers, "Behind the Shootout at Citigroup," p. 28.

160. This discussion is based on Victoria Griffith, "The People Factor in Post-Merger Integration," *Strategy + Business*, issue 20 (3rd quarter 2000), pp. 82–90.

161. Griffith, "The People Factor in Post-Merger Integration," p. 90.

Chapter 5

Competitive Assessment

No enterprise operates in a vacuum. All are confronted by others that already provide the product or service you offer or aspire to offer or that could supply the demand you might create. Careful attention to the dynamics of the competitive situation is essential to success at all stages of product life, as well as to the underlying industry environment. Competitiveness is born in the gap between managers' goals and the company's resources.[1]

"A company can outperform rivals only if it can establish a difference that it can preserve," warns Michael Porter. "It must deliver greater value to customers or create comparable value at lower cost, or do both."[2] At the heart of the competitive assessment process is this issue: can your firm "outperform" your rivals by delivering "greater value," "lower cost," or "both" in a sustained way? Preserving that competitive differential is as important as its initial creation. Each is essential for sustained success. GE's Jack Welch sums it up this way, "If you don't have a competitive advantage, don't compete."[3]

The competitive assessment process has essentially two steps: industry analysis and competitor analysis.

INDUSTRY ANALYSIS

The initial step is to identify the industry or industry segment in which you intend to compete (or in which you are already competing). Industries are identified by the customers served, the products serving them, and the firms providing the products.[4]

For United Airlines, as an example, customers are people and goods that need to travel by air from A to B, the product is the service of providing air transportation, and the firms providing that service are all carriers that also provide air transpiration along the same route structure. United's industry is transportation; the industry segment in which United and its rivals operate is air transportation. United's product (generic for product or service) is air transportation, and its customers and potential customers are people and cargo that require air transportation on its routes.

Clarity and accuracy in the identification of your industry and industry segment are vitally important for the proper identification and evaluation of your competitive environment.

Peter Drucker has spoken about the time fifty years ago when he consulted with a manufacturer of glass bottles whose principal customers were dairies, which used them as milk bottles for home delivery. The dairies were facing stiff competition from grocery stores, which had begun selling milk in wax-paper cartons at a lower price. Drucker spent time with the company attempting to understand their processes and their essential problems.

At the end of a week he asked the CEO, "What business are you in?" The CEO replied, exasperated, "The glass bottle business." Drucker said, "Ah, that's the problem. You are really in the *container* business." The firm's industry was containers and they never understood it. The company quickly adjusted to this new understanding and embarked on new applications for their products to new customers and began applying new materials to their containers. Their business exploded.[5]

Michael Porter has identified Five Forces of competition in an industry:[6]

Rivalry among Existing Firms

Rivalry among existing competitors is the most direct source of competition in an industry. Rivalry can take many forms: promotional campaigns, price reductions, new products, better customer service, increased warranties, quality improvements, and so on.

Competitive intensity is a function of the number and strength of firms in the industry, their commitment to the industry, prevailing cost structure within the industry, industry growth rate, degrees of product differentiation, and barriers to entry and exit to and from the industry. Competition will be especially strong if many firms are present, and industries with even a few strong companies will typically have more competition than where one strong firm dominates.

Large capital investment and high fixed costs in an industry will erect barriers of entry and exit and will limit participation in the industry to only a few participants. Large fixed costs simulate price competition to maintain sales volumes for efficient rates of capacity utilization. This is endemic in the auto industry during periods of sales downturns.

In growth industries all firms benefit from a growth market, reducing competitive pressure. Mature markets, however, are like a zero-sum game, where growth for one firm can only come at the expense of a rival; none are willing to relinquish market share to another, and all gains are hard-fought and costly.

Example: Commercial Aircraft Industry. For example, the commercial aircraft industry is a mature industry where there are only two global competitors: The Boeing Company and Airbus Industrie. Each company offers the airlines an airplane in each passenger class from roughly 100 seats to 400 seats. Above 400 seats Boeing presently has a monopoly with the 747, though this will change in 2006 when Airbus delivers the first A380, its new superjumbo seating up to 800 passengers.[7] In all categories today except the jumbo class, the companies fiercely compete head-to-head for every order; a sale for one company is a no-sale for the other—a zero-sum game.

Boeing's management said it well: "This market environment has resulted in intense pressures on pricing and other competitive factors. The [Boeing] Company's focus on improving processes and other cost reduction efforts is intended to enhance its ability to pursue pricing strategies that enhance its ability to maintain leadership at satisfactory margins."[8]

Each company will even take "trade-ins" of the other's planes to make a sale. In 1999, in the largest trade-in it ever made, Boeing agreed to take seventeen Airbus A340–300s from Singapore Airlines in return for Singapore's purchase of ten Boeing 777s for $1.9 billion; a month later Airbus announced it would deny parts and service to airlines that buy its used planes from Boeing.[9]

After the 1997 merger of McDonnell Douglas into Boeing, the enlarged Boeing accounted for approximately 55 percent of the world's commercial aircraft market and Airbus had 45 percent.[10] Boeing asserts it has maintained, on average, approximately a two-thirds share of the available commercial jet aircraft market.[11]

In 1998, both Boeing and Airbus lost money on their commercial aircraft. It is estimated Boeing priced their airplanes between 14 percent and 27 percent below list prices, earning a total company profit of $1.12 billion on $56 billion in sales.[12] This result, after a loss in 1997, caused Boeing's CEO to state, "Financially, 1998 did not turn out the way we planned. Far from it."[13] In 1998 Airbus Industrie lost $200 million, also having heavily discounted prices to compete for every sale in a price war that has benefited both companies' airline customers with overall price reductions of approximately 20 percent over two years.[14]

In 1999 Airbus Industrie attempted to increase output by 29 percent, to a record 295 airplanes. Its production lines struggled to accelerate to meet surging demand. "It is stretching the imagination to keep up with the throughput we've got now," warned Ian Massey, financial controller of Airbus.[15] Airbus stated it could be several years before they achieve profitability. In 1999 Airbus lost $194 million, having sold airplanes for less money than it cost to build them.[16]

For 1999 Boeing had scheduled delivery of 620 commercial jets for the year versus 563 delivered the prior year, and it met its goal. In 1997 Boeing had attempted to double production in response to heightened demand for new capacity by the world's airlines, but it failed to meet committed delivery schedules, experienced quality problems, and suffered financial loss, taking a charge of $3 billion against earnings and reporting its first yearly loss in fifty years.[17] In 1998, Boeing delivered 53 percent of its planes on time and managed to eke out $63 million in profit on $36 billion in revenue in the commercial group. For 1999, Boeing had forecast earnings of 3.5 to 4.5 percent on sales of commercial aircraft[18] and 4 to 5 percent in 2000 on reduced revenue.[19] Actual results for 1999 were earnings of $2.016 billion, which represented an operating margin of 5.2 percent on commercial aircraft, substantially beating their own forecast owing to improved production performance.[20]

This intense price competition has ripple effects throughout each company's supplier chain. Boeing's Commercial Airplane Group buys from suppliers about 1.5 billion different parts a year, representing 50 percent of the value of each new airliner. Boeing is putting intense pressure on suppliers to reduce costs and provide integrated assemblies, not just piece parts that Boeing must assemble. In return, it offers suppliers the opportunity to gain more Boeing-wide business on other commercial and military/space programs, if they perform well.[21]

Thus, the world's only commercial airplane makers are struggling to benefit profitably from one of the greatest order surges in commercial airplane history. This is an example of a "worst case" situation in a two-firm industry rivalry.

Barriers to Entry and Exit. Product differentiation can be real or apparent. Either way, the more customers exhibit preference for one firm's product, the more sheltered the product will be and the higher its firm's profitability. Strong differentiation, based on high quality, customer service, location, selection, and the like, can be a powerful barrier to entry to other firms.

There are a number of barriers to exit from an industry. (a) High fixed costs is one; selling the business or liquidating such large capital assets would likely be difficult because that capital investment represents a major barrier to entry into the industry for another firm. (b) Labor and management agreements represent a barrier to exit; labor contracts require the firm and certain key executives to continue operation for a specified time period and under stipulated conditions.

(c) The requirement to carry a full line of parts and service is another exit barrier; the industry's norm cannot be ignored by any participant without compromising customer confidence and the viability of the entire enterprise. (d) Management's determination to remain in the industry is an exit barrier. And (e) the economic and social impacts on a community from an exit can be a barrier.

Threat of New Entrants

The threat that new competitors may enter the industry stimulates competition. Firms newly entering an industry typically bring with them fresh energy, new resources, additional productive capacity, desire to build market share, and possibly a differential in products and services. All these factors challenge the firms already present in the industry with increased competitive pressure; in the face of this, prices may drop, costs may increase with more promotional activity, and profits may erode.

New potential entrants are generally aware of the risks they face entering a new industry, squaring off with existing players who usually retaliate against them, and they face a set of barriers to entry into a new industry. These two factors—threat of retaliation and entry barriers—reduce the risk of new competitors entering an industry.

What are the barriers to entry? Porter identifies eight barriers to entry as follows:[22]

- Economies of scale. Existing firms in an industry seek to operate at economically efficient levels, taking advantage of economies of scale, which declines unit cost as volume of output per unit of time increases. New entrants face incumbents that typically have these advantages. New firms therefore need to enter the industry having made substantial capital investment to achieve comparable capacity, cost, and price structure. Three things often result: overcapacity in the industry, sharp retaliation by incumbents producing price warfare, and low return on investment. For the new firm to enter without the appropriate investment and capacity it runs the risk of being the industry's high-cost producer.

- High capital investment. New entrants are faced with the need for substantial capital investment to "level the playing field" with existing firms with respect to capacity/unit cost issues. This level of investment in plant, equipment, R&D, service and support, training, working capital, promotion, and other start-up requirements is a powerful deterrent to new entrants, especially in the face of the expected sharp retaliatory actions incumbents are likely to take. The risk of not achieving acceptable return on investment is a high barrier to entry and requires a solid commitment to the business.

- Product differentiation. New entrants face existing customer loyalty to existing firms' products and brands. Overcoming these loyalties and building new ones for new products and brands is costly and risky, but it is also absolutely necessary for successful entry and a sustained presence.

- Switching costs. Customers experience costs when they switch from one supplier to another. Such costs may be clearly identified one-time, nonrecurring, or they may be less apparent and recur. Changing over from one set of standards for factory operations, computer operating systems, communications equipment, etc. are areas where switching costs are largely quantifiable. The emotional cost of leaving a reliable, familiar supplier to entrust your business to a new, untried vendor may be too great. These costs are barriers to entry.

- Access to distribution channels. Existing firms have established relationships with distribution channels. New entrants must gain access to these channels or create new ones. Costs are associated with this including promotion costs, price cuts, preferential agreements, and the like. These costs reduce the profitability of entry and constitute a barrier.

- Proprietary product technology. Incumbents typically own proprietary intellectual property associated with the products in the industry, such as patents on key processes and technologies. This is a barrier to entry that is costly or impossible to overcome.

- Learning-curve effects. Existing firms have already achieved economies of scale, having gained experience in various aspects of the business such as production operations, marketing, purchasing, etc. These firms are operating at efficient unit cost of operation. Keeping this experience proprietary is difficult, but if it can be done it constitutes a barrier to new entrants.

- Entry-deterring price. If incumbent firms are perceived to be able and willing to lower their prices in the face of new competition, this will be a barrier to new entrants, fearing below-average returns after entry into the industry.

Overcoming these powerful barriers to entry is a major challenge. Often only alliances, mergers, or acquisitions are routes available to new entrants into established industries.

Threat of Substitute Products or Services

Substitutes are different products or services that can perform the same function as existing products of firms in the industry. Making auto bodies out of plastic instead of sheet metal is a substitute. Using synthetic fiber instead of rubber for tires is a substitute. Using a phone-answering machine instead of a secretary is another.

The existence or the threat of existence of substitutes is a powerful competitive force for preventing excessive price increases. Substitutes threaten the foundation of a firm's existence because they can undermine or obsolesce an industry—like autos obsolesced buggies, phones and faxes obsolesced telegrams, and plastic largely obsolesced glass for containers. Technological advancements constantly raise the fear of potential substitutes in many industries.

Bargaining Power of Suppliers

The supplier base in any industry is another important ingredient in the competitive analysis. If the industry is characterized by a number of strong suppliers, they represent a source of competition in the industry. Suppliers have bargaining power over their customers if one or more of the following conditions is present in the industry:

- The suppliers' product is critically important to the buyer.
- There are no substitutes for the suppliers' product.
- A small number of suppliers sell to a larger number of smaller customers.
- The buyer's industry constitutes a small fraction of the suppliers' customer base.
- The suppliers' product is differentiated.
- Buyers would incur switching costs if they changed suppliers.
- Suppliers can pursue forward integration, creating outlets bypassing current buyers.

In industry conditions where suppliers are more powerful than their customers they may exercise their superior bargaining power over them to charge higher prices, to demand terms more favorable to the supplier, and in some instances to acquire a buyer both to gain a market outlet and to bypass other buyers.

Bargaining Power of Buyers

The buyer base in an industry also requires careful analysis as a source of competitive strength. In industries characterized by strong buyers and weaker suppliers, buyers can exert downward pressure on suppliers with respect to prices and other terms and conditions, such as priority timing of delivery, quality features, special service and handling considerations, and the like.

Buyers have bargaining power over suppliers if one or more of the following conditions is present in the industry:

- Buyers are few and volumes purchased are large relative to the suppliers' sales.
- Buyer's purchases are a significant part of buyer's total costs.
- Purchased products are undifferentiated and are readily available from other sources.
- Switching costs are low.
- Buyer's margins are low and constantly seek lowest supplier prices.
- Buyers can pursue backward integration.

In industries where buyers/supplier relations are asymmetrical in the buyer's favor, buyers truly hold the whip hand. In some such instances, weak suppliers seek to be acquired by a strong buyer, perhaps tiring of the lash. In industry conditions where suppliers and buyers are more equal, suppliers may become takeover targets for buyers to secure reliable supply or buyers may seek to establish more permanent relationships with critical suppliers, making them part of "the team."

Using the Five Forces analysis, the competitive environment in a given industry can be understood and evaluated on the macrolevel, providing management with insights into its available strategic alternatives as it searches for ways to attain and sustain a competitive advantage.[23]

Sources of Information

Information and data regarding industries are readily available from numerous sources. Virtually all industries have "associations" or industry groups that gather and publish industry trend data and provide it to the public free or for a nominal charge.[24] A typical example is the Aerospace Industries Association, a not-for-profit industry group located in Washington, DC. whose members are all the aerospace companies in the United States, such as Boeing, Lockheed Martin, Raytheon, etc. The AIA annually publishes statistics on composite industry sales, earnings, exports/imports, employment, etc.

Individual companies, especially the largest in an industry, routinely collect and evaluate industry-wide data for competitive analysis and other purposes. Some of these firms will share these data with students, scholars, and industry groups.

Governments, federal and state, amass data and perform trend analyses for a variety of industries: the Commerce Department tracks whole industries and industry sectors, the Labor Department collects employment information by industry, the Energy Department maintains data bases on energy companies, and the Central Intelligence Agency gathers and publishes international industry trend information. Much of this information is now available online as well as in published format.

Example: Industry Competitive Analysis of American Television. Changes within an industry are well illustrated by American television. The business model for this industry was established in the late 1940s and early 1950s: commercial television networks delivering news and entertainment via the public airwaves to home audiences paid for by advertisers.

Over the years with changes in technology, especially the introduction in 1978 of cable delivery of the signal to the household on a subscription basis and the remote channel changer, and changes in the regulatory environment permitting numerous providers to operate cable and satellite-based channels expanding viewers' choices, the underlying basis of the business model has been fundamentally altered. Other forms of electronic communication (the Internet) and entertainment (compact discs played on home PCs) have also eroded the once near-monopoly of commercial TV networks for home communications and entertainment, much like television devastated radio before it.

Using Porter's analysis, cable and satellite and the providers operating these channels represent the "threat of new entrants" as well as "substitutes" for the commercial networks. The Internet is also a "substitute." The "rivalry among existing firms," i.e., between the commercial networks, has become less and less relevant to the fundamentals of the industry because of cable. The ratings of each of the commercial networks have declined regularly since the late 1970s, from approximately 20 percent each to approximately 10 percent each twenty years later. By 1998, the four major commercial networks (ABC, CBS, Fox, and NBC) together represented only 40 percent of viewer ratings versus 80 percent twenty years earlier.

"There's a growing acceptance by everybody that the business model just doesn't make any sense any more," admitted NBC President Bob Wright. "We're going to have [to] get the 1940s' view of television kind of updated here." CBS Television President Leslie Moonves was equally candid: "The game as it was played before doesn't work. The whole way we look at our business has to be drastically different."[25] There is talk of combining two or perhaps more commercial television networks to reduce cost and more effectively compete with the 200-plus cable services available. Competition between commercial firms in the industry is no longer the main issue owing to the changes in industry fundamentals.

Recognizing this, NBC has begun its move to establish a possible new business model by buying a large stake in a technology that essentially undermines the commercial TV business model. In June 1999 NBC announced its purchase of a multimillion-dollar position in TiVo Inc., a Sunnyvale, California firm that is one of two companies marketing a technology that diverts the TV signal to a high-capacity hard disk before sending the signal to the television screen. This technology enables the viewer to record, pause, rewind, and fast-forward programs in a computer chip without videotape. Because this set-top technology enables the viewer to control his/her viewing habits by deleting commercials and recording programs for later viewing time, it has the capacity to destroy the commercial TV business model. NBC is now an owner of this technological capability that has the potential of altering the industry's fundamentals.[26]

Another important feature of the television industry business model is the contribution to the networks' profit streams of their network-owned TV stations. CBS, once the Tiffany network of the industry, fell on hard times but began recovering under Mel Karmazin's leadership. In 1998 CBS placed fourth in the four-network rating sweepstakes and so did its CBS-owned TV station group. The sixteen stations in the group contributed more than half of CBS's profits in 1998, and for a number of years that station group had underperformed the station groups of NBC, Fox, and ABC.

In 1998 CBS station group's profit improved under Karmazin to approximately $510 million, less than NBC's, which is smaller in number of stations, less than Fox's, which is slightly larger, and comparable to ABC's, which was at the 50 percent level. In July 1999, Karmazin named John Severino to the position of President of CBS's TV station division, reporting to Leslie Moonves, President and CEO of CBS Television. In the 1980s Severino had headed the ABC Television Network for five years. "The stations have been run badly for years," said Alan Bell, President of Freedom Broadcasting, owner of five CBS affiliates. "It has been a dumping ground for people who couldn't do anything else in the company." Under Karmazin, that is changing.[27] Will Sumner Redstone, CEO at Viacom, which purchased CBS for $37 billion, continue the momentum?[28]

COMPETITOR ANALYSIS

Once the industry analysis is completed, management must then tackle the competitor analysis phase of evaluating the competitive environment. This involves a thorough analysis of existing and potential competitors the firm faces in its chosen markets, which could include international markets.[29]

Sources of Information

There are numerous sources of competitive information by company, as well as within industry groups. Simply identifying all the companies competing within an industry is an important first step. One way to do this is by using the *Thomas Register of American Manufacturers*, which is in eleven volumes. Another is the *Dun and Bradstreet Reference Book*, annually updated. The *Guide to American Directories* will help steer the analyst to the correct directory for your industry.[30]

All publicly traded companies must publish annual reports to shareholders and annually file documents with the Securities and Exchange Commission, such as 8-K, 10-K, and 10-Q Reports, on their operations and financial activities. These reports are available to the public. Much of this information can be obtained through the Internet.

Another source of company competitive intelligence is industry trade shows, where anyone can gather information about companies from their displays and booths at such shows regarding new product introductions, latest technologies, specification sheets on existing products, and sometimes even customer lists. Technology data are often proudly presented in professional papers at seminars held in conjunction with trade shows and industry fairs by senior-level executives giving speeches at such events.

Autobiographies are another source of information about a company's philosophy and strategic intent. Michael Dell, in his book *Direct from Dell*, provides the reader with a wealth of insights about Dell Computer Corporation's strategic focus and business strategy. Similarly, in an earlier time, Thomas Watson, Jr., Alfred P. Sloan, and Lee Iacocca wrote of their business philosophies and strategies with respect to IBM, General Motors, and the Ford Motor Company and Chrysler.[31]

Reasons for Making Competitor Analysis

According to Michael Porter, the reasons a firm must evaluate its present and likely potential competitors are summarized as follows:[32]

- Establishing and maintaining a competitive advantage requires the firm to understand its markets, its competitors for those markets, and ways and means by which it can differentiate itself from its competitors.
- Understanding the competition will enable the firm to position itself in the market to take sustained advantage of competitors' weaknesses.
- Tracking and analyzing industry changes will enable a firm to forecast industry trends, position itself to take advantage of them, and enable the firm to compete effectively.
- Keeping abreast of technology changes and competitors' technological innovations will enable the firm to adjust to those changes or to establish or maintain a technology leadership position vis-à-vis the competition.

Elements of Competitor Analysis

Porter has identified six elements of competitor analysis:[33]

- Objectives. To the extent possible, the firm should learn and understand the strategic objectives of competitor companies. Make an evaluation of how close to achieving those objectives the key competitors are—to determine their energy, drive, and determination to completely accomplish those objectives. How well are these competitors performing relative to their objectives in terms of sales, operating income, technological innovation, market share, etc.? What is their demonstrated willingness to accept risk, their degree of aggressiveness, and the underlying values and beliefs of their management? Having answers to these questions will assist the firm in understanding competitor behavior.
- Assumptions. What assumptions have key competitors made about the state of the industry they are in and their relative position within it? These assumptions will have a major bearing on the strategic focus the firm has taken and its operating behavior. If a major competitor believes the industry is in ascent and its position is one of leadership bordering on market dominance, that firm's behavior will be vastly different from that of a company that assumes it is in a marginal position in a declining industry. These critical assumptions underlie the strategic

direction and resource allocation decisions major competitors will likely make and how they will likely respond to competitor moves.

- Past performance. On the assumption that present management will continue at major competitor companies—or that past, known management philosophies will continue to guide the behavior of new management—studying and understanding the past performance of competitors will likely yield insights into future actions. What does a competitor consider its core competencies over which it has previously demonstrated an unwillingness to lose market share? How has a key competitor historically reacted to moves by its competitors in critical arenas such as pricing policy, geographic sales territories viewed as crucial to market share, raiding of key employees, etc.? Interestingly, the Defense Department lists "past performance" as one of the factors (along with price, technological innovation, management strength, etc.) in its evaluation of proposals for contract awards.

- Managerial orientation. The types of experience and professional expertise of top management in a competitor firm will likely have a marked bearing on the degree of competitiveness, operating style, and strategic direction of the company. If the senior management is technical in background, as opposed to financial or marketing, certain styles of behavior and certain areas of company activity will tend to predominate over others. The management culture, style, and values of the competitor firm will have been formed by these functional experiences, which will likely influence future decision making and overall company behavior. On another level, what have been the successes and failures of this management team, have they learned from them, have they proven to be aggressive or passive, are they proactive or reactive, are they "maintainers" or "builders"?

- Present strategies. Understanding the present strategies of competitors will likely yield insights into their future orientation and strategic focus. Looking at each key competitor, determine as best you can what its current business strategy is relative to cost leadership, differentiation, and focus. Is it competing industry-wide or does it have a niche strategy; is it integrating vertically or horizontally; where is it seeking to position itself relative to technology advancements and applications; is it looking to acquire or be acquired? These answers will aid your firm to evaluate their moves and help you position to gain advantage.

- Competitor capabilities. Gaining knowledge of key competitors' strengths and weaknesses will assist your firm in its evaluation of those companies' underlying strategies and capacities to act. This analysis is similar to the resource audit the firm must perform on itself, as discussed earlier, except of course this time it is applied to your competitors. Fair, objective evaluations of others' strengths and weaknesses is of course difficult, but it is essential to any responsible competitive evaluation. Learning that a competitor company is severely strapped financially, or has failed in a major research project to make a technology breakthrough, would provide you with critical intelligence to second-guess the company's likely response in the marketplace to an aggressive move on your part to exploit an area of its weakness.

A competitor's position in its industry, based on a strengths/weaknesses evaluation, would also provide clues to their management's likely response to changes in industry dynamics.

Capabilities-Based Competition

"Capabilities-based competition" is a relatively recent approach to corporate strategy.[34] It also provides a new concept for competitive evaluation. After looking at the core success strategies of Wal-Mart, Canon, Honda, The Limited, and BancOne, the conclusion is reached that each firm had developed and established critically important processes that enable them to beat their competition. "Competition is now a 'war of movement' in which success depends on anticipation of market trends and quick response to changing customer needs."[35] Competition today, like the entire business environment, is less like chess and more like an interactive video game. Capabilities-based competition analysis rests on four basic principles:

1. The building blocks of corporate strategy are not products and markets but business processes.

2. Competitive success depends on transforming a company's key processes into strategic capabilities that consistently provide superior value to the customer.

3. Companies create these capabilities by making strategic investments in a support infrastructure that links together and transcends traditional SBUs and functions.

4. Because capabilities necessarily cross functions, the champion of a capabilities-based strategy is the CEO.[36]

A "capability" is a business process or a set of business processes that deliver value to customers. Few companies think of them as primary elements of strategy; they should. "Capabilities-based competitors identify their key business processes, manage them centrally, and invest in them heavily, looking for a long-term payback."[37]

An example is Wal-Mart's "cross-docking" process, which is central to its distribution and inventory replenishment system: moving whole truckloads of merchandise from a vendor delivery truck to Wal-Mart delivery trucks on the regional distribution center's loading dock, or after a brief period of warehousing, reducing inventory time and cost and speeding the goods to stores to meet customer demand.

Example: Compaq Computer Competitive Analysis. The personal computer industry provides an excellent arena to illustrate competitor analysis of its major companies, with the focus on its largest manufacturer, Compaq.

The personal computer industry was launched by Apple and IBM, using different approaches in the late 1970s and early 1980s, and by 1995, ninety million PCs were in use in the United States.[38] This is a twenty-year-old industry that has generated enormous success for its members, great wealth for its investors, and a landscape of offices and home offices equipped with the ubiquitous PC. It also enabled the explosive growth of the Internet, which gave rise to a collection of companies worth \$257 billion by early 1999. Born in 1982, Compaq Computer grew to number one in PC sales.[39]

Technology Promise. "Imagine we're back in 1981 and you're trying to see the future of technology—not because you care how it works, but because you want to be *rich*," suggests Tom Petruno, reporting on a major study by Morgan Stanley Dean Witter on IPOs in the technology industry over the past two decades.[40] In which "technology" area would you invest in 1981: (a) robots offered by Unimation in an IPO that year; (b) software as a fledgling dream of young Bill Gates, who had formed a private company called Microsoft, which went public five years later; or (c) PC hardware coming onstream from IBM?

Despite the hype at the time, the market for robots never happened, and Unimation's stock value crumbled shortly after its stellar rise at the time of the IPO; the company sold out to Westinghouse in 1983 for 9 percent less than its IPO price. Microsoft, however, was a success along with other software stocks, which by January 31, 1999 had a combined market value of \$674 billion, with Microsoft alone representing \$433 billion of that total, according to Morgan Stanley.

For the PC industry, IPOs in the decades of the 1980s and 1990s have also scored huge gains, having a market value on January 31, 1999 of \$224.5 billion, which is a 7,142-percent rise since initial public offering. IBM of course is not included in this number, not having been an IPO during this era, but Compaq, Dell, and Gateway are. (Interestingly, just 5 percent of the tech stocks that went public between 1980 and 1998 accounted for 86 percent of the total rise in shareholder value of all tech shares during that period, according to Morgan Stanley; these stocks included Microsoft, Dell, Cisco Systems, and America Online.[41])

Compaq's Early Days. In 1982, Compaq Computer Corporation was founded by a group of Texas Instruments engineers led by Joseph Canion, who approached high-tech financier Benjamin M. Rosen with the idea of making computer components. Rosen expanded their idea to make a complete computer that would be small enough to "lug" around. Rosen became Chairman of the Board and "Rod" Canion became CEO. Compaq's launch, using IBM's open architecture, was an immediate success, and the company grew.

Ten years later, in 1991, Rosen forced Canion's resignation because he resisted the idea of developing low-cost PCs, with all the operational changes that would require. Rosen appointed as CEO Eckhard Pfeiffer, who headed Compaq's European operations and believed in the need to cut costs and prices. Under Pfeiffer's leadership, Compaq was reinvented into an aggressive low-cost producer, exploiting economies of scale and adding major new products and retailers. This new model worked well for a few years.[42] But in April 1999 at Compaq's annual shareholder meeting, Rosen ousted Pfeiffer because of repeated poor earnings, and he saw that his company, as an analyst stated, "risked missing the fast-moving Internet train, potentially leaving the world's largest personal-computer maker an also-ran."[43]

During the 1990s, under Pfeiffer's direction, Compaq had become the number one PC maker in the United States, acquired Digital Equipment Corporation and Tandem Computers Inc., and expanded internationally to become the leading PC seller in the world. Toward the end of the decade, it was losing PC market share and reporting disappointing earnings. What had happened?

Compaq's Eroding Market. Total PC industry sales in the U.S. market during the mid- to late 1990s had been $4 billion to over $5 billion per quarter on quarterly unit sales of two to over three million units, according to International Data Corporation.[44] The average price for PCs sold at retail stores dropped 16 percent between February 1998 and February 1999, while the number of units sold increased less than 1 percent. The average price for a PC with a Windows operating system in February 1999 was just $947, according to PC Data Co.[45] Intense price competition continued, and International Data Corporation projected the home PC market would stay at roughly $4.1 billion per quarter in sales for the next two years. "There will be lots more PCs sold, but they will never be sold for as much money again," warned IDC. "That has huge implications for the manufacturers. They have to find other, more profitable revenue streams."[46]

By first quarter 1999, worldwide PC shipments were estimated at 25 million units, with average selling prices continuing to fall. Number one PC maker Compaq shipped 10 percent more computers than a year earlier, but its market share slid to 13.4 percent from 14.3 percent. Number two was Dell, whose shipments increased 49 percent, increasing its market share to 9.2 percent from 7.2 percent. IBM moved from second to third place, increasing its share to 8.4 percent from 7.5 percent, even though it continued to sell at a loss. Gateway was fourth.[47]

Compaq was losing ground in the PC market to Dell and Gateway, both low-cost, direct sellers, and to IBM, which then sold PCs through retail stores, online, and through reseller direct-sales channels. Compaq's distribution model of selling PCs only through retail outlets was being changed as the firm announced direct sales availability.[48]

Reasons for Compaq's Eroding Market Share. Again, what had happened to Compaq? "We lost vision, we lost empowerment, we lost speed," stated Robert W. Stearns, former chief strategist at Compaq. "We replaced it with bureaucracy and a team that has not jelled."[49] Regarding vision, Compaq had not integrated Digital Equipment Corporation fully into Compaq's business systems and strategy, had not eliminated outdated businesses such as manufacturing computer boards and outdated products such as minicomputers whose market share had not grown in years,[50] and had not put an end to DEC's proliferation of technologies. "The more difficult steps in the company integration haven't been achieved," according to Philip Rueppel, BT Alex. Brown. "There needs to be a clear direction to customers [saying] where the company is going with all its multitude of technologies."[51]

Another element of vision is customer and product focus. Should Compaq try to compete through multiple distribution channels for the consumer-PC market, while at the same time it attempts to compete with IBM to be a full-service computer manufacturer producing PCs, mainframes, and workstations? If so, it is losing customers from its DEC operation: Volkswagen, America Online, Southern [Utility] Co., and FMC's Foodtech unit all switched from DEC equipment to other suppliers, principally IBM, H-P, or Sun Microsystems.[52] Out of total 1998 sales of $31 billion, Compaq's consumer-PC sales were $4.9 billion and shrinking as unit prices fell to or below $500.[53] At that price point these product sales would not generate adequate profits, especially through resellers. "We dominate the consumer-PC business," averred Benjamin Rosen. "We feel pretty good about our competitive position. It is a good business to be in."[54]

Is it? Both Dell and Gateway, direct sellers, have grown sales volume, market share, and profits over the past few years at Compaq's expense in this market segment. Moreover, a new distribution channel opened in 1996 to the fifty million mostly lower-income American households that did not yet have PCs—door-to-door, hands-on selling, a start-up that Handtech.com initiated.[55]

Should Compaq refocus to become a full-line provider to the corporate market of Internet systems, rather than continue its consumer-PC focus via a combination of resellers and direct sales? This strategy appears to have been rejected, given the announcement in July 1999 that Compaq agreed to sell for over $2 billion most of its Alta Vista Internet portal, which it acquired as part of DEC.[56] "We still sell the bulk [of PCs] through resellers. We believe our fundamental strategy is correct," said Rosen.[57] In the first four months of 1999, Compaq's stock lost 46 percent of its value on lower-than-expected sales and profits.[58]

It appears the company has not sorted out its distribution dilemma once and for all: a mixed system of both resellers and direct sales alienates resellers and loses market share in the consumer-PC segment. For corporate sales, direct distribution will alienate resellers but will make Compaq more price competitive with Dell, which sells to corporate customers exclusively on a direct basis, giving them a 10 percent price advantage over Compaq's reseller price, according to Warburg Dillon Read.[59]

In May 1999 Compaq announced that it would refocus most of its PC sales through four of its largest wholesalers, down from the forty or so it had used in the past.[60] In March 2000, Michael Capellas, the new CEO, commented that Compaq's distribution channel dilemma remained one of its biggest weaknesses: "We still need to advance our distribution model," he said. Still, more than 80 percent of Compaq's shipments go through a middleman. This is "yesterday's model," Capellas admitted.[61]

Finally, there is the issue of management. Between 1997 and 1999, seven of the eleven senior executives at Compaq left the company under various circumstances—some were fired, some retired, some found advancement elsewhere. Those exiting included the CEO, CFO, general manager of worldwide sales, the North American chief, the manufacturing head, and the chief strategist. Compaq had become a one-way revolving door.[62] Following the CEO's firing, Benjamin Rosen, the Chairman, announced that a committee of three people would run the company on a daily basis, not as caretakers but very actively, while a CEO search was conducted. The three were Rosen, who is also involved in several other companies and resides in New York, Frank P. Doyle, a retired GE executive, and R. Ted Enole III, a Dallas mortgage executive.[63]

In July 1999 they announced the selection of Michael Capellas as the new CEO. He had joined Compaq less than a year earlier from Oracle Corporation to become Chief Information Officer.[64]

The problems with Compaq lay not, as Eckhard Pfeiffer subsequently asserted, in the PC industry only and especially in IBM's "very targeted action" to gain market share by cutting prices, but within Compaq itself.[65] As CEO for eight years, Pfeiffer built Compaq from $3.3 billion in sales and 21,000 employees to over $31 billion in sales and 69,000 employees. Part of this growth was the acquisition in June 1998 of Digital Equipment Corp. for $8.4 billion, which brought Compaq a much-needed service arm, but also brought a plethora of technologies, an expanded product line, a large bureaucracy, and heavy overheads in manufacturing segments in which they were not competitive.

Today's Competitive Situation. The PC industry had increasingly become more competitive with new, highly aggressive companies, Dell and Gateway, offering lower priced products via direct sales channels,[66] with low overheads, low cost, and stable supplier base,[67] almost no inventory (because they build the machine only after it is ordered), and solid customer rapport established over the telephone or via Internet at the time of sale.[68] Regarding inventory, Compaq's June 1999 PC inventory was eight weeks— one month's worth at its own warehouses and one month's worth at distributors.[69] Dell had less than one week of inventory on hand, and Dell had also decided to introduce an "under-$1,000" PC to directly challenge Compaq and have an active presence in that lower-price point product category, where it had previously seen no advantage in being the first mover.[70]

Also, older companies, IBM and Hewlett-Packard, aggressively priced and marketed their PCs and did an excellent job of controlling costs. IBM initiated distribution of laptops and some desktops through direct Internet sales and "direct resellers," like Value America, providing cost saving to the end user. IBM later expanded sales via the Internet, offering its entire line of PCs and small servers through a Web site, hoping to double its online sales of PCs over the next two years from about 20 percent in 1998 and to end its losses in this business sector.[71] In 1998, IBM lost $1 billion in its PC business.[72] In October 1999, IBM announced it would no longer sell PCs through retail outlets and would only offer them over the Internet, hoping to end a four-year string of losses on the product.[73] Suffering even worse losses, NEC's Packard Bell announced in late 1999 the withdrawal of its PC brand from the U.S. retail market entirely, closing its American manufacturing operations.[74]

Meanwhile, Compaq continued many of its costly overheads, failed to rationalize DEC's businesses, and confused its PC distribution system—using resellers, which necessitated heavy inventory cost, and limited direct distribution, which incensed their resellers. The industry had indeed changed, but in the late 1990s Compaq's competitors are the ones who ate its lunch by adjusting far better to changing conditions and taking advantage of Compaq's loss of focus.

At the close of 2000, the industry continued its shake-out. Five major PC rivals remained in the marketplace: Compaq, Dell, H-P, IBM, and Gateway. Since 1997, total PC sales worldwide had flattened at approximately $175 billion per year, making market share growth attainable only at competitors' expense. Dell successfully waged a price war to achieve market share growth and, owing to its low cost base, remained profitable. Compaq, with its higher costs, faced a more difficult problem making sales while trying to preserve margins and sacrificed market share in an attempt to do so. In 2000 PCs had accounted for only 13 percent of Compaq's earnings of $569 million, yet they represented 49 percent of its $42 billion in sales that year.[75] In early 2001, Compaq issued a warning that first quarter profits would fall short of expectations and announced another restructuring charge, this time to cut 7 percent of its workforce.[76]

Compaq's Dilemma. A conclusion to this analysis of Compaq's competitive situation in the PC industry is to ask a more fundamental question, which is begged by the first half of this chapter: is the PC industry, not just Compaq as a PC company, on the skids? Eckhard Pfeiffer believed the problem lay in the industry, and no less an authority than Louis Gerstner of IBM declared the PC era to be over. Michael Dell, Michael Capellas' fiercest competitor, earlier recognized this and expanded Dell Computer's product line beyond PCs: in 1995 Dell was No. 6 in desktop sales and No. 7 in notebooks, and in 1997 it was No. 5 in workstations. By 2000, Dell was No. 1 in all three U.S. markets and No. 2 in servers, behind Compaq. Dell is now developing low-cost storage systems and services to sell with its hardware.[77] The roots of Compaq's competitive problems are both company-to-company and industry-based.[78]

Today, under its new leadership, Compaq needs to do again what it did in 1991—realize its present vision is obsolete and reinvent itself totally by adopting a new vision. Capellas has stated a new vision: "EVERYTHING TO THE INTERNET."[79] Is it clear what that means? He has quite a job ahead of him and no time to lose.[80]

CONCLUSION

The competitive analysis of both the industry and the competition within the industry is an indispensable step in the business planning process. Conclusions reached from this analysis will provide a serious "reality check" for the firm's intentions, and a reexamination of your goals and even your business mission may be appropriate.

One way to approach that review is to evaluate your firm's value chain link by link in the harsh, realistic light of your competitive situation—both industry and company-to-company. After that reexamination is complete and appropriate modifications have been made to earlier portions of the plan, it is time to lay out the specific operating objectives for the enterprise, along with its pro forma.

NOTES

1. Gary Hamel and C. K. Prahalad, "Strategy as Stretch and Leverage," *Harvard Business Review*, March–April 1993, pp. 75–84.

2. Michael E. Porter, "What Is Strategy?" *Harvard Business Review*, November–December 1996, p. 62.

3. Quoted in David A. Aaker, *Developing Business Strategies*, 4th ed. (New York: Wiley, 1995), p. 195.

4. See Derek F. Abell, "Defining an Industry," in *Managing with Dual Strategies: Mastering the Present, Preempting the Future* (New York: Free Press, 1993), pp. 87–101.

5. Peter F. Drucker, as recounted by Paul Albrecht, Dean, Drucker Graduate School of Management, Claremont Graduate University, 1979.

6. Michael E. Porter, *Competitive Strategy* (New York: Free Press, 1980), pp. 3–5. Adapted with the permission of The Free Press, a Division of Simon & Schuster, Inc., from *Competitive Strategy: Techniques for Analyzing Industries and Competitors* by Michael E. Porter. Copyright © 1980, 1998 by The Free Press. See also, Michael E. Porter, *Competitive Advantage* (New York: Free Press, 1985), pp. 5–6. Adapted with the permission of The Free Press, a Division of Simon & Schuster, Inc., from *Competitive Advantage: Creating and Sustaining Superior Performance* by Michael E. Porter. Copyright © 1985, 1998 by Michael E. Porter.

7. Airbus Industrie announced the launch of a new jetliner, called A-380, having a capacity of 555 to 800 seats; *Los Angeles Times*, December 20, 2000, p. A1 and, for background, *Wall Street Journal*, November 3, 1999, p. A1.

8. *1999 Boeing Annual Report*, February 28, 2000, p. 43.

9. *Los Angeles Times*, June 19, 1999, p. C1, and July 27, 1999, p. C3.

10. Ibid., April 27, 1999, p. C3.

11. *1999 Boeing Annual Report*, p. 43.

12. Paul Nisbet, JSA Research, calculated Boeing "was $590 million in the hole" on aircraft sales alone in 1998; reported in *Los Angeles Times*, March 5, 1999, p. C2.

13. *1998 Boeing Annual Report*, February 22, 1999, p. 3. Boeing blamed its poor financial performance on manufacturing difficulties and the Asia crisis; see p. 7.

14. *Los Angeles Times*, February 26, 1999, p. C3.

15. Ibid., March 18, 1999, p. C2.

16. Ibid., March 9, 2000, p. C4.

17. Ibid., July 8, 1999, p. C2.

18. Ibid., July 18, 1999, pp. C1, C13.

19. Ibid., July 16, 1999, p. C1.

20. *1999 Boeing Annual Report*, p. 33. For 1998 Boeing reported a loss of $266 million on commercial aircraft, representing an operating margin of 0.7%, p. 33. The 1999 production figure is reported on p. 3.

21. Paul Proctor, "Boeing Shakes Up Its Supplier Chain," *Aviation Week & Space Technology*, September 27, 1999, p. 30.

22. Porter, *Competitive Strategy*, pp. 7–16. Adapted with the permission of The Free Press, a Division of Simon & Schuster, Inc., from *Competitive Strategy: Techniques for Analyzing Industries and Competitors* by Michael E. Porter. Copyright © 1980, 1998 by The Free Press.

23. See Porter, *Competitive Advantage*, p. 5, for the Five Forces chart. Adapted with the permission of The Free Press, a Division of Simon & Schuster, Inc., from *Competitive Advantage: Creating and Sustaining Superior Performance* by Michael E. Porter. Copyright © 1985, 1998 by Michael E. Porter.

24. For a roster of *all* U.S. associations by name, address, etc. see Christine Maurer and Tara E. Sheets, eds., *Encyclopedia of Associations* (Detroit: Gale Research, 1999).

25. Data and quotations are from the *Wall Street Journal*, April 19, 1999, p. B1.

26. *Los Angeles Times*, June 9, 1999, p. A1.

27. Television station group discussion is based on *Los Angeles Times*, July 7, 1999, p. C5.

28. Ibid., September 8, 1999, p. C1.

29. Michael E. Porter, "Changing Patterns of International Competition," *California Management Review* 28, no.2 (Winter 1986), in Heidi Vernon-Wortzel and Lawrence H. Wortzel, *Strategic Management in the Global Economy*, 3d ed. (New York: Wiley, 1997), Chapter 9.

30. *Guide to American Directories*, B. Klein Publishers, annual, classifies data by industry, profession, and function.

31. Thomas J. Watson, Jr., *A Business and Its Beliefs: The Ideas that Helped Build IBM* (New York: McGraw-Hill, 1963); Alfred P. Sloan, *My Years with General Motors*, edited by John McDonald (New York: Doubleday, 1963); Lee Iacocca, *Iacocca: An Autobiography* (New York: Bantam Books, 1984).

32. Porter, *Competitive Strategy*, pp. 47–64. Adapted with the permission of The Free Press, a Division of Simon & Schuster, Inc., from *Competitive Strategy: Techniques for Analyzing Industries and Competitors* by Michael E. Porter. Copyright © 1980, 1998 by The Free Press.

33. Ibid. Adapted with the permission of The Free Press, a Division of Simon & Schuster. Inc., from *Competitive Strategy: Techniques for Analyzing Industries and Competitors* by Michael E. Porter. Copyright © 1980, 1998 by The Free Press.

34. George Stalk, Philip Evans, and Lawrence E. Shulman, "Competing on Capabilities: The New Rules of Corporate Strategy," *Harvard Business Review*, March–April 1992.

35. Ibid., p. 62.

36. Ibid.

37. Ibid.

38. William J. Cook, "Software Struggle," *U.S. News & World Report*, June 19, 1995.

39. In the third quarter, 1999, Dell outsold Compaq in the U.S. PC market for the first time—their market shares being 18% and 16%, respectively; *Wall Street Journal*, October 25, 1999, p. A3.

40. Tom Petruno, "Stardate 1981: Take Me to Your High-Tech Leaders," *Los Angeles Times*, April 25, 1999, pp. C1, C4.

41. Morgan Stanley Dean Witter report on the "historical perspective on wealth creation" in technology industries, cited in Petruno, "Stardate 1981," p. C4.

42. For a discussion see Aaker, *Developing Business Strategies*, p. 220.

43. *Wall Street Journal*, April 20, 1999, pp. B1, B4.

44. *Los Angeles Times*, March 24, 1999, pp. C1, C4.

45. Ibid.

46. Roger Kay, International Data Corporation, reported in ibid., March 24, 1999, p. C4.

47. Dataquest, reported in ibid, April 24, 1999, p. C2.

48. *Wall Street Journal*, April 15, 1999, p. B7.

49. Ibid., April 20, 1999, p. A3.

50. Ibid., April 15, 1999, p. B7.

51. Ibid., April 20, 1999, p. A3.

52. Ibid., July 22, 1999, p. B4.

53. Gateway's total sales in 1998, in comparison, were $7.4 billion; *Los Angeles Times*, May 14, 1999, p. C3.

54. *Wall Street Journal*, April 20, 1999, p. A3.

55. *New York Times*, August 8, 1999, p. 4BU

56. *Los Angeles Times*, July 14, 1999, p. C3. Alta Vista was sold to CMGI for 18 percent of that company's stock, which nearly a year later was worth $5 billion. "Can Compaq Be Revived?" *Fortune*, March 6, 2000, p. 66.

57. *Wall Street Journal*, April 20, 1999, p. A3.

58. *Los Angeles Times*, April 30, 1999, p. C3.

59. *Wall Street Journal*, April 20, 1999, p. A3.

60. *New York Times*, May 10, 1999, p. C2.

61. "Can Compaq Be Revived?" *Fortune*, March 6, 2000, p. 64.

62. *Fortune*, May 24, 1999, p. 154. On June 2, 1999 John Rose, the Senior Vice President responsible for the unit that makes workstations and servers, resigned; *Los Angeles Times*, June 3, 1999, p. C3.

63. *Wall Street Journal*, April 20, 1999, p. A3; *Los Angeles Times*, April 30, 1999, p. C3.

64. Ibid., July 23, 1999, pp. C1, C6.

65. *Fortune*, May 24, 1999, p. 156.

66. By mid-1999, Dell made one-third of its sales via the Internet; *Los Angeles Times*, May 24, 1999, p. C9.

67. Dell and IBM signed a seven-year, $16 billion commitment for IBM to supply Dell computer components; ibid., March 5, 1999, p. C1.

68. In the first quarter 1999, Dell's profit jumped 42 percent on $5.5 billion in sales; consumer and small business sales were up 54 percent. Sales via the Web site increased to more than $18 million per day, accounting for 30 percent of revenue; ibid., May 19, 1999, p. C3.

69. Ibid., June 9, 1999, p. C3.

70. *Wall Street Journal*, April 9, 1999, p. B2. The inventory figure is from Eric Nee, "Refocusing Compaq," *Fortune*, March 5, 2001, p. 132.

71. Ibid., p. B5.

72. *Los Angeles Times*, May 24, 1999, p. C9.

73. *New York Times*, October 25, 1999, p. C1.

74. Packard Bell's losses were more than $1 billion each in 1997 and 1998, despite a $2 billion investment by Japan's NEC and France's Groupe Bull, which owns 12 percent of the company; *Wall Street Journal*, November 3, 1999, p. B7.

75. Eric Nee, "Refocusing Compaq," pp. 128–130.

76. *Los Angeles Times*, February 16, 2001, p. C1.

77. Betsy Morris, "Can Michael Dell Escape the Box?" *Fortune*, October 16, 2000, p. 95.

78. For further discussion, see David Kirkpatrick, "Please Don't Call Us PC," *Fortune*, October 16, 2000, p. 113.

79. "Can Compaq Be Revived?" p. 64.

80. Capellas' first formal act as CEO was to announce a 7,000-job layoff at Compaq, representing 10 percent of the workforce, taking an $800 million charge; *New York Times*, July 29, 1999, p. C1. After three months on the job, Capellas' results were not promising: Dell surpassed Compaq in U.S. PC sales for the first time ever, and Compaq's stock hit a new fifty-two-week low; *Wall Street Journal*, October 25, 1999, p. B8.

Chapter 6

Specific Objectives and Operating Plans

Having established the enterprise's vision, goals, mission, and strategy, and having completed its environmental and competitive assessments, management is now ready in this chapter to lay out the specific operating plans for the conduct of the business. These plans contain specific objectives and assign responsibility for achieving each critical task—obtaining financing, hiring, developing the organization, obtaining orders, production buildup, deliveries of goods, etc. These plans constitute the blueprints (or the road maps) for the business' operation and expansion. Later, in the next chapter, these same plans become the metric against which actual performance is measured.

Much of what follows is particularly relevant to start-up companies, those just getting underway as businesses, but there is considerable relevancy to established firms, which should undertake a periodic review of their operating plans and practices to ensure they are adequate for the changing needs of the company and reflect a true picture of the firm's genuine operational requirements. In business, as in baseball, it is always good to go back and review the fundamentals—even if just in practice.

PLAN TO MANAGE THE BUSINESS

Management's first task in this process is to plan to operate the business successfully. The task involved in preparing the master operational plan is to establish three operational guidelines, which basically communicate throughout the organization how top management wants the enterprise to function. These three master operational plans are:

- Policies: These are guides to action developed by top management for use at all levels of the enterprise. Policies are essentially "mass produced" decisions; top management decides how it wants the business to operate, establishes these decisions as "policies," and provides them to others to use as their guideline for action. Policies can be likened to "general orders" in the military—the things that you are responsible for doing all the time without the need for higher authority to give you a direct order to do them. These must of course be consistent with the prevailing culture.[1]

- Methods and Procedures: These guidelines are also like standing orders or instructions on how all levels of the organization are to perform their jobs. These establish a methodology, an order, as to how things are going to be run. They become the acceptable practices for the firm in the day-to-day conduct of its business.

- Budgets: These are the detailed operating plans expressed in monetary terms. Budgets clearly identify the resources that will be applied to particular tasks, provide those assets on a predetermined schedule, and assign accountability for their use.

Once top management has established these master operational plans, it is ready to embark on a variety of specific operating plans. How many of these are needed and to what depth they should be prepared will depend on the specific circumstances of the firm—if it is a start-up it will need an operating plan in every one of these areas; if it is an established firm it may require only some of them or modifications to existing plans.

OPERATING PLANS

What follows is a checklist of operating plans, together with a description of each.

Legal Structure Plan

This plan identifies the legal structure of the firm, whether it will be a sole proprietorship, a limited-liability company, a partnership, a joint venture, a corporation, etc. The decision with respect to the type of juridical entity the firm will be is pivotal to a number of issues concerning tax, liability, insurance, securities filings, public reporting, governmental oversight, and the like. This plan will sketch out the tasks involved in implementing the legal structure decision once management has made the decision, such as when to hire a lawyer to draw up papers, when and where to file them (in Delaware if a Delaware corporation), how much budget to set aside for these expenses, and who is responsible for implementing the task—in-house counsel, retained outside counsel, the administrative person, and so forth.[2]

Financial Plan

This operating plan identifies the sources and uses of funds.[3]

The source of funds can be one of five types: internally generated funds, borrowings from others (debt financing), selling a portion of the business to others in return for their investment (equity financing), barter, and government grants. In the case of debt financing, the amounts from each source should be indicated, the date the funds will be received, whether there are restrictions on their use as to timing or purpose, and a timeline when repayment is required (including amortized principal), together with debt service (interest cost).

Internally generated funds are of course the preferred type for financing the growth and expansion of the firm. These funds result from revenues generated by the business from any external source and have no restrictions on their use by the firm's management for any legitimate business purpose. For a start-up company or for an ongoing business whose revenues are insufficient to finance business expansion, the firm will most likely need to look for debt or equity financing, accepting the restrictions such financing may impose on the firm, or it may seek to barter goods and/or services to another firm for goods, services, or financing.

Figure 6.1 provides a checklist of the types of sources of funds for a business.

Figure 6.1
Sources of Funds

Type of Funds	Repayment Requirement/Terms
Internally Generated Funds	
Personal savings (yours and partners)	Your choice
Gifts from family members	Few or none
Revenue from ongoing operations	None, but prudent use of funds
Debt Financing	
Individuals ("angels")	Negotiated terms
Credit card borrowings	Prevailing interest rate and terms
Commercial banks	Prevailing interest rate and terms
—For secured, long-term debt	
—For working capital credit line	
Insurance companies	Negotiated terms and conditions
—For secured, long-term debt	—Could include combinations of debt, equity, and assets

Individuals (partners)	None; become part-owners
Venture capital firms	Negotiated terms
Merchant banks	Negotiated terms
—London-based banks or branches	
Mezzanine financing	Negotiated terms
—For 1-to-2-year term leading to IPO	
Investment banks	Negotiated terms
—For medium term investment	
—For underwriting securities	
Insurance companies	Negotiated terms which may include equity/debt/asset combinations
Commercial companies	Negotiated terms and conditions
—Another firm buys part of the business	

Barter

Exchange of goods/services for another's goods/services or financing[4]	Negotiated terms and conditions, which might include equity

Government Grants to Small Businesses

Federal Small Business Innovation Research program grants approximately $1 billion in early stage R&D developments having commercial potential.	Qualifications for funding: 500 or fewer employees, 51% US-owned, and organized for profit
Federal Small Business Technology Transfer Research program grants $60 million for cooperative R&D projects involving small businesses, universities, and Federally-funded research laboratories	Same

---

When raising capital, there are five primary factors to consider:

- Availability
  - —Access to capital may be limited by its availability to you, as opposed to obtaining it from a preferred source under preferred terms and conditions. For example, a start-up firm may not be sufficiently credit-worthy to borrow from

a commercial bank under favorable terms and may have to resort to equity financing, giving up part of the business to another

- Cost

  —Measure the cost of capital by its impact on earnings to the present owners, both near-term and projected future earnings

  —Do not simply measure cost by the increased expenses incurred by the need to service debt

- Risk

  —Seek sources that expose the company to the lowest risk

    —Use of "trade credit" (borrowing from suppliers) could cost loss of discounts, supplier dissatisfaction, damage to credit standing, etc.

  —Borrowed money imposes obligations on cash flow for debt service

  —Only equity capital involves no risk to the business

  —The risk taker is the investor, not the business

- Flexibility

  —Will conditions imposed by any lending source reduce flexibility in seeking further capital or in using capital generated by ongoing operations?

  —Trade credit can create dependencies on a few suppliers, locking out better prices or terms from others in the future

  —Loans may prevent securing additional debt because of prior claim against assets or other terms restricting flexibility

  —Loans may make the business overly cautious in credit extensions or inventory purchases, leading to lost sales

- Control

  —Equity investors usually gain a measure of control over the business

  —Major lenders may gain a measure of control (seats on the board)

  —Internally generated funds and trade credit produce no impact on control of the overall business by the current owners

The "use" portion of the financial plan will show how the funds are to be used: a timeline indicating the purpose for which the funds will be used, who is responsible, and the amount. For example, $50,000 is to be used in the second quarter by Purchasing to buy equipment, $10,000 to be used by Administration to lease office space per month beginning in the first quarter, and $25,000 for the first two quarters by Human Resources to recruit talent. Detailed financial plans will be developed for each business purpose, which typically are expense budgets for each operating function or department, as well as the usual aggregated income statement and balance sheet.

Budgets, which summarize the "use" of funds, are a key part of financial planning, and they become critically important in the control process, which will be discussed in the next chapter. There are three general types of budgets:[5]

- Revenue Budgets. A revenue or sales budget establishes the baseline for projecting income (especially cash) to the firm. These budgetary forecasts are then used to monitor actual performance of the enterprise using daily, weekly, or monthly sales figures as they occur. Comparing the actual data against the projected baseline provides management with a powerful indicator of whether the firm's strategy is working or corrective action is needed. Developing this budget is the marketing department's responsibility.

- Expense Budgets. The expense or cost budget allocates revenue to functional departments, and in turn each functional department (marketing, manufacturing, etc.) establishes an expense budget for its activities (direct and indirect labor, advertising, R&D, overheads, etc.). These cost budgets become the major control lever for monitoring each department's performance and correcting it if necessary. The finance department, working with general management, is responsible for developing the functional departments' budgets, based on their inputs.

- Capital Budgets. Capital budgets are a form of expense budget but because of their size and long-term significance to the firm they are broken out separately. Also, because these expenditures become part of the asset base of the company, accounting rules require their segregation. These budgets represent serious, long-term commitments of funds by management for the implementation of its strategic direction through the purchase of land, equipment, major R&D facilities and activities, etc. These budgets are critical instruments of control as the firm progresses in time toward the fulfillment of its goals, enabling managers to review progress and take remedial action if needed. General management is responsible for capital budgets, with inputs from appropriate functional departments. The rubber really meets the road in the budget process at the moment of decision with respect to capital allocations.[6]

Integrating these budgets enables management to develop pro forma income and expense statements and balance sheets.

Product Plan

This plan will identify what product(s) the firm will offer and how it will be developed and offered. The product will be identified by a generic name (aspirin, sports car, life insurance) and by brand name if one has been determined. The product plan is essentially a rollout plan for the product: a schedule indicating when it will be developed (R&D activities in a laboratory, a schedule for a movie shoot), who will be responsible for each phase of the product—basic development, application development, market launch, advertising and other promotion, outbound logistics, and delivery to distributors—and the product's price.

For start-up companies this operating plan is a key driver for all other plans because it will set the pace of activities for the entire enterprise. For mature companies, this plan will really be a new product plan, i.e., a plan to develop new, additional products, major modifications to existing products to add to the current product line, or an entirely new venture requiring a product plan.[7]

Discovery-Driven Planning. Any new venture, whether a start-up company or a major new venture by an established firm, can benefit in its product planning from "discovery-driven planning," which is "a practical tool that acknowledges the difference between planning for a new venture and planning for a more conventional line of business."[8] A five-step process is recommended:[9]

1. Start with a reverse income statement. To quickly determine the value of success.
2. Lay out all the activities needed to run the venture. Identify pro forma operational specs for sales, manufacturing, shipping, equipment, etc.
3. Track all assumptions. Keep a checklist to flag and test each assumption as the venture unfolds: revenues, profit margin, unit selling price, fixed asset investment to sales, etc.
4. Revise the reverse income statement. Insert actual performance into the earlier draft.
5. Plan to test assumptions at milestones. Establish milestones for each key event and evaluate prior assumptions against actual performance.

Discovery-driven planning, unlike platform planning typically used by established business where much is known, is a powerful tool for significant strategic undertakings fraught with uncertainty. It "forces managers to articulate what they don't know, and it forces a discipline for learning. As a planning tool, it thus raises the visibility of the make-or-break uncertainties common to new ventures and helps managers address them at the lowest possible cost."[10]

Marketing Plan

This plan identifies how, when, and by whom the product will be offered to whom—the customer—and what sales are expected when. This is a schedule of events that will determine the revenue flow to the firm and is basic to the entire planning process. Types of marketing plans differ with the industry for which they are prepared. Consumer products' plans focus on product testing with sample groups, identification of and delivery to distributors and retailers, sales training, advertising and other promotions, and direct selling. Industrial products' plans focus on trade shows and other promotional events, direct sales to original equipment manufacturers

Figure 6.2
The Five Ps for Marketing Planning

Item	Topic Addressed
Product	What is the product?
Price	How much is it; what price-point have you selected?
Promotion	How does the customer learn of it?
Place	Where can the customer buy it; what is the delivery channel?
Policy	What government policy, law, or regulation governs the product?

(OEMs), sales training, product enhancements, technological issues, and marketing to non-OEM distributors and retailers for the aftermarket.[11]

Regardless of the industry or customer focus, all marketing plans include product pricing,[12] packaging, branding, grading, standardizing, delivery, sales forecasts and anticipated revenue, technical and support services, and cost of sales (sales force salaries and commissions, sales offices expenses, advertising and other promotional costs, test market costs, etc.).

A useful way to craft a marketing plan is to begin with the Four Ps (to which experience adds a fifth P) (see Figure 6.2). Use of the Five Ps will stimulate the planner to address each of the relevant areas that require attention in the marketing plan.

Take a dealership for automobiles and light trucks as an example:

- Product: autos and light trucks (including SUVs) by brand name
- Price: the manufacturer's suggested sticker price, as the starting point for negotiations
- Promotion: marketing, advertising, trade shows, promotional events, rebates
- Place: the auto dealership
- Policy: federal laws, policies, regulations governing imports, product safety, and environmental issues; local laws governing environmental issues, EEO regulations regarding employment, OSHA regulations regarding workplace issues, sexual harassment issues, smoking regulations, etc.

In recent years some of the most significant changes in this industry have occurred in two areas: "policy"—federal laws and regulations mandating reduced emissions have led to experimentation with new or hybrid technologies to reduce air-polluting emissions,[13] and "place"—the auto dealership.

For the first time since the industry's birth nearly a hundred years ago, the distribution channel for autos and light trucks is being transformed:

local dealerships are being consolidated into nationally branded companies, like Wayne Huizenga's Auto-Nation USA. Ford Motor Company is experimenting with manufacturer-owned dealerships in test markets, and the Internet is altering the buying process by enabling purchasers to shop on the Web to obtain price quotes on selected models and even to make purchases. These changes are emerging in response to overwhelming customer distaste and dissatisfaction with the traditional distribution model and ever-declining dealer margins on cars due to intense price competition from similar-branded dealers in the same town. The auto marketing and distribution channel, historically resistant to change, is finally changing.[14]

The marketing plan needs to evaluate all five of the Ps to assess the state-of-the-art in your particular industry with respect to each of these issues and to prepare the most far-sighted approach you can develop to address each of the five "P" elements.

Operational Plan

This plan can be as comprehensive as needed to operate the business. It can include traditional issues such as location of facilities, manufacturing floor layout and sequence, tooling and equipment requirements, R&D facilities, transportation of inbound and outbound logistics, maintenance of facilities, quality assurance, scheduling, warehousing, security, etc.[15] Key traditional issues to be addressed in this plan are: use existing facilities or develop a greenfield site; make or buy,[16] purchase or lease, choice of information technology to drive the processes; keep IT in-house or outsource;[17] structure and operation of e-business activities; and start-up schedule.

Learning Organizations. The operational plan can also address some of the leading-edge operational techniques that are being employed in a number of companies with considerable success. One important technique is the "learning organization." This approach is partly based on economies-of-scale concepts, with links to time-and-motion studies of the early 1900s, to learning-curve concepts of the 1930s, and more recently to "quality circles" popularized by Japanese management.[18]

The "learning organization" approach is based on the precept that "[t]he rate at which organizations learn may become the only sustainable source of competitive advantage."[19] The organization's leader becomes the organization's teacher, building a shared vision, surfacing and testing mental models, and performing systems thinking and not just snapshots.[20] There are a number of definitions, but one expert offers this: "A learning organization is an organization skilled at creating, acquiring, and transferring knowledge, and at modifying its behavior to reflect new knowledge and insights."[21]

Example: Ford Motor Company. Ford Motor Company's President and

CEO, Jacques Nasser, is turning Ford into a "learning" company, and he is the chief teacher.[22] This concept has been fully embraced by Ford and is a major factor in the company's drive to continuously reinvent itself. One outcome of the process is Ford's decision to control distribution, which no auto maker has ever done, in order to keep close track of the pulse of the buying public and to lower the price of each new vehicle by perhaps as much as 15 percent. The idea has been used in overseas markets, has been test marketed in a few U.S. areas, and is now policy—the Ford Retail Network Strategy.[23] Nasser is seeking other ways for Ford to become more consumer-oriented.[24]

Example: BP Amoco. BP Amoco is another learning company.[25] In 1995 John Browne became CEO of British Petroleum, which is now BP Amoco and has acquired Atlantic Richfield. Under Browne's leadership and that of David Simon, his predecessor, British Petroleum was turned around and became the most profitable of the world's major oil companies, reduced its exploration and development costs, and focused its business on oil, divesting a host of noncore activities including minerals, coal, animal feed, and chickens. Browne has stated, "Learning is at the heart of a company's ability to adapt to a rapidly changing environment. It is the key to being able both to identify opportunities that others might not see and to exploit those opportunities rapidly and fully."

To advance learning, knowledge is shared through a virtual team network throughout the business in the belief that the company "has to learn better than its competitors and apply that knowledge throughout its business faster and more widely than they do."[26] Browne believes, "A clear purpose allows a company to focus its learning efforts in order to increase its competitive advantage."[27]

Example: GE. CEO Jack Welch transformed General Electric into a learning company through a series of initiatives, begun in the early 1980s with his "Work-Out" initiative, "which is based on the simple premise that those closest to the work know it best." Next, he introduced "boundaryless" behavior—removing "every organizational and function obstacle to the free and unimpeded flow of ideas" inside and outside the company. "The combination of involving everyone in the game and of responding to this flow of ideas and information turned GE into what we are today—a learning company," Welsh wrote. "By becoming a learning company we have taken market and geographic diversity, the traditional handicap of multi-business companies, and turned them into a decisive advantage—unlimited access to the most enormous supply of best ideas, information and intellectual capital the business world has to offer." This is the core of GE's "social architecture . . . the software that drives what we call the operating system of GE."[28]

e-Business Structure and Operation. Today, most companies no longer debate whether to engage in e-business, but how to do so. The debate focuses on developing an e-business structure appropriate for the firm and developing and motivating needed human resources to operate it.

A team of researchers from Booz-Allen & Hamilton discovered that there are four stages of "E-volution" through which firms typically progress on their way to achieving an appropriate e-business structure.[29] This analysis is based on interviews with twenty-five CEOs, e-business leaders around the world, and research on an additional twenty-five companies. Industries examined included financial services, health care, media and entertainment, automotive, industrials, airlines/travel/aerospace, telecommunications, computing, consumer products, and energy.

The conclusion reached is that virtually all companies pursue e-business opportunities in a strikingly consistent way, passing through four consecutive stages of development:

- Grassroots: Different e-initiatives are underway throughout the organization with little or no central direction or coordination.
- Focal Point: A lead e-commerce executive is named and a centralized e-business group is formed to set priorities and organize company-wide activities. This group devises a cohesive Internet strategy, builds a critical mass of e-awareness, and identifies e-opportunities.
- Structure and Deployment: The e-business group sets e-business opportunity priorities, deploys assets to those with the most promise, and begins to develop structures (embedded, independent business unit, IPO, or joint venture).
- Endgame: E-opportunities mature to where specific structures are formalized to support each business and nurture it. At this stage the promise of each e-opportunity is translated into an ongoing and successful e-business. This is a dynamic and iterative process that changes as the market changes, requiring a high degree of flexibility.

With the transition from each stage to the next, the firm deepens its level of commitment in budget, human resources, and management attention. Choosing the best structure for your firm is the key challenge. Typically the issue is whether to embed the e-activity in the existing business or to build a separate organization. Pivotal criteria and issues in this decision process are value creation potential, cannibalization potential, product expansion potential, potential of transforming the entire organization, speed to leverage resources and fill capability gaps, culture fit, and employee retention (i.e., need to adjust incentives.)

Internet strategy and operating structure is every company's challenge. The e-volutionary path is fast and ruthless and has Darwinian characteristics.

Human Resource Plan

This plan outlines who will work for the firm, how they will be compensated, and what kind of company it will be.

The HR plan lays out a schedule of hiring based on the critical skills needed for each phase along the growth curve of the company's functional activities: research and scientific talent, sales and marketing people, manufacturing technicians, administrators and support staff, quality assurance inspectors, etc.

As the company moves forward from design of the product to the actual production of the product, the functional needs of the firm will change and grow, and the talent requirements will change with it. There is no point hiring quality assurance inspectors before there are manufactured parts to inspect, for example. Time phasing in hiring is critical to small businesses; add to the payroll only those people needed in the numbers needed when they are needed. To avoid extremes in hiring and firing, temporary personnel services are often a good answer for nonsensitive tasks; in 1998, temporary workers filled 40 percent of all clerical and 34 percent of all industrial jobs in the United States.[30]

Compensation Policy. Compensation policy should be included in the HR plan. This should be clearly addressed as a system of rewards that meet market conditions for the skill categories to be employed by the firm. Rewards should be meaningfully linked to the individual's contribution toward achievement of the firm's strategic objectives. This can be a combination of salary and incentive compensation clearly geared to the firm's revenue, stock performance, or other objective criteria. Such linkage will motivate individuals and organizational units and promote congruence between the individual and the group in the attainment of goals. "There's a real different sense to your job" than having only a salary, said Stephen Rosen, Go2Net's product development director, one of a growing number of companies using stock options as incentive compensation.[31] "Build a company of owners,"[32] advises Michael Dell; "partner with your people— through shared objectives and a common strategy."[33]

Finally, the very nature of the company needs to be addressed as part of the HR policy. Will the company behave in a traditional employer/employee structure or will it be more collaborative in style, where the employees feel like owners, too, or are at least "engaged"? Today, employees "don't just want to work for a company. They want to belong to an organization." Such an organization is one that can capture employees' attention, engage their energy and interest, get the organization involved, and create momentum.[34] People want to belong to an organization that gives meaning to their work, shows recognition for individual accomplishments, and tells people what the company stands for.[35]

Free-Agent Employees. Bill Gates has commented to his senior staff that his principal worry is that 90 percent of the asset value of Microsoft Corporation goes home every night, and he just hopes that the next day it returns to the office.[36] In the information age, the brains of your employees are your most valuable asset. And they are portable.

One of the biggest challenges new companies have—especially high-technology companies—is attracting and holding talent. In today's "free agent" economy, highly talented high-tech experts can pick and choose where to work and where to stay. The "glue," writes Robert Reich, that holds them is money: salary, 401(k), and stock options—making the employee an "owner."

Other forms of "social glue" are participating in a mission, having meaningful work, being in a learning atmosphere for growth, having fun, engendering pride in work, and having flexible working conditions to do the job your way and to have time off when required. "This is," writes the former Secretary of Labor, "a revolutionary notion: Collaboration and mutual advantage are the essence of the organization. They can create flexibility, resiliency, speed, and creativity—the fundamental qualities of the company of the 21st century."[37] What kind of company do you want?

Administrative Plan

This plan establishes the approach management has chosen to take with respect to the administration of the firm. This includes organizational structure,[38] internal processes for booking orders, accounting, accounts receivable and payable, record-keeping system compliant with governmental regulations and industry practices, hiring and firing authority, enforcement of company rules and procedures, disciplining of infractions, etc. This plan is as important as any because it will establish the day-to-day practices that will govern the conduct of the employees and management and provide the documentation necessary for the orderly administering of the enterprise.

Other Types of Plans

This is not an exhaustive list of all the functional plans that may need to be developed for any particular firm. Advanced-technology companies would be remiss if they failed to have an Advanced-Technology Development Plan (or an Engineering Plan). An agribusiness would need a crop rotation plan based on soil conditions, climate, water supply, cost of fertilizer, and changing market demand. And a paint company might need a plan that tracked changing government air quality and other environmental regulations coupled with changing taste in colors and application techniques. The seven operational plans listed above would be needed by any type of business, and the need for additional plans would depend on specific industry conditions.

Successful companies may also want to develop investment plans and acquisition plans to grow their businesses. How to invest revenue received from success in the marketplace is a welcome task. One place to invest the internally generated funds is in the business itself—funding additional R&D activities for new products or new lines of business, the investment could be in preplanned product improvements for existing product lines, or if the business is publicly traded, investing in your own stock if you believe that is a wise course for future returns. To grow market share in nongrowth markets or to enter markets where there are high barriers to entry, acquisition planning may be the only course open.

The proper alignment of the organization with the company's strategy is critical for sustained success, enabling the firm to execute its strategy. The organizational model that the firm develops—or, more typically, that evolves over time—sets the company apart from others as much as its products. Small firms, such as a dot-com start-ups, typically have flat organizational structures, and all participants in the firm have decision rights, subject to the approval of the owner/entrepreneur. The boundaries of decision rights, as a proportion of the total business, usually diminish as the firm grows. This is a trend that forceful CEOs seek to resist, hoping to force decision making to the lowest possible level consistent with prudent control. Customizing the organizational model of the firm to achieve alignment between strategy and operating structure is becoming a critical task for any size business.[39]

Criteria for Developing Operating Plans

The process of developing these functional, operating plans is as important as the plans themselves because it will significantly impact the quality of the output of the process as well as gain buy-in by those ultimately responsible for their execution. A few suggestions are in order for how to develop these plans:[40]

- Top management must be involved in the planning process. They must determine the degree of interrelationship between the strategic plan and the various operational plans to assure consistency of purpose.

- It is ill advised to attempt to integrate or even to coordinate completely all functional plans into a single integrated plan. The result would be confusing and for implementation it would be unnecessary.

- Keep functional plans short and simple. Nothing elaborate is necessary.

- Functional managers must be kept deeply involved in making functional plans because their buy-in is needed for their execution of the plans.

- Functional managers should prepare plans for areas over which they have authority. Such plans should not be imposed on them from above because this reduces buy-in and reduces enthusiasm for execution.

- Avoid extrapolation. Start each annual planning process fresh from the beginning. Do not simply update last year's plan, for you will miss seeing newly emerging trends or problems. Treat this exercise the same as zero-based budgeting.
- Address only high-priority items in functional plans. Otherwise, preparing unimportant plans will become too burdensome.

The operational plans that the managers will develop are the vital action plans for the company. These are the plans that will be implemented and against which performance will be measured. The substance in the plans is what is important, not their format. Clarity of task assignment, its communication and accountability, is the hallmark. There are any number of ways to package and present these types of plans.[41]

Exit Criteria

All operating plans for new ventures should contain an off-ramp. Criteria should be established at the beginning of the planning process stating when and under what conditions the project will be continued or stopped. These criteria should be as objective as possible, not subjective, and all members of the top management team should buy-in to them, including the CEO.

Why is this important? When a firm invests its own or shareholder funds in an activity—a new product launch, for example—there needs to be a schedule established up front as to when and what the payoffs will be for that investment. For example, if the new product fails to generate sales of at least $x or x units by the end of year one and $xx or xx units by the end of year two, the product will be dropped. Failing to establish agreed-upon objective criteria for project abandonment at the beginning can lead to unguided behavior later, including the potential of years of bottom-line hemorrhaging while waiting for the market to embrace the new product. Executives closely identified with the new activity inevitably become ego-involved with it and will strive to protect it, sometimes at ruinous cost, hoping for vindication and ultimate success.

Example: Northrop Corporation's F-20 Tigershark. An example is Northrop (now Northrop Grumman) Corporation's F-20 Tigershark program, begun in the late 1970s and abandoned in the late 1980s.[42] Over the course of a decade, the company invested $1.2 billion of shareholder funds to perform design, engineering development, construction, and test, along with marketing, of three flying prototypes of this jet fighter intended for sale to the international market. The Carter administration provided the initial approval for the project, destined for Taiwan's air defense. The Reagan administration later stalled on giving export approval to any customer. The Bush administration ultimately chose to export the U.S.A.F.'s F-16 to Taiwan, in lieu of F-20s. No F-20s were ever sold.

Northrop shut down the F-20 program only when it had become abundantly clear that the U.S. government wanted no competition for its own F-16 inventory product to be exported or to be introduced into the U.S. inventory even in a secondary capacity, like training. The principal sponsor of the F-20 within the company was the CEO, who doggedly pursued it even after two of the three prototypes crashed. No opposition to it within the company was tolerated.

No objective criteria were established at any time during the project for determining its failure and termination. The government's influence over the market forced that decision. Building a weapon system on spec is universally viewed as a bad idea as a result of the F-20 write-off.

CONCLUSION

The specific objectives that management has identified in its various operational plans will become the action plans that various managers will now implement. Periodic reviews should be held with top management to evaluate performance, which will be tracked on these plans during their implementation. It is these management reviews that form the essential core of the control process.

NOTES

1. For definitions of "policies," see George A. Steiner, *Top Management Planning* (New York: Macmillan, 1969), pp. 264–66.

2. For a discussion see William L. Megginson, Mary Jane Byrd, Charles R. Scott, Jr., and Leon C. Megginson, *Small Business Management*, 2d ed. (Toronto: Irwin, 1997), Chapter 4; for an overview of small business–government relations see Chapter 23.

3. For useful forms and formats, see Harold J. McLaughlin, *The Entrepreneur's Guide to Building a Better Business Plan: A Step-by-Step Approach* (New York: Wiley, 1992), Chapters 3, 4, 7, and 8; examples of small business plans are included.

4. Venture capital firms have begun bartering services (e.g., advertising) for equity; *Wall Street Journal*, August 3, 1999, p. B2.

5. For a discussion of the budget process, see James H. Donnelly, Jr., James L. Gibson, and John M. Ivancevich, *Fundamentals of Management* (Plano, TX: Business Publications, Inc., 1981), p. 74ff.

6. See John A. Boquist, Todd T. Milbourn, and Anjan V. Thakor, "How Do You Win the Capital Allocation Game?" *Sloan Management Review*, winter 1998, p. 59ff.

7. For project planning, see Steven C. Wheelwright and Kim B. Clark, "Creating Project Plans to Focus Product Development," *Harvard Business Review*, March–April 1992.

8. Rita Gunther McGrath and Ian C. MacMillan, "Discovery Driven Planning," *Harvard Business Review*, July–August, 1995, p. 44.

9. This discussion is based on ibid., pp. 50–52.

10. Ibid., p. 54.

11. For suggestions on marketing planning, see David S. Hopkins, *The Marketing Plan* (New York: The Conference Board, 1985).

12. See Robert J. Dolan, "How Do You Know When the Price Is Right?" *Harvard Business Review*, September–October 1995. Dolan offers an eight-step process.

13. For example, Ford Motor Company and BMW have each announced they are developing an experimental car powered by hydrogen-burning internal combustion engines; Ford alone is spending $400 million on this effort to reduce emissions. *Los Angeles Times*, August 17, 1999, p. C3.

14. Evan R. Hirsh, Louis F. Rodewig, Peter Soliman, and Steven B. Wheeler, "Changing Channels in the Automotive Industry," *Strategy & Business*, issue 14, 1st quarter 1999.

15. Megginson, Byrd, Scott, and Megginson, *Small Business Management*, Chapter 6.

16. See Ravi Venkatesan, "Strategic Sourcing: To Make or Not to Make," *Harvard Business Review*, November–December 1992.

17. See N. Venkatraman, "Beyond Outsourcing: Managing IT Resources as a Value Center," *Sloan Management Review*, spring 1997.

18. David A. Aaker, *Developing Business Strategies*, 4th ed. (New York: Wiley, 1995), p. 222.

19. Ray Stata, Analog Devices, quoted in Peter M. Senge, "The Leader's New Work: Building Learning Organizations," *Sloan Management Review*, reprint of vol. 32, no. 1, fall 1990, p. 1. For a discussion see Peter M. Senge, *The Fifth Discipline* (New York: Doubleday, 1990).

20. Senge, "The Leader's New Work," p. 5.

21. David A. Garvin, "Building a Learning Organization," *Harvard Business Review*, July–August 1993, p. 80. Italics deleted.

22. Suzy Wetlaufer, "Driving Change: An Interview with Ford Motor Company's Jacques Nasser," *Harvard Business Review*, March–April 1999. For the "learning approach," see Noel Tichy, "The Teachable Point of View: A Primer," in *Harvard Business Review*, March–April 1999, pp. 82–83.

23. *Los Angeles Times*, February 19, 1999, pp. C1, C4. General Motors announced it will buy dealerships to sell directly to customers; *Wall Street Journal*, September 29, 1999, p. A3.

24. See "Remaking Ford," *Business Week*, October 11, 1999, pp. 132–42.

25. Steven E. Prokesch, "Unleashing the Power of Learning: An Interview with British Petroleum's John Browne," *Harvard Business Review*, September–October 1997.

26. Ibid., p. 148.

27. Ibid., p. 150.

28. *1999 Annual Report of the General Electric Company*, February 11, 2000, pp. 2–3. For a discussion of the learning operating system at GE, see pp. 3–4.

29. This section is based on the following: Jill Albrinck, Gil Irwin, Gary Neilson, and Dianna Sasina, "From Bricks to Clicks: The Four Stages of E-volution," *Strategy + Business*, issue 20, 3rd quarter 2000, pp. 62–72.

30. *Los Angeles Times*, May 29, 1999, pp. A1, A20–21.

31. Go2Net, Charles Schwab, and Texas Instruments are three of 350 companies

surveyed by William M. Mercer Co., of which 35 percent provide stock options to most employees, reducing employee turnover dramatically. *Wall Street Journal*, May 18, 1999, p. A1.

32. Michael Dell, *Direct from Dell* (New York: HarperCollins, 1999), p. 121.

33. Ibid., p. 108.

34. Christopher A. Bartlett and Sumantra Ghoshal, "Changing the Role of Top Management: Beyond Strategy to Purpose," *Harvard Business Review*, November–December 1994, p. 86.

35. Developing and maintaining a well-recognizable corporate image and favorable reputation is a vital strategic resource for several of the firm's stakeholders, including employees; see Edmund R. Gray and John M. T. Balmer, "Managing Corporate Image and Corporate Reputation," *Long Range Planning*, 31, no. 5 (October 1998).

36. Private conversation with a Microsoft senior staffer, October 1998.

37. Robert B. Reich, "The Company of the Future," *Fast Company*, November 1998, p. 150.

38. For a discussion of types of organizational structures, based on the view that strategy is a determinant of structure and process, see Peter Lorange, *Strategic Planning and Control* (Cambridge, MA: Blackwell Business, 1993), p. 53ff.

39. See Jeffrey W. Bennett, Thomas E. Pernsteiner, Paul F. Kocourek, and Steven B. Hedlund, "The Organization vs. the Strategy," *Strategy + Business*, issue 21, 4th quarter 2000, p. 77.

40. Based on George A. Steiner, *Strategic Planning* (New York: Free Press, 1979), pp. 211–13.

41. See, for example, Wilbur Cross and Alice M. Richley, *The Prentice-Hall Encyclopedia of Model Business Plans* (Paramus, NJ: Prentice-Hall Press, 1998). This book contains sixty model business plans. See also Eric Berthelette and Frank Kresen, eds., *The Entrepreneur's Planning Handbook*, rev. ed. (Denver, CO: Entrepreneurial Education Foundation, 1997). Also, Jill E. Kapron, *Biz Plan Builder* (Cincinnati, OH: South-Western College Publishing, 1995).

42. This discussion is based on the author's personal experience and observations.

Chapter 7

Control and Review

In this chapter the plan lays out the processes by which management will control and review the implementation of the plan, based on the operational plans developed in the previous chapter.[1] It is important to establish the control and review process plan before beginning implementation so that the plan will be complete, and all levels of management will understand the rules of the game before the game actually begins. All parties need to know in advance what will be expected of them and on what basis their performance will be measured and evaluated. More fundamentally, structure and control systems must be aligned to strategy at all levels of the firm for consistency of purpose and execution.[2]

This chapter provides the means for management to monitor the firm's progress during the execution of its plans. By this means, using periodic reviews (e.g., weekly, quarterly, yearly), management can track and evaluate its performance as the plan rolls out and can identify areas needing more of its attention—to control and direct the operation of the enterprise.[3]

STEPS FOR ESTABLISHING EFFECTIVE CONTROL AND REVIEW PROCESSES

Basic steps involved in establishing an effective control and review process are these:

1. Establish specific business goals in the operating plans. Take the various operational plans developed in the last chapter and lay them out in this chapter as the foundation for your control and review process.

2. Distribute the goals over time. Establish periodic reviews for each operational plan as appropriate—weekly, monthly, quarterly, annually. Distributing these goals over time periods becomes the "standard of performance" for the firm. Knowing that everything cannot be measured, managers should choose their standards with care, answering the basic question: what is it management wishes to measure?[4]

3. Measure actual performance against planned performance. At each established time interval, record the measurement of performance (dollars of sales, units of goods delivered, number of people hired, etc.) of each operational plan.

4. Evaluate performance. Compare the actual performance against the planned performance and note deviations. Do deviations fall within acceptable limits of difference or unacceptable difference? Look for causal factors. What caused the deviation—internal performance or external factors? Diagnose deviations to find underlying causes.

5. Determine corrective action. Decide what needs to be done to equalize actual performance with planned performance. Strengthen deficient areas of operation. If these cannot be strengthened, change the plan sufficiently to reflect the realities of the situation, without at the same time losing motivational momentum if possible. If over time it becomes clear that the plan cannot be implemented, execute the previously determined exit strategy, provided the failure to implement meets the criteria in the exit plan.

Measurement Systems

Measurement is central to an effective control and review process. How you measure and what you measure are key issues needing decision. There are a number of traditional performance measurement systems that have been used and perfected for decades.[5] Most of these compare actual performance against the previously decided standard, usually the operational plan, to help management control ongoing operations.

These metrics primarily employ financial systems.[6] Why financial? They are usually regarded as consistent, reliable, and provide accountability. They directly relate to the firm's primary objective of making a profit, thereby focusing performance measurement in consonance with organizational objectives.

Criticisms are that financial performance measures lack sufficient variety to provide decision makers a needed range of information and have a lack of focus and robustness for internal management and controls.[7] Some of these controls simply do not fit a particular management's style.[8] Another criticism is that financial controls typically deal with events only after they have taken place, whereas management needs to take action to correct a situation before it gets out of control. This is especially true of longer-term strategies.

STRATEGIC MANAGEMENT

To overcome some of the shortcomings of financially focused management control systems, to provide more comprehensive control mechanisms, and to enable management to "get ahead" of problems before they become uncontrollable disasters, the concept of strategic management has emerged.[9] Traditional approaches to strategic management view this as one useful technique in a hierarchy of control mechanisms, enabling management to intervene during a plan's implementation to take needed corrective action. This approach is useful in small companies as well as large.[10]

The traditional strategic management approach is based on four factors:[11]

1. having measurable performance standards consistent with strategic objectives;
2. measuring performance against the selected standards, which requires a reliable flow of information regarding performance;
3. evaluating performance, which essentially is variance analysis—normal variance between planned and actual performance and variance between the firm's performance and an external standard of excellence (benchmarked peer firm); and
4. taking corrective action—either realign performance with strategic objectives or reevaluate objectives in light of changes in the business environment.

Leveraging off this traditional approach, a number of innovations to strategic management have been developed. Prahalad and Hamel developed the idea that core competencies of an organization are the bedrock of its strategy, that the strategy is stated in its "strategic architecture," and the strategic architecture (the strategic plan) should become the primary mechanism of control—enabling alignment of performance with goals and communicating and learning within and beyond the organization.[12] This strategic architecture approach would promote the fulfillment of the following specific purposes:

- state the firm's strategic vision in terms of combinations of existing competencies and developing or acquiring new ones
- reinforce strategic focus on competencies to ensure all major decisions are consistent with developing and preserving competencies
- discipline behavior in all operating units to the standard—does an action contribute to core competencies?
- align culture, structure, and management behavior to the uniform frame of reference of competence—as an instrument of integration and coordination
- identify deficiencies that would inhibit the organization's ability to develop new competencies
- facilitate learning within the organization and promote strategic awareness.

The concept of strategic architecture "represents the convergence of competency and control." It is an "ideal mechanism" for control and to focus alignment, and it provides many benefits to management.[13]

Steering Control

Another particularly useful strategic management technique is the concept of "steering control," which was developed by Yavitz and Newman also to provide management with a robust, forward-looking strategic control mechanism.[14] This approach employs a four-step process to assure that management is able to use this "advance warning" system, which involves long lead times between strategy decision and strategy fulfillment and which requires constant scanning and data inputs.

The four steps of strategic "steering control" are:

- Observe progress on strategic initiatives. Identify the critical factors for the plan's successful implementation and monitor only these over time; do not mix the critical factors with other, less critical elements of current operations.

- Monitor external environment. The assumptions that had been made about the overall business climate may be altered over time by ongoing events; keep a close watch on those critical factors that could have a serious impact on the company's performance in the achievement of the strategy.

- Conduct milestone reviews. Regularly scheduled reviews of performance against the plan are needed, as well as nonscheduled reviews when events warrant, such as a major success or failure in the plan's implementation, critical changes in the external business environment, a new move by a competitor, etc. Revise the plan accordingly.

- Maintain integrity of the process. The three prior points relate to the evaluation of the plan against performance. This final step assures the integrity of the control process itself by asking pertinent questions at each review: are enough resources allocated to the plan's implementation, is the reward system adequate to motivate people, is the organization capable of facilitating change needed to achieve the plan's success, is the relationship between the strategy and the organization's resources clear?

Strategic Performance Measurement

Another recent development also intended to overcome criticisms and weaknesses of financial-based control systems is called "strategic performance measurement."[15] This approach "focuses on one output of strategic planning: senior management's choice of the nature and scope of the contracts that it negotiates, both explicitly and implicitly, with its stakeholders. The performance measurement system is the tool the company uses to monitor these contractual relationships."[16]

Figure 7.1
Example of Balanced Scorecard Approach

Financial Perspective		Customer Perspective		Internal Perspective	
Goals	*Measures*	*Goals*	*Measures*	*Goals*	*Measures*
Survive	Cash flow	New	% of sales	Technology	Manufacturing
Succeed	Sales growth	products	from new	capability	geometry vs.
Prosper	Increased		products		competition
	market				
	share				
	& ROE				

Two types of stakeholders are identified: environmental stakeholders (customers, owners, the community—the external environment that defines critical elements of the competitive strategy) and process stakeholders (employees and suppliers—the group that plans, designs, and operates the processes to make and deliver the products to its customers). The interplay between and among these sets of stakeholders is coordinated vertically and horizontally, monitored, and measured.

An additional performance measurement technique is the "balanced scorecard" approach.[17] This approach includes financial measures that tell results of actions already taken and complements these with operational measures on customer satisfaction, internal processes, and the innovation and improvement activities underway—operational measures that drive future financial performance. For each "goal" there is a "measure" from a particular perspective.

Figure 7.1 is a sample of the balanced scorecard approach.[18]

This approach, like reading dials on a dashboard, provides management with a quick and easy way to read results and make an assessment of ongoing performance against the strategic plan. The process has been put to work in a number of situations with success.[19] It can also be used as a strategic management system.[20]

Strategic Audit

A final strategic measure is the "strategic audit," which a board of directors can establish to strengthen its oversight capability. This would be a formal process to assist directors in their periodic review of the company's strategy without undermining the authority of the CEO.[21] Boards, not management, must establish the criteria to be used, choose the metrics to be employed, and control the databases.

Typically, financial metrics should be employed because they facilitate discussion in terms all parties understand. Appropriate performance measures include cash flow return on investment (CFROI), net economic value added (EVA), and total of shareholders' return on investment (TSR). Outside consultants can be retained to help develop the metrics, and it is a good idea to involve the company's public auditors. If this activity is low-key and pursued in a spirit of mutual respect between the Board and the CEO, the process can facilitate an ongoing, constructive dialogue. Using such a process, the Board would communicate to shareholders "their shared commitment to orderly and effective governance."[22]

TYPES OF MEASUREMENT

All control systems are based on measurement. Generally speaking, there are two types of measurement systems: results measures and process measures.[23] Results measures track a particular function's activities and some track cross-functional activities; the latter are mostly financial measures, like revenues, debt, margins, capital assets, and the like. These results measures tell where you are but not how you got there or what you should do about it.

Process measures track tasks and activities across an organization that produce results. Team-based organizations require the use of such measures, which monitor entire activities, like product development or product delivery to customers. What multifunctional teams need is performance measurement systems that will maximize the effectiveness of teams. Companies are increasingly using integrated product teams (IPTs) to develop new products or new models of existing products. These teams are composed of representatives from the key functional departments (engineering, marketing, finance, manufacturing, purchasing, etc.) and key suppliers. These teams' performance must be measured to ensure appropriate, timely outputs.

Four criteria for team-oriented performance measurement systems are identified:[24]

1. The primary purpose of a measurement system should be to help a team, not top management, gauge progress. The system is mainly a tool for telling the team when to take corrective action; it can also provide a means for top management to intervene if the team encounters problems it cannot solve alone.

2. An empowered team must take the lead in designing its own measurement system. Senior managers need to ensure that the system developed is consistent with the overall company strategy.

3. The measurement system must track the value-delivery processes that cut across several functions, such as product development, order delivery, and customer service. Since teams are designed for cross-functional process

work, tasks that cut across several functions, their measurement systems must reflect this team mission.

4. Only a handful of measures should be adopted by a team. The team's principal task is to get the job done, not to measure itself. Therefore, if too many measurements are assigned, the time and energy of the team will be consumed in control processes versus accomplishing the assigned task. A few good, simple measures, like a "team dashboard," are appropriate.[25]

Whatever measurements you select, they will include milestones. These are "dates certain" by which time critical tasks should be accomplished or certain events should have occurred. Such metrics are necessary and expected both by top management and project leaders as well as by functional heads for ongoing activities.

For new ventures, "milestone planning" is becoming a familiar technique for tracking progress. One caution that this technique raises is to postpone major commitments of resources until evidence from previous milestone events signals that the risk of taking the next step is warranted.[26] "Conventional planning approaches tend to focus managers on meeting plan, usually an impossible goal for a venture rife with assumptions. It is also counter-productive—insistence on meeting plan actually prevents learning. Managers can formally plan to learn by using milestone events to test assumptions."[27] This overall process using milestone planning for managing and controlling new ventures is "discovery-driven planning."

CONTROL CRITERIA

Peter Drucker has identified seven criteria for effective control in a business; these are especially important for strategic control. Drucker's control criteria are:[28]

- Economical. The fewer controls used, the more effective each will be. Less is best.

- Meaningful. Focus control on significant activities, not marginal ones. Control should relate to key objectives and priorities related to them.

- Appropriate. Controls should be relevant and appropriate to the type and nature of the phenomena being measured—quantifiable and measurable in units of measurement (dollars, gallons, pounds, numbers of people, etc.) significant to the items in question.

- Congruent. Measurements should be consistent with events being measured. Avoid the pitfall of false precision where phenomena cannot be measured precisely.

- Timely. Frequency of measurement and reporting on results should relate to the essential nature of the events being measured, not too frequently or too infrequently; data should be collected, reported, and communicated promptly.

- Simple. Complex controls confuse people and divert attention to the methodology, away from the activities being controlled; keep controls cost-effective.

- Operational. Control should relate to actions and should reach those who can act upon the information, showing cause/effect relationships, to permit redirection if appropriate to achieve planned objectives.

Building on Drucker's criteria, the following additional tests of an effective control process should also be included:

- Single-person accountability. Controls should identify the locus of responsibility for a task and assign accountability to that individual. Sufficient authority and resources need to be assigned to the responsible person to permit success.
- Fairness. Control mechanism assigned to an individual should be acceptable to that person; accountability and responsibility should be in balance.
- Auditability. Management should ensure that its control processes include the capability to review records—especially financial records—later in time in sufficient detail and accuracy to permit their audit. Proper accounting standards should be met.

An additional control metric that management may wish to use is benchmarking with other firms in your industry or with industry averages. These types of measurements afford insights into how well your firm is doing in its industry—e.g., market share, overall sales growth—compared with other important firms in the same industry. A pitfall of this metric is the distraction it creates by focusing management's attention on only the existing players in an industry and may cause management to ignore potential new rivals or substitutes that may emerge.

CONTROL SYSTEMS

For multinational corporations and multinational subsidiaries, unique control systems will most likely be needed.[29] Why? Firms that have operations in several different countries are exposed to the national variables of each, such as political risk, financial and monetary policy changes, and numerous cultural and other environmental differences. Management's control task in this multinational context is highly challenging. There are numerous control mechanisms available, some of which work well in combination. One approach is to have strongly centralized strategic control from headquarters using a variety of administrative mechanisms.[30] Other approaches stress the linkages between the firm's organizational structure and its organizational control.[31] Still other approaches feature a political risk model,[32] an economic risk model,[33] and a three-dimensional model combining political, economic, and cultural risk factors.[34]

Examples: Control Disasters. How much control is enough? Clearly the control processes must be sufficient to prevent disasters such as these:

Figure 7.2
Four Levers of Control

Potential	Organizational Blocks	Managerial Solution	Control Lever
To contribute	Uncertainty about purpose	Communicate core values and mission	Belief systems
To do right	Pressure or temptation	Specify and enforce rules of the game	Boundary systems
To achieve	Lack of focus or resources	Build and support clear targets	Diagnostic control systems
To create	Lack of opportunity or fear of risk	Open organizational dialogue to encourage learning	Interactive control systems

Kidder, Peabody & Company lost $350 million when a trader allegedly booked fictitious profits.

Sears, Roebuck and Company took a $60-million charge against earnings after admitting it recommended unneeded auto repairs to customers.

Standard Chartered Bank was banned from trading on the Hong Kong stock exchange after being implicated in an improper securities scheme.[35]

The ultimate disaster is perhaps this: a twenty-eight-year-old trader in Barings Bank's Singapore office made unauthorized futures trades that lost $1.38 billion and led to England's oldest commercial bank's collapse in 1995.[36]

The cost to companies from such disasters can be enormous—in fines, business losses, theft, reputations, missed opportunities, and bankruptcies. Managers need to erect control systems to protect against such abuses and losses.

At the same time, given today's dynamic and highly competitive marketplace, risk-averse management techniques may stifle employee creativity and entrepreneurship. A balance is needed that reconciles the conflict between over- and undercontrolling—a proper equilibrium between control and empowerment.

Four Levers of Control

To achieve balance, Robert Simons suggests a system having Four Levers of Control[37] (see Figure 7.2).

Each of the four control levers has a purpose for harnessing employees' creativity and provides a solution to a particular "block" in the organization:

- Diagnostic system controls allow managers to ensure that important goals are being achieved efficiently and effectively. Like the dials on the control panel of an airplane's cockpit, these alone are not adequate for effective control; they monitor progress toward targets, like revenue growth and market share. They can also stimulate pressures leading to abuse, such as Nordstrom's $15 million settlement of claims that supervisors pressured sales associates to underreport hours on the job to boost sales per hour performance, a metric of their emphasis on customer service.

- Belief system controls empower individuals and encourage them to search for new opportunities, communicating core values and inspiring everyone to commit to the organization's purpose. These systems imbed the basic philosophy of the business into a control system, like Johnson & Johnson's credo, that passionately articulates the company's responsibility to customers, employees, communities, and stockholders. They helped J&J weather the Tylenol crisis, but they were insufficient to prevent it. These systems are by themselves not enough to ensure management control, but they leaven the organization toward fulfilling the mission.

- Boundary system controls establish the rules of the game and identify actions and pitfalls that must be avoided. These systems set the bounds for behavior—the list of "don'ts" that are punishable. These controls are the organization's brakes. In 1985 when General Electric was "suspended" as a federal government contractor, with $4.5 billion in contracts at risk, for improper cost allocations on those contracts, CEO Jack Welch strengthened internal controls to prevent a recurrence.

- Interactive system controls enable top management to focus on strategic uncertainties, to learn about threats and opportunities as competitive conditions change, and to respond appropriately. These systems depend on frequently updated, reliable information on items of significance that can be discussed face-to-face with key managers. USA Today uses this system each Friday when reports are delivered to senior managers giving a picture how they have done the previous week, showing account-specific data, changing industry conditions, advertising strategies of key customers, and year-to-date information.

These four control systems powerfully reinforce one another and provide balance between creativity and control for today's businesses.

CONCLUSION

Operational plans developed in the previous chapter are the principal mechanisms for control and review of the enterprise, through management's periodic monitoring of actual performance against those plans.

The successful business will neither over- nor undercontrol itself. Proper balance is needed, and some experimentation may be required to find the right proportions to stimulate growth and creativity, while at the same time maintaining effective management oversight. Legal and industry requirements for accountability, auditability, and financial reporting must of course be included in the control system adopted.

Beyond meeting these requirements, the control processes should primarily be an aid to top management (and product teams) in pursuit of the accomplishment of its strategic and operating objectives. Anything imposed on the organization beyond meeting these needs may impede its performance, may stifle creativity, and may be counterproductive. Success cannot be achieved and sustained without controls; too many controls or too complex controls may undermine it.

NOTES

1. Drucker carefully distinguishes between control and controls: "Control is direction. Controls pertain to means, control to an end. Controls deal with facts, that is, with events of the past. Control deals with expectations, that is, with the future." Peter F. Drucker, *Management: Tasks, Responsibilities, Practices* (New York: Harper & Row, 1973), p. 494. For his discussion, see pp. 494–98.

2. For a discussion of matching structure and control to strategy, see Charles W. L. Hill and Gareth R. Jones, *Strategic Management: An Integrated Approach*, 5th ed. (Boston: Houghton Mifflin, 2001), pp. 450–83.

3. For a discussion see William H. Newman, *Constructive Control: Design and Use of Control Systems* (Englewood Cliffs, NJ: Prentice-Hall, 1975).

4. George A. Steiner, *Strategic Planning* (New York: Free Press, 1979), pp. 267–69.

5. Robert N. Anthony, *Planning and Control Systems: A Framework for Analysis* (Boston: Harvard University, Graduate School of Business Administration, 1965). William Trafers Jerome III, *Executive Control: The Catalyst* (New York: Wiley, 1961).

6. For example, Fred Weston and Eugene F. Brigham, *Essentials of Managerial Finance*, 7th ed. (Hinsdale, IL: Dryden Press, 1985).

7. Anthony A. Atkinson, John H. Waterhouse, and Robert B. Wells, "A Stakeholder Approach to Strategic Performance Measurement," *Sloan Management Review*, spring 1997, p. 25.

8. Cortlandt Cammann and David A. Nadler, "Fit Control Systems to Your Managerial Style," *Harvard Business Review*, January–February 1976.

9. For a discussion, see Aime Heene, "The Nature of Strategic Management," *Long Range Planning* 30, no. 6 (December 1997), pp. 933–38.

10. Philip Waalewijn and Peter Segaar, "Strategic Management: The Key to Profitability in Small Companies," *Long Range Planning* 26, no. 2 (April 1993).

11. See J.A.F. Stoner, *Management*, 2d. ed. (London: Prentice-Hall, 1982). Also, A. A. Thompson and A. J. Strickland, *Strategic Management: Concepts and Cases* (Boston: Irwin, 1990).

12. C. K. Prahalad and Gary Hamel, "The Core Competence of the Corporation," *Harvard Business Review*, May–June 1990, pp. 79–91.

13. David C. Band and Gerald Scanlan, "Strategic Control through Core Competencies," *Long Range Planning* 28, no. 2 (April 1995), p. 112.

14. This discussion of "steering control" is from Boris Yavitz and William H. Newman, *Strategy in Action* (New York: Free Press, 1982), pp. 206–18.

15. This discussion is based on Atkinson, Waterhouse, and Wells, "A Stakeholder Approach to Strategic Performance Measurement," pp. 25–35.

16. Ibid., p. 26.

17. Robert S. Kaplan and David P. Norton, "The Balanced Scorecard—Measures that Drive Performance," *Harvard Business Review*, January–February 1992.

18. Adapted from ibid., p. 76.

19. Robert S. Kaplan and David P. Norton, "Putting the Balanced Scorecard to Work," *Harvard Business Review*, September–October 1993.

20. Robert S. Kaplan and David P. Norton, "Using the Balanced Scorecard as a Strategic Management System," *Harvard Business Review*, January–February 1996.

21. Gordon Donaldson, "A New Tool for Boards: The Strategic Audit," *Harvard Business Review*, July–August 1995.

22. Ibid., p. 107.

23. This discussion is based on Christopher Meyer, "How the Right Measures Help Teams Excel," *Harvard Business Review*, May–June, 1994, pp. 95–96.

24. Christopher Meyer, "How the Right Measures Help Teams Excel," *Harvard Business Review*, May–June 1994, pp. 95–103.

25. For the "team dashboard" discussion, see ibid., pp. 98–99.

26. Ian C. MacMillan, *Corporate Venturing* (Boston: Harvard Business School Press, 1993). Cited in Rita Gunther McGrath and Ian C. MacMillan, "Discovery-Driven Planning," *Harvard Business Review*, July–August 1995, p. 54.

27. Ibid.

28. Drucker, *Management: Tasks, Responsibilities, Practices*, pp. 498–504.

29. Robert D. Hamilton III, Virginia A. Taylor, and Roger J. Kashlak, "Designing a Control System for a Multinational Subsidiary," *Long Range Planning 29*, no. 6 (December 1996).

30. Yves Doz and C. K. Prahalad, "Headquarters Influence and Strategic Control in MNCs," *Sloan Management Review*, fall 1981, and C. K. Prahalad and Yves Doz, "Patterns for Strategic Control within Multinational Corporations," *Journal of International Business Studies*, fall 1984.

31. William Ouchi, "The Relationship between Organizational Structure and Organizational Control," *Administrative Science Quarterly*, March 1977.

32. J. Simons, "A Theoretical Perspective on Political Risk," *Journal of International Business Studies*, winter 1984.

33. D. Leassard, *International Financial Management* (New York: Wiley, 1979).

34. Hamilton, Taylor, and Kashlak, "Designing a Control System for a Multinational Subsidiary," pp. 863–66.

35. Robert Simons, "Control in an Age of Empowerment," *Harvard Business Review*, March–April 1995, p. 80.

36. *Los Angeles Times*, July 5, 1999, p. C2; the trader, Nick Leeson, was released from a Singapore prison in 1999 after serving three and one-half years.

37. This discussion is based on Robert Simons, "Control in an Age of Empowerment," *Harvard Business Review*, March–April 1995, pp. 80–88.

Chapter 8

Implementation

This chapter reminds the makers of the plan that their plan should in fact be executed and provides a mechanism for doing so, and it provides managers with tools to diagnose and deal with problems when they occur during its execution. The rollout of the plan is quite simple. It involves presentation of the business plan to top management, their review and changes, incorporation of changes, and their issuance of go-ahead orders for its implementation on an agreed-upon schedule.[1] The plan has no chance of success if there is no attempt to execute it. The chapter also presents criteria and a process for changing strategy later.

HAVE COURAGE: DO IT!

All the work that has gone before leads to this final step: implementation. This part of the planning process actually requires the greatest courage of all. For the entrepreneur, you are now faced with actually having to do something—put money at risk, put yourself into the action mode, hire people, lease office space, bid farewell to the safety and comfort of your present job, go out and face a customer, restructure your life, and all the rest. For the start-up and the corporate planner, your plan cannot be a success unless it is put to work.

If you believe in your plan, you should execute it. After all, why have you bothered to expend all the effort to develop the plan if you are simply going to let it languish? Go ahead, take the risk of being a success.

MASTER IMPLEMENTATION SCHEDULE

A master implementation schedule may be needed as part of the planning process.[2] This chart would simply identify on a time-line schedule each person or department responsible for implementing each of the operating plans identified earlier. This is a chart that the CEO would use to announce the implementation assignments, launch their rollout, and monitor the performance of each responsible party. This chart would be strictly top-level; it would *not* duplicate the individual operating plans for each department. It would be the CEO's plan of plans.

Use the Plan

In large corporations, at this stage of the planning process, after the plan has been presented and approved, it is often put in an attractive binder and placed on a bookshelf in the CEO's office as tangible proof that, yes, we do have a business plan at this company. And there, like other trophies, it collects dust.

The plan should be used. The plan has become the road map for the firm, and like all maps it should be consulted regularly to determine the proper course for the enterprise and to verify progress. It is an operating guide. It does you no good if it becomes simply a monument to a process that is now finished; the planning process is never finished—it is continuous.

To assure it is used, the plan should be in a loose-leaf binder or online, readily available to everyone who needs to use it on a regular basis to help with current decision making. At the end of the year the document should be as dog-eared as the "yellow pages" from frequency of use. Make your plan a working document to help you and others do your work. It is essential that everyone knows the strategy for everyone to effectively execute it.

"There are few original strategies in banking," Sir John Bond, Chairman of HSBC Holdings PLC, said. "There is only execution."[3] Executing against a strategy is a priori essential to the success of the strategy. Many businesses excel at strategic development and fail miserably at implementing it. Few fail at both, but when they do the results make headlines.

Example: AT&T. AT&T provides an example of a major company that attempted in a short time period a strategic refocus that required precision in execution and failed in both strategy and performance.

During the second half of the 1990s America's largest telecommunications company transformed itself from a "long-distance" telephone company into an "any distance, any service" telecommunications company—a distinctly different business model—by adopting a strategy that stimulated the following actions:[4]

(a) divesting assets that did not fit the strategy to raise capital for the new strategy—spinning off Lucent Technologies and NCR Corporation, and selling Universal Card Services;

(b) investing $11.3 billion to purchase Teleport Communications Group to speed AT&T's entry into the local business telephone market;

(c) reducing the workforce by 18,000 people in 1998 alone to reduce cost;

(d) investing $10 billion in a joint venture with British Telecom to provide communications services around the world;

(e) investing $5 billion to acquire IBM's global data network, accompanied by a record-setting outsourcing contract to manage IBM's global networking;

(f) acquiring a total of $115 billion in cable assets to become the largest cable and broadband operator in the United States,[5] the largest investments being $47 billion to purchase Tele-Communications, Inc., $58 billion for Media One cable company,[6] and establishing joint ventures with Time Warner to access additional homes through their cable operations; and

(g) investing $1.5 billion to purchase Vanguard Cellular Systems to extend AT&T's wireless footprint in the eastern United States to serve an additional 625,000 customers.

In 1998, AT&T's revenues were $53.2 billion and its net income was $6.3 billion. With all these changes brought about by its new global "any distance, any service" strategy, which is a wholly new business model for this venerable company, the main task before it became implementation—for wired local service, wired long-distance service, wireless "anywhere" service, video cable service, broadband video/data/voice cable service, and global voice and data service.

"For AT&T in 1999, the big challenge is to execute the strategy we've put in place," wrote C. Michael Armstrong, AT&T's first outside Chairman and CEO. "We have the strategy. We have the assets. And we have the people. How well we put all this together for our customers will be what sets us apart."[7] Executing the strategy became the major challenge, given the enormity of the task to transform this one staid, highly regulated, "widows and orphans" style of company into a fast-paced, highly innovative, complex, multiservice, management-driven company with global reach. Few large companies have ever attempted to alter themselves so thoroughly, so quickly as AT&T. "[T]his is the toughest time in our transformation," admitted Armstrong, ". . . the execution of our strategy."[8]

AT&T's challenge was to execute. Every wire, every fiber-optic cable, every circuit, every software interface, every line of software code everywhere in the world had to be properly connected and programmed to every other wire, cable, and circuit to assure that they had "put all this together for our customers" correctly. How well did AT&T execute?[9]

The 1999 results, Armstrong believed, showed the company was "delivering." Michael Armstrong wrote, "We set the strategy. We backed it up with investments. And now we're delivering results." The "strategy is not just doable—it's being done." For 1999 revenues were up 17 percent to $62.3 billion, but net income was down 14.8 percent to $5.4 billion. Importantly, the company had network reliability of 99.99 percent. "Because we know that however elegant the strategy, it's results that count."[10]

The results were devastating. By October 2000 it had become clear that not only had AT&T failed to focus its efforts to deliver, but also the underlying strategy was a failure. During the previous twelve months, AT&T stock had fallen from its all-time high by more than 60 percent in value, the company had accumulated $61 billion in debt to fund its acquisitions, and it was failing to deliver value at an increasing rate in its core businesses—exhibiting, admitted the company, a "systemic decline."[11] Wall Street had had enough, and so had Armstrong.

He announced on October 25, 2000 the breakup of AT&T into four companies, ending his dream and Theodore Vail's, the legendary early 20th-century executive who cobbled together AT&T into America's leading company, of providing one-stop communication service for every customer.[12] This breakup signals a strategic failure in American business of the first magnitude, based on a change strategy begun too late, having insufficient focus, an inability to execute, and loss of customer focus. "It's really the end of an icon . . . , it's the death of [a] corporate giant," said a Wall Street analyst.[13]

During Armstrong's then three-year tenure as AT&T's Chairman and CEO, he bet a big part of the farm on cable, seeking to use that as a wire route into homes across America, following AT&T's loss of the other wire in 1984 with the breakup of the company into six Baby Bells for local phone service plus AT&T for long distance. He also bet heavily on the technologies needed to upgrade the cables to have broadband capability. Simultaneously, he bet another part of the farm on wireless technology, becoming through acquisition one of the country's largest wireless operators. This undercut other parts of his strategy when he offered free long-distance wireless service to new subscribers, eroding the wired long-distance core of the company. There simply was not enough money or time to deliver on this mixed, nonfocused strategy to an ever-impatient Wall Street. This "waffling wrecked havoc" on the company's stock price, reaching a string of fifty-two-week lows throughout the year 2000. "The revenues are falling so fast that they can't protect the margins anymore," added a Merrill Lynch analyst at the time.[14]

AT&T's problems had as much to do with execution as they did with business strategy and the business mix it produced. Value has to be delivered through performance, and three of the four businesses that emerged after October 2000 are deeply flawed. The consumer services portion is viewed as a dog, and business services and cable/broadband are suspect. Only wireless has an optimistic future; the wireless piece of the business represented about half of AT&T's total market cap of $90 billion (less debt) at the time of the breakup announcement.[15]

Execution requires people to perform. After the 1984 breakup and especially following the enactment of the 1996 Telecommunications Act, which deregulated the telephone industry, AT&T had to face a new business atmosphere for which it had no experience and for which it was clearly unprepared: competition. For a previously regulated company in a heavily regulated industry, that transition was too great a challenge for its people.

Compounding the problem was the go-slow corporate culture of this 114-year-old company, where employees used to try to fit the mold of "Bell Heads," a powerful pressure to conform and seek consensus. In the fiercely competitive post-1996 telecommunications world, the requirement was for change, speed, and innovation—characteristics that AT&T never acquired. "The corporate culture," said a former Justice Department lawyer who helped break up AT&T, "of traditional companies like AT&T just couldn't adapt quickly enough."[16]

What are the prospects for the four new AT&T companies? On the day of the breakup announcement, the analyst community was mixed. Some urged their clients to buy, others to hold, and stunningly one major investment firm sent out a rare "sell" bulletin for a Dow Jones stock.[17] Two months later, for the first time in its history, AT&T cut its dividend—by 83 percent, and it issued another earnings warning.[18] Failure to execute a flawed strategy is a double-barreled prescription for defeat.

DIAGNOSING PROBLEMS: VALUE CHAIN ANALYSIS

No plan is flawless. And no plan is executed flawlessly. How do you anticipate problems in the plan, and how do you identify the locus and causes of problems during execution, so as to be able to take appropriate action?[19]

One approach to this diagnosis/prescription task begins with an analysis of the firm's value chain.[20] Build into the plan a thorough understanding of the firm's sequence of primary activities that add value and competitive advantage by their being performed by the firm.[21] This can be accomplished anywhere in the plan managers feel comfortable. A recommended location is in the implementation chapter because it is during the execution phase of the plan that these performance-management challenges arise.

Michael Porter's generic value chain is shown in Figure 8.1.[22]

Support activities associated with all these links in the value chain are:

Firm infrastructure: overhead activities that support the entire chain

Human resource management: recruiting, hiring, training, compensating, and management development activities

Figure 8.1
The Generic Value Chain

Inbound logistics	Operations	Outbound logistics	Marketing and Sales	Service

Technology development: activities to improve the product and the process
Procurement: the function of purchasing inputs for the firm's use

The five generic categories of primary activities are undertaken by any firm in any industry. Porter defines them as follows:[23]

- Inbound Logistics. Activities associated with receiving, storing and disseminating inputs to the product, like material handling, warehousing, inventory control, etc.
- Operations. Activities associated with transforming inputs into the final product, like machining, assembly, testing, packaging, equipment maintenance, printing, etc.
- Outbound Logistics. Activities associated with collecting, storing, and physically delivering the product to the buyer, like warehousing of finished product, material handling, order processing, delivery vehicle operations, scheduling, etc.
- Marketing and Sales. Activities associated with providing a means by which buyers can purchase the product and inducing them to do so, like advertising, promotion, sales force, channel selection and channel relations, pricing, etc.
- Service. Activities associated with providing service to enhance or maintain the product's value, like installation, repair, parts supply, training, product adjustment, etc.

Once managers understand their firm's value chain well, they can execute the plan they have crafted with confidence that when problems in execution arise they will be equipped with insight as to where the problem lies in the sequence of activities and what the true underlying problem is. Having performed this diagnosis, they can then take appropriate remedial action.

Example: Small High-Tech Companies. For example, small high-technology firms classically have a myopic focus on technology issues in their formative stage of life. The firm's founders, like William Hewlett and David Packard, could be scientists or engineers previously employed by another company who strike out on their own to establish a company to develop and produce a product based on a "better idea" they have invented. Little "business" judgment is used at this stage because they are focused on the R&D activities, tinkering in the lab (or the garage). This phase of the value chain is in the "technology" support role—inventing the product.

Later, after the product is invented and the owners want to mass-produce and sell it, they have to address "business" issues—identify the customer and make the product known to him, figure out how to make the product, what parts to purchase or make in-house, what price to charge, how to deliver the product, how to install and service it. These "business" issues run the gamut of the value chain. They also run the gamut of the "support" activities—the owners need to establish a physical location, hire people having certain job skills, establish a parts-purchasing procedure, hire a delivery company, etc. All these "business" tasks are "management" tasks.[24]

Once the operation is established and production has begun, new sets of problems arise—problems associated with actual production operations, like parts shortages, skilled labor shortages, training, quality control, warehousing, inventory control, accounts payable, etc. These are no longer R&D problems in the "technology" area of activity; they are "operations" problems in the value chain itself, with linkage to "inbound logistics" and "outbound logistics."

Can these "new sets" of problems be anticipated—identified ahead of time? This is one of the major values of comprehensive planning—identification in advance of management challenges at each step of the value chain process. As a start-up firm moves from R&D to production operations, the challenges it will face are absolutely anticipatable.

A solid implementation plan will address these in advance of their happening, to prevent their occurrence if possible or to accurately diagnose and remedy them as they occur. How? By planning to hire enough skilled labor to produce the product when the orders come in. By planning to lease enough floor space for the machinery and equipment that will be needed to produce sufficient throughput to meet projected sales and delivery schedules. By planning to advertise on the Internet to attract customers and their orders in sufficient volume to meet cash-flow requirements to pay vendors, employees, and yourself. These management tasks are able to be identified and scheduled by planning—especially by planning for the successful launch of a new product or model of an existing product.

Plan to have enough trained people to produce the product, enough factory capacity to produce it, enough sales people and advertising to stimulate the orders, and enough management to operate and control the business.

Example: IBM and the Introduction of the PC. Transition from R&D to production is a problem that does not happen only at small companies. One of the classic examples of failure to adequately plan for the successful transition from R&D to production is IBM's invention in 1980–81 of the open-architecture personal computer.[25] The company spent large sums of money and talent assets to invent their PC—which was accomplished on a one-year compressed schedule. But once it was invented, they failed to invest enough resources to produce it in the quantities that the marketplace demanded after the product was launched. IBM could not supply enough product to resellers to meet demand because they had not planned for the PC's enormous success in the marketplace. Others quickly took advantage of IBM's inadequate production capacity and filled the demand, using IBM's own open architecture.

If it had not been for IBM's initial failure to plan fully to exploit its first mover advantage by securing market domination, together with the "open-architecture" design, which allowed others to replicate it, Compaq, Dell, and the other "IBM compatible" brand names would not have been born— or would not have had the wide-open opportunity that IBM handed them to satisfy surging demand. IBM achieved a brilliant tactical success for itself with the invention of their PC, but it made a massive strategic mistake for itself by failing to plan for its market dominance.

Plan for success, not for partial success. And plan to exploit success by having enough product to satisfy customer demand that you have stimulated.

CHANGING STRATEGY

Determining the need for change is a major management challenge.[26] Managers often fail to see the need to change a strategy that has proven successful in the past, even though it is no longer appropriate or has become obsolete.[27] What is not being addressed here is a situation where "tinkering and kludging" with organizational structure or internal processes could be sufficient to produce marginal benefits of "change without pain."[28] Rather the focus here is on fundamental change—repositioning resulting from a strategic shift, a situation that may require an internal insurrection.[29]

One observer believes firms go through stages or life cycles: conception, initiation, beginning operations, initial success, expansion, crossroads, and maturity and/or reconception.[30] Strategic reassessment at any stage of the firm's life cycle is difficult, especially at "maturity and/or reconception," and incumbent management typically lacks the energy and skills necessary to identify this need, much less have the skills needed to develop a strategic refocus and to implement it.

Firms are most vulnerable to competitive challenge and need to refocus strategy when they are experiencing significant downturns, or, oddly, when they are at the peak of success—feeling they have "arrived" at market dominance and have achieved an unassailable position of strength. This is never the case. Constant and systematic reevaluation of your firm's strengths and weaknesses, its opportunities and threats is mandatory for continuing success. A feeling of invulnerability is hubris.

The challenge of redefining strategy and implementing a redefined strategy is never easy. Whatever new strategy is chosen, its success depends on its implementation.[31] Successful implementation may in turn depend on "intangible assets" being in place and used well. "[T]he key intangible asset is the capacity to carry through the changes implied by the strategy and if necessary transform the strategy through use." This is the critical factor "linking management change to competitive success."[32]

A change-agent leader is most likely needed at this stage in the life of the firm, especially if the firm appears at the moment to be successful with the present strategy. The change-agent leader can come from within the firm or from outside. Jack Welch, an insider, recognized the need for change when he assumed the leadership of General Electric, when to most appearances the firm was an icon of success. Louis Gerstner, an outsider, performed this role at IBM, brought in not because the firm was in the midst of success but because it was obvious to everyone it needed to refocus to avoid more failure. C. Michael Armstrong was brought in to AT&T to perform this role, but the plan was begun too late, the strategy was fundamentally flawed, and it was poorly executed. AT&T is being broken up as a result, signaling one of the greatest corporate failures in American history. When Rick Thoman, an outsider from IBM, was brought in as CEO to shake up Xerox, a corporate civil war began, which the insiders won, and Xerox continued to tank when Thoman "retired" a year later.[33]

A new, more competitive strategy is needed when:

- sales stagnate relative to the competition,
- costs of operations are increasing and market share is decreasing,
- sales are flat or growing marginally but profits are squeezed,
- external conditions alter negatively to the firm's positioning, especially to its core products,
- the business model has eroded or obsolesced, or
- the firm's leadership loses energy or the will to innovate and compete.

In the last case, new strategic focus needs to be coupled with fresh leadership.

The new strategy must not be a reflection of management's biases based on the firm's past success, nor can it be based on ignorance of either internal factors or the realities of the external context—the marketplace and the competition. First and foremost, the new strategy has to be grounded on fundamentally honest assessments of internal and external realities. Second, the new strategy can be a success only if management allocates the resources necessary and sufficient to fully implement the new strategy. Aligning resources to fit strategies is especially challenging in mature firms, where vested interests and departmental barons jealously guard assets to preserve the present model. Change-agent leadership is needed to cut through these Gordian knots.

Example: Levi Strauss. Privately held Levi Strauss, a "mature" company needing "reconception," faced up to the need for a change-agent leader in

1999. The inventor of blue jeans 150 years earlier confronted a serious set of issues: loss of half its market share (from 50 percent to 25 percent) in jeans from 1990 to 1999, loss of ground to trendier cuts of jeans (wide-leg and cargo pants) from The Gap and Tommy Hilfiger for high-end customers, loss of ground to private-label brands at J. C. Penney and Wal-Mart for lower-priced product, and increased cost of U.S.-based manufacturing operations. Sales and profits plunged and debt soared to the point where in May 2000 the company stated in an extraordinary SEC filing that it will be "difficult for us to successfully execute our business strategy or to compete in the worldwide apparel industry."[34]

To address these issues, in recent years Levi Strauss closed twenty-nine plants in North America and fired 18,500 workers to reduce cost as demand for its jeans fell. Next, it searched for a new Chief Executive to revitalize the company; after eight months, Philip Marineau, president of PepsiCo's North American beverage unit where he had revitalized that brand, was hired as Levi Strauss' new president and CEO. The fact that Robert Haas, whose family controls the company, stepped aside as CEO to become Chairman signaled the depth of the need for change. Finally, the company decided to alter its business model to focus on designing and marketing products, rather than production, much as Nike does.[35] Marineau, known as a first-rate marketer, is the type of "outsider" change-agent leader needed at Levi Strauss.

Strategic Refocus

Any company seeking to change direction, particularly if it plans to use a new product to provide the platform for the refocus, needs to heed a few cautions, in addition to normal market and competitive considerations. First, be certain the new product (and perhaps the new markets and distribution channels it requires) is consistent with the firm's core competencies and the firm leadership's core values. Second, does the firm have the internal resources (human, material, and capital) to undertake the new business lines and products alone, or (possibly no longer qualifying for additional debt) will it require equity participation from outside, thus diluting its ownership and control of the new product and possibly the firm itself?

Third, will the inclusion of the new product within the firm's existing product line and business model be an acceptable strategic "fit"?[36] Finally, be certain management is comfortable with the "endgame," i.e., the new strategic position where the repositioning will place the firm, assuming a successful new product launch.

Northrop Grumman Corporation's experience with a transit bus program illustrates these points.[37] Facing a serious downturn it its traditional Defense Department business with the ending of the Cold War, this aerospace company decided to test the applicability of its core competencies for other markets by using its advanced technology to design nondefense products for other government customers. The company won contracts in the early 1990s to design, develop, and build six prototype transit buses for the Los Angeles Metropolitan Transportation Authority, using local and federal transportation funds.

After five years of work, the company proved its core competencies could be applied to this nondefense product, the prototypes were a success, and the Los Angeles transit authority wanted to buy a large quantity of production vehicles. The company, however, which had never committed to produce the buses (only to design and develop them), concluded it lacked the resources by itself to produce the buses at the needed high rate of production, lacked in-depth knowledge of the transit bus marketplace and business model, and lacked the desire to undertake the production program.

In the end, Northrop Grumman decided not to build the buses and could find no other company willing to do so, either alone or in a working arrangement with Northrop Grumman. The "end game" of this venture was that Northrop Grumman's management, by the late 1990s, had decided to reposition as a pure defense industry player, and the endgame the transit bus would have positioned the company in did not "fit" that strategy. The bus project was shelved.

Clayton Christensen has developed a practical, three-stage process to assist top management in implementing strategic refocus.[38]

Stage One: Identify the driving forces in the company's competitive environment. Driving forces are the fundamental, root causes of the issues the company needs to address: economic, demographic, technological, or competitive factors in the company's environment that represent threats or opportunities. This process is needed to ensure that the correct problems are being identified; answers to the wrong questions are pointless.

A useful technique for achieving this is for the management group to develop hypotheses of the problem areas during brainstorming sessions. Next, test and evaluate these hypotheses through mapping—a visual, iterative tool for discovering correct root causes of phenomena affecting the company.[39] Mapping enables managers to plot the most critical issues on a conceptual level, freeing everyone from the need to collect exact numbers, to focus their analysis on the driving issues, and to expose and examine their underlying assumptions explicitly.

Stage Two: Formulate a strategy that addresses the driving forces. This stage has three steps. First, managers brainstorm ideas for what needs to be done and develop strategy initiatives for each driving force, putting them in priority order. Second, plot these initiatives on a matrix to see how they fit together. Third, develop maps to make explicit how each functional group will contribute to achieving the chosen strategy.

Stage Three: Create a plan for implementation of the strategy. This plan defines specifically how money and other resources must be spent over time to implement the selected strategy. Elegantly conceived strategies often fail because managers do not define programs and projects throughout the company that are required to implement high-level strategy statements. Allocating resources mirroring the strategy on a project-by-project basis across the company enables managers to translate strategy into action using this deliberate mechanism to implement change.[40]

Christensen concludes with this observation, "The process of defining and periodically reassessing driving forces and the strategies required to address them must be repeated in a way that is not perfunctory. If companies make these tasks an integral part of their annual planning process, their managers will become competent strategic thinkers." The linkage between strategy and innovation in the project-planning process will enable senior managers "to develop competence in implementing strategic change."[41]

Identifying the need for, choosing, and implementing strategic redirection requires leadership. That leadership must recognize the need for redirection, adopt a mechanism for finding the best new course, and methodically drive the implementation of change throughout the organization's structure—project by project, department by department. This is the work of an obdurate, determined change-agent leader.

CONCLUSION

Having prepared the master implementation schedule, it is time to get started executing it. The business plan will now serve both as a guide to the future and as an operating mechanism for getting you there successfully. Keep in mind the day will come when the underlying strategy will have to be changed, probably by someone else.

NOTES

1. See John Harrison, *Strategic Management: Concepts and Cases* (Cincinnati: South-Western College Publishing, 1997).

2. For a discussion of implementing strategy with respect to resources, budgets, policies, best practices, etc., see Arthur A. Thompson, Jr. and A. J. Strikland III, *Strategic Management: Concepts and Cases*, 10th ed., (New York: McGraw-Hill, 1998), Chapters 9 and 10.

3. Quoted in Jeffrey W. Bennett, Thomas E. Pernsteiner, Paul F. Kocourek, and Seven B. Hedlund, "The Organization vs. the Strategy," *Strategy + Business*, issue 21, 4th quarter 2000, p. 70.

4. *AT&T Annual Report 1998*, March 9, 1999, pp. 1–3.

5. *Wall Street Journal*, October 26, 2000, p. B4.

6. *AT&T Midyear Report*, 1999, p. 3.

7. *AT&T Annual Report 1998*, p. 5.

8. *AT&T Midyear Report*, July 25, 2000, p. 1.

9. First-half 1999 results compared with first-half 1998 were: revenues $29.7 billion, up from $26 billion; operating income $5.1 billion, up from $945 million; *AT&T Midyear Report*, 1999, p. 5.

10. *AT&T Annual Report 1999*, March 17, 2000, inside cover, pp. 1, 3, and 11.

11. *Wall Street Journal*, October 26, 2000, p. A1.

12. Ibid., pp. A–12, B1, C1.

13. Ibid., p. B1.

14. Ibid., p. B4.

15. In December, 2000 AT&T sold 16 percent of its wireless business for $9.8 billion to NTT DoCoMo, Japan's largest wireless company having thirty million customers; *Los Angeles Times*, December 1, 2000, p. C3.

16. *Wall Street Journal*, October 26, 2000, p. A12.

17. *Los Angeles Times*, October 26, 2000, pp. C1, C10.

18. The *Wall Street Journal*, December 21, 2000, p. A3. AT&T's 2000 4th quarter operating profit declined by 42% on 3% rise in revenue; *Los Angeles Times*, January 30, 2001, p. C3.

19. For a discussion of diagnosis of the need for strategic change, see Joseph N. Fry and J. Peter Killing, *Strategic Analysis and Action* (Englewood Cliffs, NJ: Prentice-Hall, US/International Ed., 1986), Chapter 12; for a discussion of tactics for strategic change, see Chapter 13.

20. Michael E. Porter, *Competitive Advantage* (New York: Free Press, 1985), pp. 36–53. Adapted with the permission of The Free Press, a Division of Simon & Schuster, Inc., from *Competitive Advantage: Creating and Sustaining Superior Performance* by Michael E. Porter. Copyright © 1985, 1998 by Michael E. Porter.

21. For a discussion of the benefits the "natural value chain" analysis provides firms in the rigorous reconceptualization of their business, see Leonard O'Sullivan and J. Michael Geringr, "Harnessing the Power of Your Value Chain," *Long Range Planning* 26, no. 2 (April 1993), pp. 59–68.

22. Adapted from Porter, *Competitive Advantage*, p. 37. Adapted with the permission of The Free Press, a Division of Simon & Schuster, Inc., from *Competitive Advantage: Creating and Sustaining Superior Performance* by Michael E. Porter. Copyright © 1985, 1998 by Michael E. Porter.

23. Ibid., pp. 39–40. Adapted with the permission of The Free Press, a Division of Simon & Schuster, Inc., from *Competitive Advantage: Creating and Sustaining Superior Performance* by Michael E. Porter. Copyright © 1985, 1998 by Michael E. Porter.

24. See Carl Hanoman, *The Complete Small-Business Source Book* (New York: Random House, 1999).

25. This discussion is based on Hale C. Bartlett, *Cases in Strategic Management for Business* (New York: Dryden Press, 1988), "IBM Case," pp. 89–127.

26. See the discussion on implementing strategic change in Charles W. L. Hill and Gareth R. Jones, *Strategic Management: An Integrated Approach*, 5th ed. (Boston: Houghton Mifflin, 2001), pp. 484–512.

27. In this context, "strategy" is "the All-Embracing S-Word." Eddie Obeng, *Putting Strategy to Work* (London: Pitman, 1996), p. 140.

28. Eric Abrahamson, "Change without Pain," *Harvard Business Review*, July–August 2000, pp. 75–79.

29. Gary Hamel, "Waking Up IBM: How a Gang of Unlikely Rebels Transformed Big Blue," *Harvard Business Review*, July–August 2000, pp. 137–46. For a seven-step playbook on how to start an insurrection, see p. 142.

30. Steven C. Stryker, *Plan to Succeed: A Guide to Strategic Planning* (Princeton, NJ: Petrocelli Books, 1986), pp. 37–43.

31. Michael Beer and Russell A. Eisenstat, "The Silent Killers of Strategy Implementation and Learning," *Sloan Management Review*, summer 2000, pp. 20–40.

32. Andrew Pettigrew and Richard Whipp, "Managing the Twin Processes of Competition and Change, The Role of Intangible Assets," in Peter Lorange, Bala Chakravarthy, Johan Roos, and Andrew Van de Ven, eds., *Implementing Strategic Processes: Change, Learning and Co-operation* (Oxford, UK: Blackwell Business, 1993), p. 3.

33. Anthony Bianco and Pamela L. Moore, "Downfall: The Inside Story of the Management Fiasco at Xerox," *Business Week*, March 5, 2001, pp. 82–92.

34. *Los Angeles Times*, May 5, 2000, p. C1. In March 2001 Levi Strauss reported a 7% decline in quarterly profits on 8% decline in sales; ibid., March 21, 2001, p. C2.

35. Ibid., September 8, 1999, pp. C1, C15.

36. Michael E. Porter, "What Is Strategy?" *Harvard Business Review*, November–December 1996, pp. 70–75.

37. This discussion is based on José de la Torre and Wesley B. Truitt, "Northrop Grumman and the Advanced Technology Transit Bus Program," in José de la Torre, Yves Doz, and Timothy Devinney, *Managing the Global Corporation: Case Studies in Strategy and Management* 2d ed. (New York: Irwin/McGraw-Hill, 2001), pp. 259–71.

38. This discussion is based on Clayton M. Christensen, "Making Strategy: Learning by Doing," *Harvard Business Review*, November–December 1997, pp. 141–56.

39. For a discussion of mapping, see ibid., pp. 144–48.

40. For a discussion of project-planning tools, see Steven C. Wheelwright and Kim B. Clark, "Creating Project Plans to Focus Product Development," *Harvard Business Review*, March–April 1992. See also Anil Khurana and Stephen R. Rosenthal, "Integrating the Fuzzy Front End of New Product Development," *Sloan Management Review*, winter 1997.

41. Christensen, "Making Strategy: Learning by Doing," p. 156.

Selected Bibliography

ANNUAL REPORTS

America Online Annual Report 1999. June 1999.
AT&T Annual Report 1998. March 9, 1999.
AT&T Annual Report 1999. March 17, 2000.
AT&T Midyear Report, 1999.
Bank of America. *1998 Summary Annual Report*. (Undated)
Bell Atlantic 1999 Annual Report. March 2000.
Boeing Annual Report, 1998. February 22, 1999.
Boeing Annual Report, 1999. February 28, 2000.
Cisco Systems, 2000 Annual Report. August 2000.
The Coca-Cola Company. *Letter to Share Owners*. July 1, 1999.
The Coca-Cola Company *1997 Annual Report*. February 19, 1998.
The Coca-Cola Company *1998 Annual Report*. February 18, 1999.
The Coca-Cola Company *2000 Annual Report*. February 15, 2001.
Delphi Automotive Systems. *Investor Facts*. 1999.
Delphi Automotive Systems 1999 Annual Report. March 27, 2000.
E. I. du Pont de Nemours and Company, 1998 Annual Report. March 1, 1999.
E. I. du Pont de Nemours and Company, 1999 Annual Report. March 1, 2000.
General Electric Company, 1998 Annual Report. February 12, 1999.
General Electric Company, 1999 Annual Report. February 11, 2000.
General Motors Corporation. *Stockholder News*. March 1997.
General Motors Corporation. *Stockholder News*. September 1999.
General Motors Corporation. *Stockholder News*. March 2001.
General Motors Corporation 1996 *Midyear Report*. September 10, 1996.
General Motors Corporation 1998 Annual Report. January 20, 1999.

General Motors Corporation 1999 Annual Report. February 25, 2000.
IBM 1999 Annual Report.
McDonald's Corporation 1998 Annual Report, The Annual. March 15, 1999.
McDonald's Corporation 1999 Annual Report, The Annual. March 15, 2000.
Motorola, Inc. *1998 Summary Annual Report.* (Undated)
Philip Morris Companies, Inc., 1998 Annual Report. February, 24, 1999
Philip Morris Companies, Inc., 1999 Annual Report. February 22, 2000.
Raytheon Company 1998 Annual Report. February 24, 1999.

ARTICLES FROM JOURNALS AND NEWSPAPERS

Abrahamson, Eric. "Change without Pain." *Harvard Business Review*, July–August 2000.
Albrinck, Jill, Gil Irwin, Gary Neilson, and Dianna Sasina. "From Bricks to Clicks: The Four Stages of E-volution." *Strategy + Business*, issue 20, 3rd quarter 2000.
Alexander, Marcus. "Planning for Planners." *Long Range Planning* 28, no. 3 (June 1995).
Alexander, Robert J. "Castro, Latin America and United States Policy," in Robert A. Goldwin, ed. *Beyond the Cold War.* Chicago: Rand McNally, 1963.
Argus Update. February 1999.
Atkinson, Anthony A., John H. Waterhouse, and Robert B. Wells. "A Stakeholder Approach to Strategic Performance Measurement." *Sloan Management Review*, spring 1997.
Baetz, Mark C. and Christopher K. Bart. "Developing Mission Statements which Work." *Long Range Planning* 29, no. 4 (August 1996).
Baker, Edward F., Jr. "Strategic Planning in a U.S. Federal Agency." *Long Range Planning* 25, no. 5 (October 1992).
Band, David C. and Gerald Scanlan. "Strategic Control through Core Competencies." *Long Range Planning* 28, no. 2 (April 1995).
Banks, Howard. "General Electric—Going with the Winners." *Forbes.* March 26, 1984.
Bartlett, Christopher A. and Meg Wozny. "GE's Two-Decade Transformation: Jack Welch's Leadership." Harvard Business School, Case No. 9–399–150, Rev. January 6, 2000.
Bartlett, Christopher A. and Sumantra Ghoshal. "Changing the Role of Top Management: Beyond Strategy to Purpose." *Harvard Business Review*, November–December 1994.
Beer, Michael and Russell A. Eisenstat. "The Silent Killers of Strategy Implementation and Learning." *Sloan Management Review*, summer 2000.
Bennett, Jeffrey W., Thomas E. Pernsteiner, Paul F. Kocourek, and Steven B. Hedlund. "The Organization vs. the Strategy." *Strategy + Business*, issue 21, 4th quarter 2000.
Bennis, Warren. "The Leader as Storyteller." *Harvard Business Review*, January–February 1996.
Bernal, Richard L. "From NAFTA to Hemispheric Free Trade." *Columbia Journal of World Business* 29, no. 3 (Fall 1994).

Bianco, Anthony, and Pamela L. Moore. "Downfall: The Inside Story of the Management Fiasco at Xerox." *Business Week*, March 5, 2001.

Boquist, John A., Todd T. Milbourn, and Anjan V. Thakor. "How Do You Win the Capital Allocation Game?" *Sloan Management Review*, winter 1998.

Bowman, Cliff and Andrew Kakabadse. "Top Management Ownership of the Strategy Problem." *Long Range Planning* 30, no. 2 (April 1997).

Bradley, Gene E. "How to Work in Washington: Building Understanding for Your Business." *Columbia Journal of World Business* 29, no. 1 (spring 1994).

Brandenberger, Adam M. and Barry J. Nalebuff. "The Right Game: Use Game Theory to Shape Strategy." *Harvard Business Review*, July–August 1995.

Business Week. August 24–31, 1998.

———. "The 21st Century Economy." August 24–31, 1998.

Cammann, Cortlandt and David A. Nadler. "Fit Control Systems to Your Managerial Style." *Harvard Business Review*, January–February 1976.

Campbell, Andrew, "Mission Statements." *Long Range Planning* 30, no. 6 (December 1997).

———. "Tailored, Not Benchmarked: A Fresh Look at Corporate Planning." *Harvard Business Review*, March–April, 1999.

Campbell, Andrew and Marcus Alexander. "What's Wrong with Strategy?" *Harvard Business Review*, November–December 1997.

"Can Compaq Be Revived?" *Fortune*, March 6, 2000.

Christensen, Clayton M. "Making Strategy: Learning by Doing." *Harvard Business Review*, November–December 1997.

Christensen, Clayton M. and Michael Overdorf. "Meeting the Challenge of Disruptive Change." *Harvard Business Review*, March–April 2000.

Clarkberg, Marian. "Report to the American Association for the Advancement of Science." *Los Angeles Times*, January 24, 1999.

"A Clean Technology Powers Up." *Business Week*, May 8, 2000.

Collins, James C. and Jerry I. Porras. "Building Your Company's Vision." *Harvard Business Review*, September–October 1996.

Collins, Jim. "Turning Goals into Results: The Power of Catalytic Mechanisms." *Harvard Business Review*, July–August 1999.

Congressional Quarterly Almanac, 1978. Washington, DC: Congressional Quarterly News Features, 1979.

Cook, William J. "Software Struggle." *U.S. News & World Report*, June 19, 1995.

Copeland, Tom. "Cutting Costs without Drawing Blood." *Harvard Business Review*, September–October 2000.

Costello, Bill. "Make Money by Thinking the Unthinkable." *The Futurist* 33, no. 5 (May 1999).

Courtney, Hugh, Jane Kirkland, and Patrick Viguerie. "Strategy under Uncertainty." *Harvard Business Review*, November–December, 1997.

Crainer, Stuart. "The Days of Futurists Past." *Strategy + Business*, issue 20, 3rd quarter 2000.

David, Laura. "Consumer Product Survey of America." Buffalo, NY: Consumer Research Center, February, 1999.

de Geus, Arie. "Planning as Learning." *Harvard Business Review*, March–April 1988.

de la Torre, José and Wesley B. Truitt, "Northrop Grumman and the Advanced

Technology Transit Bus Program," in José de la Torre, Yves Doz, and Timothy Devinney, *Managing the Global Corporation: Case Studies in Strategy and Management*, 2d ed. New York: Irwin/McGraw-Hill, 2001.

Dolan, Robert J. "How Do You Know When the Price Is Right?" *Harvard Business Review*, September–October 1995.

Donaldson, Gordon. "A New Tool for Boards: The Strategic Audit." *Harvard Business Review*, July–August 1995.

Doz, Yves L. "Strategic Management in Multinational Companies." *Sloan Management Review*, winter 1980.

Doz, Yves and C. K. Prahalad. "Headquarters Influence and Strategic Control in MNCs." *Sloan Management Review*, fall 1981.

Drozdow, Nancy and Vincent P. Carroll. "Tools for Strategy Development in Family Firms." *Sloan Management Review*, fall 1997.

Drucker, Peter F. "Beyond the Information Revolution." *Atlantic Monthly*, October 1999.

———. "Change Leaders." *Inc.*, June 1999.

———. "Long-Range Planning." *Management Science* 5 (April 1959).

———. "Managing Oneself." *Harvard Business Review*, March–April 1999.

Eade, John M. "A Productive Population." *Argus Update*, March 1999.

Easton, David. "An Approach to Political Systems." *World Politics* 9 (1957).

Eller, Claudia and James Bates. "FedEx Chief Banks on Film-Making Package." *Los Angeles Times*, March 14, 2000.

"En Garde, Wal-Mart." *Business Week*, September 13, 1999.

Erskine, Hazel Gaudet. "The Polls: Defense, Peace, and Space." *Public Opinion Quarterly* XXV, no. 3 (fall 1961).

Farkas, Charles M. and Suzy Wetlaufer. "The Ways Chief Executive Officers Lead." *Harvard Business Review*, May–June 1996.

Feinstein, Charles H. "Pessimism Perpetuated: Real Wages and the Standard of Living in Britain during and after the Industrial Revolution." *Journal of Economic History* 58, no. 3 (September 1998).

Ferdows, Kasra. "Making the Most of Foreign Factories." *Harvard Business Review*, March–April 1997.

Flanigan, James. "Can Coke Avoid Mistakes and Reach Its Potential." *Los Angeles Times*, March 11, 2001.

———. "Ireland on Web Points Way for Global Business." *Los Angeles Times*, July 25, 1999.

Fortune, September 27, 1999.

Frost and Sullivan. "World Contraceptive and Infertility Drug Markets." *Los Angeles Times*, April 15, 1999.

Fuhrmann, Henry. "Ford Offered the Masses Freedom of Movement." *Los Angeles Times*, October 25, 1999.

Fulghum, David A. "F-22 Headed for Reprieve from Congressional Ax." *Aviation Week & Space Technology*, August 9, 1999.

The Futurist. Bethesda, MD: World Future Society. Quarterly editions.

Garvin, David A. "Building a Learning Organization." *Harvard Business Review*, July–August 1993.

Goffee, Robert and Gareth Jones. "Why Should Anyone Be Led by You?" *Harvard Business Review*, September–October 2000.

Goleman, Daniel. "Leadership that Gets Results." *Harvard Business Review*, March–April 2000.

Gray, Edmund R. and John M. T. Balmer. "Managing Corporate Image and Corporate Reputation." *Long Range Planning* 31, no. 5 (October 1998).

Greening, Daniel W. and Daniel B. Turban, "Corporate Social Performance as a Competitive Advantage in Attracting a Quality Workforce." *Business & Society* 39, no. 3 (September 2000).

Griffith, Victoria. "The People Factor in Post-Merger Integration." *Strategy + Business*, issue 20, 3rd quarter 2000.

Halal, William E., Michael D. Kull, and Ann Leffmann. "Emerging Technologies: What's Ahead for 2001–2030." *The Futurist*, November–December 1997.

Hall, Peter. "Modeling the Post-Industrial City." *Futures* 29, no. 4/5 (May/June 1997).

Hamel, Gary. "Strategy as Revolution." *Harvard Business Review*, July–August 1996.

———. "Strategy Innovation and the Quest for Value." *Sloan Management Review*, winter 1998.

———. "Waking Up IBM: How a Gang of Unlikely Rebels Transformed Big Blue." *Harvard Business Review*, July–August 2000.

Hamel, Gary and C. K. Prahalad. "Competing for the Future." *Harvard Business Review*, July–August 1994.

———. "Strategy as Stretch and Leverage." *Harvard Business Review*, March–April 1993.

Hamilton, Robert D., III, Virginia A. Taylor, and Roger J. Kashlak. "Designing a Control System for a Multinational Subsidiary." *Long Range Planning* 29, no. 6 (December 1996).

Harvey, Michael. "The Selection of Managers for Foreign Assignments: A Planning Perspective." *Columbia Journal of World Business* 31, no. 4 (Winter 1996).

Hastings, Donald F. "Lincoln Electric's Harsh Lessons from International Expansion." *Harvard Business Review*, May–June 1999.

Heene, Aime. "The Nature of Strategic Management." *Long Range Planning* 30, no. 6 (December 1997).

Hill, Terry and Roy Westbrook. "SWOT Analysis: It's Time for a Product Recall." *Long Range Planning* 30, no. 1 (February 1997).

Hirsh, Evan R., Louis F. Rodewig, Peter Soliman, and Steven B. Wheeler. "Changing Channels in the Automotive Industry." *Strategy + Business*, issue 14, 1st quarter 1999.

Hogarty, Thomas F. "Gasoline: Still Powering Cars in 2050?" *The Futurist* 33, no. 3 (March 1999).

"Is the World Big Enough for Jurgen Schrempp?" *Fortune*, March 6, 2000.

Johnson, Jeff. "Environment and the Bottom Line." *Chemical & Engineering News*, June 21, 1999.

Kahn, Jeremy. "Wal-Mart Goes Shopping in Europe." *Fortune*, June 7, 1999.

Kaplan, Robert S. and David P. Norton. "The Balanced Scorecard—Measures that Drive Performance." *Harvard Business Review*, January–February 1992.

———. "Having Trouble with Your Strategy? Then Map It." *Harvard Business Review*, September–October 2000.

———. "Putting the Balanced Scorecard to Work." *Harvard Business Review*, September–October 1993.

———. "Using the Balanced Scorecard as a Strategic Management System." *Harvard Business Review*, January–February 1996.

Kapoor, Vikas and Arnab Gupta. "Aggressive Sourcing: A Free-Market Approach." *Sloan Management Review*, fall 1997.

Katzenbach, Jon R. "The Myth of the Top Management Team." *Harvard Business Review*, November–December 1997.

Khurana, Anil and Stephen R. Rosenthal. "Integrating the Fuzzy Front End of New Product Development." *Sloan Management Review*, winter 1997.

Kirkpatrick, David. "Please Don't Call Us PC." *Fortune*, October 16, 2000.

Kobrin, Stephen J. "Assessing Political Risk Overseas," in P. Grub and D. Khambata. *The Multinational Enterprise in Transition: Strategies for Global Competitiveness*, 4th ed. Princeton, NJ: Darwin Press, 1993.

Kotkin, Joel. "The Valley Unmasked." *Los Angeles Times*, July 18, 1999.

Labich, Kenneth, "Nike vs. Reebok, a Battle for Hearts, Minds and Feet." *Fortune*, September 18, 1965.

Langeler, Gerard H. "The Vision Trap." *Harvard Business Review*, March–April 1992.

Leamer, Edward E. "Cyclically, We're Back to the Past." *Los Angeles Times*, December 6, 2000, p. B9

Liedtka, Jeanne M., Mark E. Haskins, John W. Rosenblum, and Jack Weber. "The Generative Cycle: Linking Knowledge and Relationships." *Sloan Management Review*, fall 1997.

Luehrman, Timothy A. "What's It Worth?" *Harvard Business Review*, May–June 1997.

Magretta, Joan. "Growth through Global Sustainability: An Interview with Monsanto's CEO, Robert B. Shapiro." *Harvard Business Review*, January–February 1997.

"The Man Who Would Be Welch." *Business Week*, December 11, 2000.

"Management by Morgan." *Fortune*, March 1934.

Markides, Constantinos. "Strategic Innovation." *Sloan Management Review*, spring 1997.

Massing, Michael. "Taking on Big Tobacco." *Washington Monthly*, October 1999.

McClelland, David C. and David H. Burnham. "Power Is the Great Motivator." *Harvard Business Review*, January–February 1995.

McGrath, Rita Gunther and Ian C. MacMillan. "Discovery Driven Planning." *Harvard Business Review*, July–August 1995.

McTavish, Ron. "One More Time: What Business Are You In?" *Long Range Planning* 28, no. 2 (April 1995).

Mehta, Stephanie N. "Great Balls of Wire!" *Fortune*, November 13, 2000.

Meyer, Christopher. "How the Right Measures Help Teams Excel." *Harvard Business Review*, May–June 1994.

Mintzberg, Henry. "Crafting Strategy," in Henry Mintzberg and James Brian Quinn. *The Strategy Process: Concepts, Contexts, Cases*. 3d ed. Upper Saddle River, NJ: Prentice-Hall, 1996.

———. "The Fall and Rise of Strategic Planning." *Harvard Business Review*, January–February 1994.

———. "Generic Business Strategies," in Henry Mintzberg and James Brian Quinn. *The Strategy Process: Concepts, Contexts, Cases.* 3d ed. Upper Saddle River, NJ: Prentice-Hall, 1996.

Moore, John. "British Privatization—Taking Capitalism to the People." *Harvard Business Review*, January–February 1992.

Morgan Stanley Dean Witter. "Report: Historical Perspective on Wealth Creation." *Los Angeles Times*, April 25, 1999.

Nee, Eric. "Refocusing Compaq." *Fortune*, March 5, 2001.

Newman, William H. "Shaping the Master Strategy of Your Firm." *California Management Review* 8 (spring 1967).

Nisbet, Paul. JSA Research Report on Boeing. *Los Angeles Times*, March 5, 1999.

Norton, Rob. "Luck of the Irish." *Fortune*, October 25, 1999.

O'Brien, Timothy L. "Reed Announces Plans to Step Down as Co-Chief of Citigroup." *New York Times*, February 29, 2000.

Ohmae, Kenichi. "Putting Global Logic First." *Harvard Business Review*, January–February 1995.

O'Sullivan, Leonard and J. Michael Geringr. "Harnessing the Power of Your Value Chain." *Long Range Planning* 26, no. 2 (April 1993).

Ouchi, William. "The Relationship between Organizational Structure and Organizational Control." *Administrative Science Quarterly*, March 1997.

Packard, Kimberly O'Neill and Forest Reinhardt. "What Every Executive Needs to Know about Global Warming." *Harvard Business Review*, July–August 2000.

Paul, Ronald N., Neil B. Donavan, and James W. Taylor. "The Reality Gap in Strategic Planning." *Harvard Business Review*, May–June 1978.

Petruno, Tom. "Stardate 1981: Take Me to Your High-Tech Leaders." *Los Angeles Times*, April 25, 1999.

Pettigrew, Andrew and Richard Whipp. "Managing the Twin Processes of Competition and Change, the Role of Intangible Assets," in Peter Lorange, Bala Chakravarthy, Johan Roos, and Andrew Van de Ven, eds. *Implementing Strategic Processes: Change, Learning and Co-operation.* Oxford, UK: Blackwell Business, 1993.

Porter, Michael E. "Changing Patterns of International Competition." *California Management Review* 28, no. 2 (winter 1986).

———. "What Is Strategy?" *Harvard Business Review*, November–December 1996.

Prahalad, C. K. and Gary Hamel. "The Core Competence of the Corporation." *Harvard Business Review*, May–June 1990.

Prahalad, C. K. and Yves Doz. "Patterns for Strategic Control within Multinational Corporations." *Journal of International Business Studies*, fall 1984.

Proctor, Paul. "Boeing Shakes Up Its Supplier Chain." *Aviation Week & Space Technology*, September 27, 1999.

Prokesch, Steven E. "Unleashing the Power of Learning: An Interview with British Petroleum's John Browne." *Harvard Business Review*, September–October 1997.

Puri, Shaifali. "Deals of the Year." *Fortune*, February 17, 1997.

Quinn, James Brian. "Strategies For Change," in Henry Mintzberg and James Brian Quinn. *The Strategy Process: Concepts, Contexts, Cases.* 3d ed. Upper Saddle River, NJ: Prentice-Hall, 1996.

Reich, Robert B. "The Company of the Future." *Fast Company*, November 1998.

"Remaking Ford." *Business Week*, October 11, 1999.

Resetar, Susan A. "Technology Forces at Work." Washington, DC: RAND Science & Technology Policy Institute, June 1999.

Robock, Stefan H. "Political Risk: Identification and Assessment." *Columbia Journal of World Business*, July–August, 1971.

Rohwer, Jim. "GE Digs Into Asia." *Fortune*, October 2, 2000.

Sahlman, William A. "How to Write a Great Business Plan." *Harvard Business Review*, July–August 1997.

Salzman, Marian and Ira Matathia. "Lifestyles of the Next Millennium: 65 Forecasts." *The Futurist*, June–July 1998.

Schoemaker, P.J.H. "Scenario Planing: A Tool for Strategic Thinking." *Sloan Management Review*, 36, no. 2 (winter 1995).

Schollhammer, Hans. "Long-Range Planing in Multinational Firms." *Columbia Journal of World Business* VI, no. 5 (September–October 1971).

Schwartz, Nelson D. "Still Perking after All These Years." *Fortune*, May 24, 1999.

Sealey, Peter. "How E-Commerce Will Trump Brand Management." *Harvard Business Review*, July–August 1999.

Sellers, Patricia. "Behind the Shootout at Citigroup." *Fortune*, March 20, 2000.

———. "Crunch Time for Coke." *Fortune*, July 19, 1999.

Sells, Bill. "What Asbestos Taught Me about Managing Risk." *Harvard Business Review*, March–April 1994.

Senge, Peter M. "The Leader's New Work: Building Learning Organizations." *Sloan Management Review*, fall 1990.

Simons, J. "A Theoretical Perspective on Political Risk." *Journal of International Business Studies*, winter 1984.

Simons, Robert. "Control in an Age of Empowerment." *Harvard Business Review*, March–April 1995.

Singh, Jasbinder. "Making Business Sense of Environmental Compliance." *Sloan Management Review*, spring 2000.

Stalk, George, Philip Evans, and Lawrence E. Shulman. "Competing on Capabilities: The New Rules of Corporate Strategy." *Harvard Business Review*, March–April 1992.

Stein, Nicholas. "The World's Most Admired Companies." *Fortune*, October 2, 2000.

Stewart, Thomas A. "Getting Real about Going Global." *Fortune*, February 15, 1999.

Taylor, Alex, III. "Kings of the Road." *Fortune*, June 7, 1999.

Taylor, Bernard. "The Return of Strategic Planning—Once More with Feeling." *Long Range Planning* 30, no. 3 (June 1997).

Tetzeli, Rich. "Surviving Information Overload." *Fortune*, July 11, 1994.

Tichy, Noel. "The Teachable Point of View: A Primer." *Harvard Business Review*, March–April 1999.

Venkatesan, Ravi. "Strategic Sourcing: To Make or Not to Make." *Harvard Business Review*, November–December 1992.

Venkatraman, N. "Beyond Outsourcing: Managing IT Resources as a Value Center." *Sloan Management Review*, spring 1997.

Vishwanath, Vijay and Jonathan Mark. "Your Brand's Best Strategy." *Harvard Business Review*, May–June 1997.

von Hippel, Eric, Stefan Thomke, and Mary Sonnack. "Creating Breakthroughs at 3M." *Harvard Business Review*, September–October 1999.

Waalewijn, Philip and Peter Segaar. "Strategic Management: The Key to Profitability in Small Companies." *Long Range Planning* 26, no. 2 (April 1993).

Wack, Pierre. "Scenarios: Shooting the Rapids." *Harvard Business Review*, November–December, 1985.

———. "Scenarios: Uncharted Waters Ahead." *Harvard Business Review*, September–October, 1985.

Wetlaufer, Suzy. "Driving Change: An Interview with Ford Motor Company's Jacques Nasser." *Harvard Business Review*, March–April 1999.

Wheelwright, Steven C. and Kim B. Clark. "Creating Project Plans to Focus Product Development." *Harvard Business Review*, March–April 1992.

Yip, George. "Who Needs Strategic Planning?" *Journal of Business Strategy* 6 (fall 1985).

BOOKS

Aaker, David A. *Developing Business Strategies*. 4th ed. New York: Wiley, 1995.

Abell, Derek F. *Defining the Business*. Englewood Cliffs, NJ: Prentice-Hall, 1980.

———. *Managing with Dual Strategies: Mastering the Present, Preempting the Future*. New York: Free Press, 1993.

Acheson, Dean. *Sketches from Life of Men I Have Known*. New York: Harper & Brothers, 1959.

Amey, Lloyd R. *Corporate Planning: A Systems View*. New York: Praeger, 1986.

Anderson, Carol H. and Julian W. Vincze. *Strategic Marketing Management: Meeting the Global Marketing Challenge*. Boston: Houghton Mifflin, 2000.

Ansoff, H. I. *Corporate Strategy*. New York: Wiley, 1965.

———. *The New Corporate Strategy*. New York: Wiley, 1988.

Anthony, Robert N. *Planning and Control Systems: A Framework for Analysis*. Boston: Harvard University, Graduate School of Business Administration, 1965.

Anthony, William P. *Practical Strategic Planning: A Guide and Manual for Line Managers*. Westport, CT: Quorum Books, 1985.

Barney, Jay B. *Gaining and Sustaining Competitive Advantage*. Reading, MA: Addison-Wesley Publishing Co., 1997.

Baron, David P. *Business and Its Environment*. 2d ed. Upper Saddle River, NJ: Prentice-Hall, 1996.

Barry, Frank, ed. *Understanding Ireland's Economic Growth*. New York: St. Martin's Press, 1999.

Bartlett, Hale C. *Cases in Strategic Management for Business*. New York: Dryden Press, 1988.

Baughman, James P., George C. Lodge, and Howard W. Pifer III. *Environmental Analysis for Management*. Homewood, IL: Irwin, 1974.

Bennis, Warren. *On Becoming a Leader*. Reading, MA: Addison-Wesley, 1989.

Berthelette, Eric and Frank Kresen, eds. *The Entrepreneur's Planning Handbook*. Rev. ed. Denver, CO: Entrepreneurial Education Foundation, 1997.

Boycko, Maxim, Andrei Shleifer, and Robert Vishny. *Privatizing Russia*. Cambridge, MA: MIT Press, 1995.

Branch, Taylor. *Parting the Waters: America in the King Years, 1954–63*. New York: Simon & Schuster, 1988.

Bryson, John M. *Strategic Planning for Public and Nonprofit Organizations*. San Francisco: Jossey-Bass, 1988.

Burns, James MacGregor. *Leadership*. New York: Harper & Row, 1978.

Casti, John L. *Would-Be Worlds: How Simulation Is Changing the Frontiers of Science*. New York: Wiley, 1997.

Chandler, Alfred D., Jr. *Strategy and Structure*. Cambridge, MA: MIT Press, 1962.

Coates, Joseph, Jennifer Jarratt, and John Mahaffie. *Future Work: Seven Critical Forces Reshaping Work and the Workforce in North America*. San Francisco: Jossey-Bass, 1990.

Collier, P. and D. Horowitz. *The Fords: An American Epic*. New York: Summit Books, 1987.

Collins, Jim and Jerry I. Porras. *Built to Last: Successful Habits of Visionary Companies*. New York: HarperBusiness, 1994.

Cross, Wilbur and Alice M. Richley. *The Prentice-Hall Encyclopedia of Model Business Plans*. Paramus, NJ: Prentice-Hall, 1998.

Davies, Norman. *Europe: A History*. New York: Oxford University Press, 1996.

de la Torre, José, Yves Doz, and Timothy Devinney. *Managing the Global Corporation: Case Studies in Strategy and Management*. 2d ed. New York: Irwin/McGraw-Hill, 2001.

Dell, Michael. *Direct from Dell: Strategies that Revolutionized an Industry*. New York: HarperCollins, 1999.

Donnelly, James H., Jr., James L. Gibson, and John M. Ivancevich. *Fundamentals of Management*, Plano, TX: Business Publications, Inc., 1981.

Drucker, Peter F. *The Age of Discontinuity*. New York: Harper & Row, 1969.

———. *The Concept of the Corporation*. New York: John Day, 1946.

———. *Management Challenges for the 21st Century*. New York: Harper Business, 1999.

———. *Management: Tasks, Responsibilities, Practices*. New York: Harper & Row, 1973.

———. *The New Realities*. New York: Harper & Row, 1989.

Easton, David. *The Political System*. New York: Knopf, 1960.

Elliott, Derek Wesley. *Finding an Appropriate Commitment: Space Policy Development under Eisenhower and Kennedy*. Washington, DC: George Washington University, unpublished Ph.D. dissertation, 1992.

Ergang, Robert. *Europe from the Renaissance to Waterloo*. Boston: D. C. Heath, 1954.

Farkas, Charles M. and Philippe De Backer. *Maximum Leadership: The World's Leading CEOs Share Their Five Strategies for Success*. New York: Holt, 1996.

Feist, William R., James A. Heely, Min H. Lu, and Roy L. Nersesian. *Managing a Global Enterprise: A Concise Guide to International Operations*. Westport, CT: Quorum Books, 1999.

Freeze, Gregory L. *Russia, a History*. New York: Oxford University Press, 1997.

Fry, Joseph N. and J. Peter Killing. *Strategic Analysis and Action*. U.S./international ed. Englewood Cliffs, NJ: Prentice-Hall, 1986.

Gardner, Howard. *Leading Minds: An Anatomy of Leadership*. New York: Basic Books, 1995.

Gates, Bill. *Business @ the Speed of Thought*. New York: Warner Books, 1999.

Goldwin, Robert A., ed. *Beyond the Cold War*. Chicago: Rand McNally, 1963.

Grant, Robert M. *Contemporary Strategy Analysis*. 3d ed. Oxford, UK: Blackwell Publishers, 1998.

Griffin, Ricky W. and Michael W. Pustay. *International Business: A Managerial Perspective*. Reading, MA: Addison-Wesley, 1996.

Grub, P. and D. Khambata. *The Multinational Enterprise in Transition: Strategies for Global Competitiveness*. 4th ed. Princeton, NJ: Darwin Press, 1993.

Guide to American Directories. (no city) B. Klein Publishers, 1999.

Halberstam, David. *The Reckoning*. New York: Morrow, 1986.

Hanoman, Carl. *The Complete Small-Business Source Book*. New York: Random House, 1999.

Harrison, John. *Strategic Management: Concepts and Cases*. Cincinnati, OH: South-Western College Publishing, 1997.

Hill, Charles W. L. and Gareth R. Jones. *Strategic Management: An Integrated Approach*. 5th ed. Boston: Houghton Mifflin, 2001.

Hitt, Michael A., Duane Ireland, and Robert E. Hoskisson. *Strategic Management: Competitiveness and Globalization*. 3d ed. Cincinnati, OH: South-Western College Publishing, 1999.

Holloway, Clark. *Strategic Planning*. Chicago: Nelson-Hall, 1986.

Hopkins, David S. *The Marketing Plan*. New York: The Conference Board, 1985.

Iacocca, Lee. *Iacocca: An Autobiography*. New York: Bantam Books, 1984.

Jerome, William Trafers, III. *Executive Control: The Catalyst*. New York: Wiley, 1961.

Johnson, Paul. *Modern Times: The World from the Twenties to the Eighties*. New York: Harper & Row, 1983.

Kaplan, Robert S. and David P. Norton. *The Strategy-Focused Organization*. Boston: Harvard Business School Publishing, 2000.

Kapron, Jill E. *Biz Plan Builder*. Cincinnati, OH: South-Western College Publishing, 1995.

Leassard, D. *International Financial Management*. New York: Wiley, 1979.

Leontiades, James C. *Multinational Corporate Strategy: Planning for World Markets*. New York: Lexington Books, 1985.

Lorange, Peter. *Strategic Planning and Control*. Cambridge, MA: Blackwell Business, 1993.

Lorange, Peter, Bala Chakravarthy, Johan Roos, and Andrew Van de Ven, eds. *Implementing Strategic Processes: Change, Learning and Co-operation*. Oxford, UK: Blackwell Business, 1993.

MacMillan, Ian C. *Corporate Venturing*. Boston: Harvard Business School Press, 1993.

Maurer, Christine and Tara E. Sheets, eds. *Encyclopedia of Associations*. Detroit: Gale Research, 1999.

McCartney, Scott. *ENIAC*. New York: Walker, 1999.

McClellan, James E. and Harold Dorn. *Science and Technology in World History*. Baltimore, MD: Johns Hopkins University Press, 1999.

McLaughlin, Harold J. *The Entrepreneur's Guide to Building a Better Business Plan: A Step-by-Step Approach*. New York: Wiley, 1992.

Megginson, William L., Mary Jane Byrd, Charles R. Scott, Jr., and Leon C. Megginson. *Small Business Management: An Entrepreneur's Guide to Success*. 2d ed. Toronto: Irwin, 1997.

Michael, Robert. *Strategy Pure and Simple II*. Rev. ed. New York: McGraw-Hill, 1998.

Mintzberg, Henry. *The Rise and Fall of Strategic Planning*. Englewood Cliffs, NJ: Prentice-Hall, 1994.

Mintzberg, Henry and James Brian Quinn. *The Strategy Process: Concepts, Contexts, Cases*. 3d ed. Upper Saddle River, NJ: Prentice-Hall, 1996.

Morrison, Ian and Greg Schmid. *Future Tense: The Business Realities of the Next Ten Years*. New York: Morrow, 1994.

Nader, Ralph. *Unsafe at Any Speed*. New York: Grossman, 1965.

Naisbitt, John. *Megatrends*. New York: Warner Books, 1984.

Nevins, Allan, ed. *The Burden and the Glory*. New York: Harper & Row, 1964.

Newman, William H. *Constructive Control: Design and Use of Control Systems*. Englewood Cliffs, NJ: Prentice-Hall, 1975.

Obeng, Eddie. *Putting Strategy to Work*. London: Pitman, 1996.

O'Connor, Rochelle. *Facing Strategic Issues: New Planning Guides and Practices*. New York: Research Report from The Conference Board, Report No. 867, 1985.

———. *Planning under Uncertainty: Multiple Scenarios and Contingency Planning*. New York: Conference Board, Inc., 1978.

O'Donnell, Michael. *Writing Business Plans that Get Results: A Step-by-Step Guide*. Chicago: Contemporary Books, 1991.

O'Hara, Patrick. *The Total Business Plan*. 2d ed. New York: Wiley, 1995.

Oksenberg, Michel, Michael D. Swaine, and Daniel C. Lynch. *The Chinese Future*. Los Angeles: Pacific Council on International Policy and RAND Center for Asia/Pacific Policy, 1997.

Orey, Michael. *Assuming the Risk: The Mavericks, the Lawyers, and the Whistle-Blowers Who Beat Big Tobacco*. Boston: Little, Brown, 1999.

Parry, J. H. *The Age of Reconnaissance: Discovery, Exploration and Settlement, 1450–1650*. Berkeley, CA: University of California Press, 1981.

Pearce, John A. and Richard B. Robinson, Jr. *Strategic Management*. Homewood, IL: Irwin, 1982.

Peters, Thomas J. and Robert H. Waterman, Jr. *In Search of Excellence*. New York: Warner Books, 1984.

Pipes, Richard. *The Formation of the Soviet Union*. Rev. ed. Cambridge, MA: Harvard University Press, 1997.

Popper, Steven W., Caroline S. Wagner, and Eric V. Larsen. *Industry Views Critical Technologies*. Santa Monica, CA: RAND Corporation, MR-1008-OSTP, 1998.

Porter, Michael E. *Competitive Advantage: Creating and Sustaining Superior Performance*. New York: Free Press, 1985.

———. *The Competitive Advantage of Nations*. New York: Free Press, 1998.

———. *Competitive Strategy: Techniques for Analyzing Industries and Competitors.* New York: Free Press, 1980.

———. *On Competition.* Boston, MA: Harvard Business School Publishing, 1998.

Quinn, James Brian. *Strategies for Change: Logical Incrementalism.* Homewood, IL: Irwin, 1980.

Roney, C. W. *Assessing the Business Environment: Guidelines for Strategists.* Westport, CT: Quorum Books, 1999.

Root, Franklin. *International Trade and Investment.* 7th ed. Cincinnati, OH: International Thompson Publishing, 1994.

Schlesinger, Arthur M., Jr., ed. *The Almanac of American History.* New York: Barnes and Noble Books, 1993.

Schumpeter, Joseph A. *Capitalism, Socialism, and Democracy.* New York: Harper & Brothers Publishers, 1950.

Senge, Peter M. *The Fifth Discipline.* New York: Doubleday, 1990.

Slater, Robert. *Jack Welch and the GE Way.* New York: McGraw-Hill, 1999.

Sloan, Alfred P., with John McDonald, ed. *My Years with General Motors.* New York: Doubleday, 1963.

Steiner, George A. *Strategic Planning: What Every Manager Must Know.* New York: Free Press, 1979.

———. *Top Management Planning.* New York: Macmillan, 1969.

Steiner, George A., John B. Miner, and Edmund R. Gray. *Management Policy and Strategy.* 3d ed. New York: Macmillan, 1986.

Stoner, J.A.F. *Management.* 2d ed. London: Prentice-Hall, 1982.

Struik, Dirk J. *Yankee Science in the Making.* New York: Dover Publications, 1991.

Stryker, Steven C. *Plan to Succeed: A Guide to Strategic Planning.* Princeton, NJ: Petrocelli Books, 1986.

Thomas, Hugh. *Cuba, or the Pursuit of Freedom.* New York: Da Capo Press, 1998.

Thompson, Arthur A. Jr. and A. J. Strickland III. *Strategic Management: Concepts and Cases.* 10th ed. New York: McGraw-Hill, 1998.

van der Heijden, Kees. *Scenarios: The Art of Strategic Conversation.* New York: Wiley, 1996.

Vernon-Wortzel, Heidi and Lawrence H. Wortzel. *Strategic Management in the Global Economy.* 3d ed. New York: Wiley, 1997.

Vincze, Julian W. and Carol H. Anderson. *Cases in Strategic Marketing Management.* Boston: Houghton Mifflin, 2000.

Ward, J. L. *Keeping the Family Business Healthy: How to Plan for Continuity, Growth, Profitability, and Family Leadership.* San Francisco: Jossey-Bass, 1988.

Watson, Thomas J., Jr. *A Business and Its Beliefs: The Ideas that Helped Build IBM.* New York: McGraw-Hill, 1963.

Weston, Fred and Eugene F. Brigham. *Essentials of Managerial Finance.* 7th ed. Hinsdale, IL: Dryden Press, 1985.

Wickens, Peter. *The Road to Nissan.* London: Macmillan, 1987.

Womack, James P., Daniel T. Jones, and Daniel Roos. *The Machine that Changed the World.* New York: Rawson Associates, 1990.

Yavitz, Boris and William H. Newman. *Strategy in Action.* New York: Free Press, 1982.

Yip, George S. *Total Global Strategy: Managing for Worldwide Competitive Advantage*. Englewood Cliffs, NJ: Prentice-Hall, Business School Ed., 1995.

GOVERNMENT DOCUMENTS AND GOVERNMENT OFFICIALS

Central Intelligence Agency. *The World Factbook*. Washington, DC: GPO. Annual eds.

Hayghe, Howard. U.S. Bureau of Labor Statistics. Telecon. September 23, 1999.

Institute of International Finance, Inc. *Capital Flows to Emerging Market Economies*. Washington, DC, 1999.

International Monetary Fund. *World Economic Outlook, May 2000*. Washington, DC.

Kennedy, John F. *Public Papers of the Presidents of the United States, 1961*. Washington, DC: GPO, 1962.

Organization for Economic Co-operation and Development. *OECD Economic Outlook, 2000*. Washington, DC, December 1999.

United Nations. *Economic Survey of Europe, 1999, No. 3*. Economic Commission for Europe. New York, 1999.

U.S. Department of Commerce, Bureau of Economic Analysis. *Survey of Current Business*. August 1999.

U.S. Department of Commerce, Bureau of the Census. *U.S. Industry & Trade Outlook, 2000*. Washington, DC, 2000.

U.S. Federal Reserve Bank of San Francisco. "Western Economic Developments." August 1999.

U.S. Federal Reserve System. *Bulletin*. Washington, DC: GPO. Monthly eds.

The World Bank. *The World Bank Atlas*. Washington, DC: The World Bank Group. Annual eds.

The World Bank. *World Development Indicators*. Washington, DC: The World Bank Group. Annual eds.

The World Competitiveness Yearbook. Lausanne, Switzerland.: IMD. Annual eds.

PUBLIC LECTURES

Grillo, Michael, Head of Production, DreamWorks SKG. Speech to Western Academy of Management, Redondo Beach, CA, March 25, 1999.

McAleese, Mary, President of Ireland. "Ireland Today." Speech to Los Angeles World Affairs Council. Cited in Los Angeles World Affairs Council, *World Affairs Journal*. November 1999.

Ohmae, Kenichi, Professor. Lecture to Faculty at Anderson Graduate School of Management, UCLA, February 11, 1997.

Smith, John F., Jr., Chairman and Chief Executive Officer, General Motors. Speech to Los Angeles World Affairs Council, Beverly Hills, CA, May 19, 2000.

WEB SITES FOR ECONOMIC DATA

European Union: European Central Bank. www.ecb.int/
European Union: Main Site. www.europa.eu.int/index.en.htm

The Federal Reserve Board: Statistics. www.federalreserve.gov/releases/

International Monetary Fund: Annual Reports (2000 in English). www.imf.org/
external/pubs/ft/ar/2000/eng/index.htm

Organization for Economic Cooperation and Development: Macroeconomic Reports. www.oecd.org/eco/surv/www.htm

United Nations: International Trade Center. www.intracen.org/infobase.htm

United Nations: Regional Commissions. www.un.org/partners/business/reg.htm

U.S. Department of Commerce, Bureau of Economic Analysis: National Accounts
Data. www.bea.doc.gov/bea/dn1.htm

U.S. Treasury Department: Import/Export Data. www.customs.treas.gov/impoexpo/
impoexpo.htm

World Bank Group: Annual Reports (2000). www.worldbank.org/html/extpd/
annrep/index.htm

Index

About the Author

WESLEY B. TRUITT is Executive-in-Residence at the College of Business Administration, Loyola Marymount University, Los Angeles, where he teaches business planning to MBA and Executive MBA students. He is also Adjunct Professor at the Anderson Graduate School of Management at UCLA and Principal of Truitt Consulting, which assists organizations with business planning and strategic positioning.